THE PERCEPTION OF SPACE IN THE OLD TESTAMENT

An exploration of the methodological problems of its investigation,
exemplified by a study of Exodus 25 to 31

Promotor: Prof.Dr. J.C. de Moor
Copromotor: Prof.Dr. C. Houtman
Referent: Prof.Dr. E. Talstra·

THE PERCEPTION OF SPACE IN THE OLD TESTAMENT

An exploration of the methodological problems of its investigation,
exemplified by a study of Exodus 25 to 31

JOHAN BRINKMAN

Kok Pharos Publishing House
Kampen – The Netherlands

This study was defended as a dissertation for the doctorate at the University of Kampen.
Supervisor was Prof.Dr. J.C. de Moor.

CIP-GEGEVENS KONINKLIJKE BIBLIOTHEEK – DEN HAAG

© 1992 Kok Pharos Publishing House
Kampen, The Netherlands / J.M. Brinkman
Cover bij Dik Hendriks
ISBN 90 390 0003 4
NUGI 632

PREFACE.

Working at a dissertation is like making a journey through unknown territory. Sometimes, the environment looks familiar and one feels at ease, in particular when one discovers others travelling in the same direction. Sometimes, however, it looks strange and one does not feel very comfortable, especially when no other people are visible.

Fortunately, I was never completely alone during my journey. The idea of making it originated during a series of lectures of Professor Dr. J.C. de Moor in 1978. Since then, he has provided stimulating and encouraging supervision. Even at times when he and I got the impression that I had lost my way, he remained available for giving advice and practical support. I am extremely grateful for everything I learnt from him and for his continuous friendship.

Professor Dr. C. Houtman, my copromotor, was involved in the final leg of my journey. By his criticism he showed me a number of pitfalls on my way, for which I want to thank him in particular.

Dr. E. Talstra of the Free University at Amsterdam was prepared to act as external referent and I highly appreciate his interest in the result of my journey.

Many other people provided help underway. Of them, I mention in particular: the staff of the libraries of the Theological University Kampen and the Hendrik Kraemer Institute in Oegstgeest, who helped me in collecting the necessary literature, Peterjan van der Wal, who helped me in using a text processing system on the computer, and Paul Harder, Joy Lapp and Paula Skreslet, who corrected my use of the English language. In 1984, the Reformed Church of IJsselmuiden-Grafhorst gave me a three months leave in order to work at my investigation. The Missionary Board of the Dutch Reformed Church for which I have worked since 1989, allowed me to spend part of my time on it and provided substantial and stimulating support in other respects. I greatly acknowledge all this assistance.

In addition, I realize that I did not start my journey fully unprepared. My study of chemistry and psychology at the Free University at Amsterdam and of theology at the Theological University at Kampen gave an adequate basis, and I wish to honour all members of the teaching staff of both institutions of whom I had the privilege to be a student.

Above all, however, I am aware of the fact that my journey in 'scientific land' would not have been possible, had I not received the permanent love of those people who are very near to me and with whom I share my daily life on this planet. First of all, I think of my wife and children; in addition, I mention my relatives and friends and all those whom I met in my work as a pastor in IJsselmuiden and Arnhem and as a lecturer in Cairo. On one hand, scientific

5

work requires a certain level of isolation; on the other hand, somebody involved in it is in permanent need of indispensable spiritual support 'from outside' and I am grateful that I received so much of that not only during the journey of my dissertation but also in many other areas.

In this connection, I confess that this support 'from outside' not only involves human sources, but also relates to Him, whose Word I am trying to serve, and whose Son I am trying to follow, because, according to the gospel of John, He forms the "only reliable way of life."

CONTENTS

1.INTRODUCTION.

1.1. Background of the investigation.

This study seeks to contribute to our knowledge of the role of space in the Old Testament. For modern man the experience of space seems to be important and comprehensive. In addition it seems to be narrowly connected with that of time. But what about the people of the Old Testament? Did space play a similar role for them?

When in the eighteenth century Kant considered the problems of aesthetics and human knowledge, he formulated the crucial role of both time and space as epistomological categories. Since then there have been ongoing discussions on detailed aspects of their functioning as such. But regardless of the various positions which have been taken in this respect, there is one thing which seems to have been accepted generally, viz. , that time and space, and aspects connected with them, do play an important role when people think, speak, write, express themselves, about whatever topic possible. It is recognized that there are differences; some matters require more spatial and temporal 'involvement' than others, and also regarding the distribution of the two factors, there are clear distinctions. But there appears to be general agreement on the idea that human cognition, and its expressions and manifestations in the broadest sense, cannot be studied adequately without paying attention to both time and space.

This idea also had its influence on the investigation of ancient civilisations. When we study the people belonging to them, and the results and manifestations of their culture which are available to us, we are bound to take into account that these have spatial and temporal aspects. Groenewegen-Frankfort even published a monograph which especially considers the aspects of space and time in the art of the ANE.[1]

So it does not come as a surprise that the role which time and space play in the Old Testament and its world have been the object of (scientific and aesthetic) study. In his course on images of reality in the world of the Bible, De Moor paid attention to the way in which history is approached in the ANE and the Bible.[2] As part of the fulfilment of the requirements for the 'doctoraal examen theologie' in 1979, I researched the literature on the role of time and space in the Old Testament. On the basis of this search a few things can be said:

- The objective of many publications in this field is to devise a picture of how people of Old Testament times perceived and experienced time and space, and

---

1   Groenewegen-Frankfort, 1951.
2   De Moor, 1977 - 78.

11

how the resulting temporal and spatial perception and experience influenced their ideas and utterances about all kinds of things, including religious matters.
- There is a lot of controversy regarding the proper method of investigation necessary to arrive at such a picture; as a consequence a well-founded (and generally accepted) picture of time- and space-experience in the Old Testament does not exist.
- The study of the role and experience of time has received much more attention than the study of space and its aspects.
This last point prompted the decision to study the role of space in the Old Testament in order to try to improve our knowledge of it. As the first step of such a study, a careful investigation of the relevant literature is needed. This will enable us to describe what is known at the moment. It will also allow us a deeper insight into the methodological problems involved. It should be borne in mind that these latter problems do not relate to the role of space only, but also to that of time, since both fields have many things in common.
But prior to this first step of our study, it seems wise to include an introductory survey of the role of space and spatial relations in modern, Western science and culture, since it will be undertaken by somebody who is living in the climate determined by them, and consciously and unconsciously undergoes their influence.
This survey, which within the framework of the present study has to remain only superficial, will be given in the next paragraph of this introductory chapter.
The objective of our study will be outlined in more detail in paragraph 1.3. , whereas the final paragraph of this introductory chapter gives in advance a brief description of the various chapters of this thesis.

1.2. Space and spatial relations in Western science and culture; an introductory survey.

In the preface to his monumental, two-volume treatise on the history of the problems of space in philosophy and science, Gosztonyi points to the fact that space and time belong to the facts of life which from ancient times have bothered mankind. At certain periods of history the interest was predominantly with space, while in other eras it was time that received the most attention.[1]
Whereas at the beginning of the twentieth century the problems of time were in the foreground, in its second half the interest in space increased considerably. In addition to the popular attention which resulted from the conquest of long distances, both terrestrial and extra-terrestrial, Gosztonyi mentions four reasons that have scientific background for this increase in interest in the problems of space:
1. The newly developed general relativity theory in physics and recent discoveries in astronomy led to questions concerning the structure of the

---

[1] Gosztonyi, 1976, p. 29.

universe.

2. The discovery of non-Euclidean geometry, already made in the nineteenth century, put into question the traditional Euclidean picture of space, and prompted philosophers to investigate the consequences of this discovery, and to develop alternative models for space.

3. Ethnological research demonstrated that many 'primitive people' exhibit an experience of space which seems to be different from that of Western culture in many aspects.

4. In psychiatry, the occurrence of very anomalous ways of perceiving and experiencing space was brought to light.

From this list it is clear that the problems of space in Western culture and science relate to a wide variety of scientific disciplines, such as mathematics, geometry, physics, physiology, sense-psychology, psychiatry, ethnology, etc.[1]

This variety is reflected in the detailed historical survey of space and its problems, which forms the main part of the book by Gosztonyi. It is noteworthy that already in his report of the ancient Greek philosophy, which forms the starting-point for his review, the author puts heavy emphasis on the relation between the concept of space and the picture of nature and cosmos, and the use of mathematics, in particular of geometry, in giving shape to this relation.

This heavy emphasis on the physical aspects of space is maintained throughout the whole of his historical survey, up to the rise of modern physics with its concept of space-time as an n-dimensional multiple.

Space, as experienced by man in common life, did not become a matter of scientific and philosophical reflection until the nineteenth century, when the investigation of the detailed working of the human perceptual apparatus got off the ground. In line with this development, the phenomenological philosophy of the early twentieth century gave attention to space as perceived and experienced by man. More recent thinkers in the second half of this century included emotional and 'existentialist' factors in this experience and investigated the 'lived space' (erlebte Raum).

As a result of these developments, contemporary interest in space is somewhat confusing. In the introduction to his treatise, Gosztonyi lists twenty-nine examples of 'adjectival spaces', such as: experience-space (Erlebnisraum), tempered space (gestimmte Raum), perceptional space, body-space, geometrical space, physical space, orientated space, etc.[2]

Quite often these particular types of space are used by authors in a very personal and special way, and terminological problems contribute to the existing confusion. Therefore, it is not easy to determine whether all these different approaches to space, and the resulting kinds of spaces, have something in

---

1   see o.c. , p. 30.
2   o.c. , p. 34 - 51.

common, which might be considered to be characteristic for the Western approach to the problem of space.

Perhaps a common factor in all Western involvement with space might be found in the search for spatial structure. It is quite understandable that this makes sense in the study of physical space, while using different types of mathematical space as models for it. Geometrical space, i.e. space seen as an entity the parts of which are structured according to geometrical relations, plays an important role in Western approach and use of space. But also in the case of 'experienced space,' it is remarkable that many scholars try to describe it in terms of order and structure. From the authors discussed by Gosztonyi we mention as examples, Ströker, who uses the central role of the body as orientational point for the human consideration of space, and Voss, who describes as fundamental for the 'total experience of space' two principal human spatial experience, namely that of heaven and that of earth.[1]

It may be that Gosztonyi, who gave the concluding chapter of his treatise the title "The structure of space," is to a certain extent pre-occupied with searching for structure and order in space; he does not discuss Gölz, who in his monograph on "Dasein und Raum" emphasizes the paradox of human existence in space. He sees this paradox in the fact that on one hand the essence of our existence is decisively determined by our 'spatial condition,' whereas on the other hand we seem to be unable to consider ourselves just as things located in space.[2] With this paradox, Gölz is pointing to one of the fundamental problems in human experience of space already recognized earlier in history, viz., that in one sense human beings are bound to space, but in another sense they seem to transcend it.

In addition, there are other problems which originate from recent developments, a few of which should be mentioned:

1. Up to this century, time and space were considered to be related, though clearly separated, categories. Developments in modern physics and astronomy have led to devising the concept of 'space-time,' in which time and space have been incorporated into one multi-dimensional whole. So far, this concept has proved to be very useful in accounting for certain phenomena on the micro-scale (atomic physics) and on the macro-scale (astronomy). In addition, the question arises as to what extent it influences the 'existential experience of space' of modern man.

2. The fact that at present so many notions of space are being used (see above) makes people wonder whether each of these refers to a 'different space,' or whether there exists one underlying 'fundamental space.' In addition, the older problem of the 'reality' of space, of its independent existence, continues to occupy scholars. For from the 'physical side,' another paradox is becoming

---

1   o.c. , p. 928 - 943.
2   Gölz, 1970, p. 255.

14

apparent; on one hand the distribution of matter in the universe is dependent on the geometrical properties of space, but at the same time matter seems to determine the curvature and 'density properties' of space.[1] Thus it looks as if matter and space, in some way or another, are strongly interrelated. But this phenomenon makes the question of the 'independent existence' of space the more pertinent.

3. We encounter a similar problem when we speak about the structure of space. It looks as if the geometrical structure of space is something 'found' in nature by mankind, when investigating space, whereas the order or structure of 'existential space' is something which can be attributed to the 'constitutional activity' of the human mind while investigating this aspect of space. At the same time, it should be borne in mind that geometrical models also originate from human intelligence and reflect his attempts to explain the natural phenomena he observes. The question of the reality of these structures can be asked. Some philosophers deny them any reality at all, and consider them only as human explanatory models, e.g. Sklar.[2] Others, like Gosztonyi, if we understand him correctly, assume some kind of existence for structures and connect them with 'activity' (Wirkung) of space.[3]

These examples illustrate how space and its problems figure in modern Western science and philosophy. It should be emphasized once more that this brief paragraph is not intended as an exhaustive survey of this field, but only as a kind of reminder at the beginning of an investigation into some aspects of the role of space in the world of the Old Testament. Some idea of the role of space in our own world is useful since we may expect that it will influence the results of our investigation.

Of course, one may wonder to what extent the detailed and sometimes highly theoretical work on space, e.g., in modern physics or sense psychology, influences in practice the everyday modern experience of space. At the same time, modern communication media are able to overcome many barriers, not only of physical distances but also of 'psychological distances.' There may be more influence than superficially expected.

In addition, awareness of the modern Western view of space, with its many unsolved questions and diversified approaches, may help us to be as open as possible towards experience and perception of space in other cultures.

1.3. The objective of the study.

In the first paragraph of this chapter we described the subject area of our study as: "the role of space in the Old Testament." We now proceed with a more detailed account of its objective in which we should keep in mind that the

---

1   Gosztonyi, 1976, p. 713.
2   Sklar, 1974, p. 415 - 17.
3   Gosztonyi, 1976, p. 1245.

description used above presupposes elements which are typical for a Western approach to space:

1. On one hand, space is seen as an individual aspect of human existence, occasionally even as a more or less separate 'object' in the world; in both cases science tries to devise models in order to describe its structure.

2. At the same time, there seems to be a growing awareness that space cannot be studied on its own, but should always be investigated in the light of its fundamental function and more extensive role for both the material and non-material world.

In addition, a distinction is usually made between the perception and the experience of space. Perception is described as: "(formal) process by which we become aware of changes (through the senses of sight, hearing, etc.); act or power of perceiving."[1] In experimental psychology which investigates this process, it is assumed that one of its main elements is the physical stimuli originating from objects in the world which are received by the human sense organs. At the same time, it is clear that it is more than simply the registering of sensory information. Factors involved include: quality of sense organs, level of attention, previous knowledge of the world, ability of pattern recognition, etc.[2] Experience is seen as the "process of gaining knowledge or skill by doing and seeing things; knowledge or skill so gained."[3] Experience then, is the broader of the two concepts. It is not restricted to the senses and connected functions, but covers the whole of human activities. As a consequence, it results not only in knowledge but also in the capability to act accordingly.

A complete and sharp distinction between the two is not possible; it looks as if they represent extremes of a continuum. It further seems reasonable to consider perception as fundamental to experience.

These considerations help us to delineate in more detail the objective of our investigation. As outlined in paragraph 1.1., its subject area is the role of space in the Old Testament. From our previous, preliminary literature review, we know that little attention has been paid to the perception of space in the Old Testament. Hence, we decided to concentrate on this aspect and make it the particular target area of our study. This decision will determine the angle from which we look at what is known at present and examine the methodological issues involved. At this stage, before having completed the initial step of searching the literature in more detail, the objective of our study can be formulated as follows: to investigate and describe how space was perceived in the Old Testament.

If this objective can be realized, we would like to make a preliminary attempt to relate this picture of the perception of space in the Old Testament to two

---

1   Hornby, 1981, s.v.
2   see Anderson, 1980, p. 21 - 59.
3   Hornby, 1981, s.v.

other phenomena:
- the experience of space in the Old Testament in the broader sense of the word.
- the perception of space in other cultures of the ANE.
Bearing in mind the close connection between the world of the Bible and its cultural environment, we may expect that the perception of space in the Old Testament is influenced by the corresponding phenomenon in the ANE. In the initial phase of our study, we made an exploratory search of the literature of this latter area hoping to find information which might be relevant for the methodological issues which we discovered to exist in the former field. But it appeared that in this area much use is made of pictorial and material sources, which are not available to the same extent for the investigation of the perception of space in the Old Testament. As a result, both the methods used and the scope of the results obtained in the two areas differ considerably. This made us decide to use the Old Testament as the main basis for our investigation. But at the end, we will consider its results in the light of relevant data on the ANE in general, including archaeological and metrological evidence from Israel.

1.4. The contents of this thesis.
Having outlined the objectives of our study, we conclude this introductory chapter by giving a brief description of its contents. At the same time, it provides a preliminary impression of the means we used to achieve our objective.
This chapter is followed by a survey of the role of space and spatial relations in general in current theological reflection on the Old Testament. In fact, this is an area which falls outside the subject area of our study, but we decided to include it, because we wondered if the low level of attention to the experience of space in the Old Testament, which we had found earlier, was an indication of a very limited role of space in the study of the theological ideas of the Old Testament. If this were true, our study in this field would be a more or less isolated event. However, we were able to review a number of publications which illustrate the importance of spatial concepts for the theology of the Old Testament.
In chapter 3 we start our study with reporting the results of our search of the literature of the science of the Old Testament. From our earlier search we had obtained the impression that as far as the Old Testament is concerned, only publications which direct themselves to the broader concept of space experience have appeared. The distinction between perception and experience has not been made, so we decided to include all publications on the experience of space in the Old Testament. In our report, however, we emphasized the aspects concerning the perception of space.
An initial evaluation revealed that only very diverse statements can be found, which sometimes lack the support of data obtained by adequate research. A properly founded, coherent picture of space perception in the Old Testament does not seem to be available. In addition, the confusion regarding methodology

which we expected to find, appears to exist indeed, which made an adequate assessment of the state of the art impossible. In order to obtain more clarity in these methodological issues, we made an additional survey of a number of recent publications on the general application of modern linguistic developments to the study of the Old Testament. However, it did not provide sufficient means to clarify this confusion.

The main source of the controversy on methodology is the questionable position of the Linguistic Relativity Hypothesis, which forms one of the basic ideas in the interdisciplinary field covering the relation between language and cognition. We decided to explore the position of this hypothesis by examining the literature of linguistics, psychology, and anthropology. At the end of chapter 4, in which we present the results of this search, we conclude that a number of fundamental questions relating to the interaction of language, world, and cognition are at stake.

As a consequence, we decided to study in more detail a few aspects of the philosophy of language as well. The result of this enquiry is reported in chapter 5. At the end of that chapter we condense the findings of our research outside the field of Old Testament study into a model which helps us to evaluate what is known of the perception of space in the Old Testament, and to obtain some clarity in the methodological issues involved.

The use of the model in this sense is the topic of the first part of chapter 6 and this confirmed our preliminary impression that no properly founded picture of the perception of space in the Old Testament is available. Hence, in the second part of this chapter we give an outline of a method for further study, which is also based on this model. Since this method included the detailed investigation of a relevant text of the Old Testament, it was necessary to choose one. At the end of chapter 6 we give the reasons for our choice of the tabernacle text of Exodus 25 to 31 as the 'test area' for assessing our methodological ideas and exploring how far they will bring us in formulating a well-founded picture of the perception of space in the Old Testament.

Before we started our 'experimental work' on Exodus 25 to 31, we wanted to obtain some idea of the role these chapters play in recent research of the Old Testament, so we carried out a literature search on this topic, the results of which are reported in chapter 7.

After all this preparatory work, chapter 8 describes how we applied the method outlined in chapter 6 to Exodus 25 to 31, and its last paragraph contains a description of some elements of the perception of space in the Old Testament, which was the objective of our study.

The final chapter discusses these elements in the light of previous research, and tries to put them together into a coherent picture. It also contains a preliminary attempt to relate this picture to two other areas: the experience of space in the Old Testament in general, and the perception of space in other cultures of the ANE.

At the end of this introductory chapter we would like to make three comments:

1. From this short summary of our study it is clear that methodological issues play an important role in our investigation. We therefore decided to include the word 'methodological' in the title of this thesis.

2. Because of the great amount of work required in connection with methodological problems, our investigation of the Old Testament itself had to remain limited. In fact, our study has been mainly an exploration of how far we could get in obtaining a well-founded picture of the perception of space in the Old Testament. It is only at the end that we are able to formulate a number of its elements.

3. Now that we have summarized the course of our study, which has been carried out over a number of years, and described its various steps in a more or less systematic way in this publication, the idea might come up that everything has been performed in a nice and chronological order. This has not been the case. As with much scientific work, there has constantly been a movement forwards and backwards, within all the steps and aspects of the investigation. This could be seen as an example of the close relationship between time and space.

2. SPACE AND SPATIAL RELATIONS
IN CURRENT REFLECTION ON THE THEOLOGY
OF THE OLD TESTAMENT.

2.1. Introduction

In paragraph 1.1 we already reported that in a preliminary literature search we had found that the study of the experience of time and temporal relations in the Old Testament had received much more attention than the corresponding study of space and spatial relations. Apparently this is caused by the fact that scholars put heavy emphasis on the role of history in the theological thinking of the Old Testament. A good example is Von Rad, who in the second volume of his epoch-making treatise on the theology of the Old Testament, included a separate section on "Israel's ideas of time and history and the prophetic eschatology."[1]

But not only he: many before him and following him saw history as the main entry to discuss and explain the characteristics of the faith of Israel. So it is not surprising to discover that two surveys of current research in Old Testament theology contain separate chapters on this subject.[2]

This does not mean that space and spatial relations did not receive any attention at all. The following examples illustrate this point. In his discussion of the meaning of the cult as one of the institutions of the covenant, Eichrodt spent quite some effort in investigating the holy places and the spatial concepts connected with them.[3] Along similar lines, Jacob, who considered the 'living God' as the central theme of the theology of the Old Testament, discussed space and spatial relations under several headings: the manifestations of God, esp. his face, creation, and the institutions in which holy places play a central role.[4]

So, whereas space and spatial concepts have not been out of sight completely, it must be said that in general, history has been considered to be the central factor in the theology of the Old Testament. And, leaving aside the question whether the concept of history does not contain spatial aspects as well, the temporal aspects were studied most extensively.

The heavy emphasis on history as the central theological concept of Israel's faith has not remained unchallenged. In 1967 Albrektson published a study titled "History and the Gods," in which he showed that the idea of historical events as divine revelation is not quite as distinctive for the Old Testament as commonly

---

1   Von Rad, 1975, p. 108 - 133.
2   Hasel, 1975, p. 57 - 75; Reventlow, 1982, p. 65 - 137.
3   Eichrodt, 1959.
4   Jacob, 1955.

thought: " ... it is part of the common theology of the ancient Near East."[1] He claimed that "the specific content of the Hebrew faith .... is, in the last resort, derived from what the Old Testament represents as a divine revelation through the word. This is why the exaggerated emphasis on historical events as a distinctive and supreme medium of revelation, which is characteristic of much contemporary Old Testament theology, requires modification."[2]

In addition, in the last two decades, a few publications have appeared, in which space or concepts with strong 'spatial components,' rather than history, have been given the main role in the theology of the Old Testament.

In view of the objective of our investigation, we want to discuss in this chapter a number of these publications, in order to get some idea of the role which space and spatial aspects play, when they are being seen as central, or at least as important factors, in the theology of the Old Testament. In the following paragraphs we will review publications by Heschel, Tesfai, Terrien, Levenson and Gorman.

In each case we start by presenting the results and views of the author, as much as possible by means of quotations from his publication. And we end by making a number of preliminary remarks. In the final paragraph of this chapter we will summarize what we have found regarding the role of space in the theology of the Old Testament.

2.2. A.J.Heschel: The sabbath, a palace in time.

This publication is not so much a theological investigation, but rather a "profound, scholarly, and beautiful meditation."[3] It is included in this survey because of the characteristic way in which it describes the role of time and space and their relationship, in the faith of Israel.

In his prologue Heschel considers technical civilisation as "man's conquest of space." He acknowledges that this is certainly one of the aspects of human life, but he continues: "Life goes wrong when the control of space, the acquisition of things of space, becomes our sole concern."[4] According to him "even religions are frequently dominated by the notion that the deity resides in space, within particular localities like mountains, forests, trees or stones, which are, therefore, singled out as holy places; the deity is bound to a particular land; holiness a quality associated with things of space, and the primary question is: Where is the god?"[5]

Now his intention is not "to deprecate the world of space .... Time and space are interrelated. To overlook either of them is to be partially blind. What we plead

---

1   Albrektson, 1974, p. 114.
2   o.c. p. 122.
3   Heschel, 1951 , back cover.
4   o.c. , p. 3.
5   o.c. , p. 4.

against is man's unconditional surrender to space, his enslavement to things. We must not forget that it is not a thing that lends significance to a moment; it is the moment that lends significance to things.

The Bible is more concerned with time than with space. It sees the world in the dimension of time. It pays more attention to generations, to events, than to countries, to things; it is more concerned with history than with geography. To understand the teaching of the Bible, one must accept its premise that time has a meaning for life which is at least equal to that of space; that time has a significance of its own."[1]

In line with this biblical concern, Heschel sees Judaism as "a religion of time aiming at the sanctification of time."[2] He believes it to be very significant that when in the Bible the word qadosh, holy, "a word which more than any other is representative of the mystery and majesty of the divine," is used for the first time, "it is applied to time: 'And God blessed the seventh day and made it holy.' ..... When history began, there was only one holiness in the world, holiness in time. When at Sinai the word of God was about to be voiced, a call for holiness in man was proclaimed: 'Thou shalt be unto me a holy people.' It was only after the people had succumbed to the temptation of worshipping a thing, a golden calf, that the erection of a Tabernacle, of holiness in space, was commanded. The sanctity of time came first, the sanctity of man came second, and the sanctity of space last. Time was hallowed by God; space, the Tabernacle, was consecrated by Moses."[3]

It is remarkable that in his subsequent explanation of the meaning of the Sabbath, Heschel frequently uses spatial terms to describe it. He calls it a "palace in time which we build,"[4] an expression which he comments as follows: "The seventh day is like a palace in time with a kingdom for all. It is not a date but an atmosphere. It is not a different state of consciousness but a different climate; it is as if the appearance of all things somehow changed. The primary awareness is one of our being within the Sabbath rather than of the Sabbath being within us. We may not know whether our understanding is correct, or whether our sentiments are noble, but the air of the day surrounds us like spring which spreads over the land without our aid or notice. .... The difference between the Sabbath and all other days is not to be noticed in the physical structure of things, in their spatial dimension. Things do not change on that day. There is only a difference in the dimension of time, in the relation of the universe to God. The Sabbath preceded creation and the Sabbath completed creation; it is all

---

1   o.c. , p. 6 - 7.
2   o.c. , p. 8.
3   o.c. , p. 9 - 10.
4   o.c. , p. 15.

of the spirit that the world can bear."[1]

After having described the characteristics of human civilisation ("the splendor of space"), Heschel comes to represent his ideas on time. He starts with an allegory: "At the beginning time was one, eternal. But time undivided, time eternal, would be unrelated to the world of space. So time was divided into seven days and entered into an intimate relationship with the world of space. With every single day, another realm of things came into being, except on the seventh day. The Sabbath was a lonely day. It may be compared to a king who has seven sons. To six of them he gave his wealth, and the youngest one he endowed with nobility, with the prerogative of royalty. The six older sons who were commoners found their mates, but the noble one remained without a mate."[2] In line with this allegory Heschel remarks that Israel was destined to be a helpmate for the Sabbath, which explains its great role in Jewish life.

In his next chapter Heschel discusses the personification of the Sabbath which is common among Jews. He considers it to be a personification of a special kind: "The idea of the Sabbath as a queen or a bride is not a personification of the Sabbath but an exemplification of a divine attribute, an illustration of God's need for human love; it does not represent a substance but the presence of God, His relationship to man."[3] By considering the Sabbath in this way Heschel is able to describe what happens on its arrival as follows: "And the world becomes a place of rest. An hour arrives like a guide, and raises our minds above accustomed thoughts. People assemble to welcome the wonder of the seventh day, while the Sabbath sends out its presence over the fields, into our homes, into our hearts. It is a moment of resurrection of the dormant spirit in our souls."[4]

Consequently the author sees the Sabbath in the light of eternity, and asks: "What is the Sabbath? Spirit in the form of time. With our bodies we belong to space; our spirit, our souls, soar to eternity, aspire to the holy. The Sabbath is an ascent to the holy. It gives us the opportunity to sanctify time, to raise the good to the level of the holy, to behold the holy by abstaining from profanity."[5]

Continuing this line of thought Heschel is able to write a few pages later: "The Sabbath is all holiness. ..... It is the world of souls: spirit in the form of time."[6]

To the epilogue of his meditation he gave the title "To sanctify time." Here he contrasts two approaches to time: "Time to us is a measuring device rather than a realm in which we abide. .... Fundamental to the consciousness of time is the distinction between earlier and later. .... To the common mind the essence of time is evanescence, temporality. The truth, however, is that the fact of

---

1   o.c. , p. 21.
2   o.c. , p. 51.
3   o.c. , p. 60.
4   o.c. , p. 66.
5   o.c. , p. 75.
6   o.c. , p. 82.

evanescence flashes upon our minds when porting over things of space. It is the world of space that communicates to us the sense for temporality. Time, that which is beyond and independent of space, is everlasting; it is the world of space which is perishing. Things perish within time; time itself does not change. We should not speak of the flow or passage of time but of the flow or passage of space through time. It is not time that dies; it is the human body which dies in time. Temporality is an attribute of the world of space, of things of space. Time which is beyond space is beyond the division in past, present and future."[1]

This distinction between time and space he carries forward on to the final pages of his book. "Time, then, is otherness, a mystery that hovers above all categories. It is as if time and the mind were a world apart. Yet, it is only within time that there is fellowness and togetherness of all beings.

Every one of us occupies a portion of space. He takes it up exclusively. The portion of space which my body occupies is taken up by myself in exclusion of anyone else. Yet, no one possesses time. There is no moment which I possess exclusively. This very moment belongs to all living men as it belongs to me. We share time, we own space....."[2]

And he ends: "Creation is the language of God, Time is His song, and things of space the consonants in the song. To sanctify time is to sing the vowels in unison with Him.

This is the task of men: to conquer space and sanctify time.

We must conquer space in order to sanctify time....

Eternity utters a day."[3]

Heschel's publication prompts us to make the following remarks:

1. It is clear that he sees time as central to the Bible. But there is a big difference with the Western approach referred to in the previous paragraph. There the important position of time originates from its central role in the concept of history which is considered to be the dominating area of divine revelation in the Old Testament.

2. Heschel arrives at the central position of time, by connecting time with concepts such as holiness, spirit, eternity. It is this heavily-loaded idea of time to which he assigns the main role in the Bible.

3. To a certain extent Heschel emphasizes the contrast between time and space. It might be said even that he transfers the contrast between spirit and matter into that between space and time. But at the same time he uses much spatial terminology when he describes the characteristics of his concept of time.

4. It is clear that in such an approach, in order to prevent confusion, terminological and conceptual aspects require careful consideration.

---

1   o.c. , p. 96 - 97.
2   o.c. , p. 99.
3   o.c. , p. 101.

2.3. Y.Tesfai: Is history central to the Old Testament?

The object of the doctoral dissertation by Tesfai is "to examine the assertion that history is central to the Old Testament, and to set forth a programmatic statement which corrects the imbalance of emphasis on history and which offers an alternative."[1] In the first two chapters he explores the question whether history and the concept of time which goes with it, are the main interest of the Old Testament. On the basis of his investigation he concludes it does not, and he subsequently develops a view of time which is not based on the modern concept of history but is more in line with the approach of the Old Testament. With clear reference to Eccl. 3: 1 - 15, he presents this new picture of time under the heading "Times as pockets of experience," and summarizes it as follows:

"These texts from the various books of the Old Testament show that in the first place, times are differentiated by the nature of the experience to which they point, as set down by the Preacher. Their most important element is that they point to the nature of what happens. Times thus refer to the pockets of human experience bound together by means of some uniting factor such as the person or people undertaking the experience. Primarily, they are reference to experience. As such, they have a quantity which has its own limits, whether big or small. In the second place, these times are given by Yahweh alone. He alone administers them and determines how and when they occur."[2]

According to him, in this view "the difference between chronological and 'realistic' time does not obtain. An automatic succession of days simply cannot be imagined." .... It "precludes and is vehemently opposed to that rigid understanding of time as an irreversible, unceasing, forward bound line." It permits such flexibility that it "shatters the rigidity that Old Testament scholars impose upon it in the name of history."[3] These pockets of time are not so much parts of a movement which acquires its meaning only in terms of its goal, but "they may be more accurately comprehended in terms of space. This may be supported by the fact that some of the terms which are used as expressions of time are used to express categories of space as well. Such words as רחוק עולם, קדם,, and מועד, can be used to refer to both time and space, thus showing the interrelationship of time and space."[4]

He concludes that "on the whole the Old Testament is not interested in a more or less straight-lined time and the relationship of events to it...... The phrases convey meaning only in connection with other events because, in the Old Testament, events are identified in relationship to each other. They are not hung on the pegs of an imaginary, fixed line, so to speak. ... It is no cause for surprise then that the bulk of the Old Testament exhibits relatively little interest in both

---

1 Tesfai, 1975, p. 1.
2 o.c. , p. 44.
3 o.c. , p. 45 - 46.
4 o.c. , p. 47 - 48.

history and chronology."[1]

In a discussion of the 'credo' of Deut. 26, which has been used by Von Rad as the main fundament of his theology of the Old Testament, Tesfai remarks that this credo has its main setting in the cult, so "the dichotomy that von Rad wants to maintain between cult and history lacks any foundation in this case."[2] According to him the events referred to in the credo must in the first place be considered as "pockets of human experience. As such they are not inexorably bound to follow one another. Their relationship to one another is not one of cause and effect, and there is no inevitability to their connection. Instead, their linkage is flexible, for they are attached to each other loosely. They may be comprehended in figurative terms as seeds scattered over a field of human experience, in this case the life of Israel. Their position in the field does not necessarily have to be sequential. They may be related to each other in many and varied ways. Such a flexibility of the relationship of one event to another is well suited to the cultic understanding. ..... Such a segmented, we may say in that sense spatial, understanding of the events is necessitated and supported by the fact that the confession is made while in celebration of space. .... In fact .... it is space, in this case the land, which gives rise to the confession."[3]

In the final chapters of his book he explores the relation between Yahweh and space. By extensive quotations from all parts of the Old Testament he shows that the concept of the land is a basic concern to the Old Testament. At the end of the chapter concerned, he summarizes his findings as follows: "Space in the form of land was not peripheral to the life and thought of Ancient Israel; on the contrary, it was integral to both. Within it both Yahweh and the people were intimately related. So far as the extant evidence goes, it is clear that the land is part and parcel of the faith of Ancient Israel. The people's relation to the land is not interpreted just in terms of the use of the land, but rather in terms of its being an integral part of the faith of Ancient Israel. The land belongs to Yahweh and he alone gives it to the people; it occupies a major share of God's promise to his people. But even when it is given to them, he keeps watch over it in a very jealous manner. It is where he dwells, and where Israel is to enjoy his presence. If the people are not responsible towards the land and toward the covenant with God, it follows that they are expelled from it. The land, then, is at the centre of the life and faith of Ancient Israel."[4]

In a subsequent chapter, Tesfai examines the role of two other concepts with spatial connotations: temple and city. In this connection he also pays attention to the cult, and emphasizes the importance of space for it: "We must go so far as

---

1   o.c. , p. 50 - 51.
2   o.c. , p. 54.
3   o.c. , p. 55.
4   o.c. , p. 80.

to say that, without space, cult cannot take place."[1] A further subject he deals with is 'the presence of Yahweh': "The most important questions in the life of Ancient Israel revolved around the presence and the absence of Yahweh: How is Yahweh present? Where is he present? If he is present, how can his presence be celebrated? When he is present, how does he make himself known? To such significant questions, the cult with its personnel and objects gave the answers."[2]

The conclusion at the end of this chapter is very clear: "Yahweh's presence through the medium of space and his dwelling in a particular place - the temple, the city and the land - has a profound significance for the entire fabric of the life of Ancient Israel."[3]

And in the final conclusion of his publication he writes: "The foregoing study has been an attempt to show that the difficulty with the historical frame of reference arises because of a misunderstanding of the faith of Ancient Israel and of its traditions. So far as Israel was concerned, history was not the dominating center of the faith and certainly not the all-determining factor in her life, as has been maintained. Rather, an approach to the Old Testament which takes space as an interpretative principle succeeds in gaining a better understanding of the Old Testament. Even time ought to be viewed in terms of space.

The main concern of the Old Testament is the presence of Yahweh, which is mediated through space, and the meaning and consequences of that presence. Space is thus indispensable for coming to terms with the faith of Israel. Such places as the temple, the city and the land were variously used as the dwelling places of Yahweh. He is seen there; he reveals himself there; and he is worshipped there."[4]

Having completed our review of the thesis by Tesfai we would like to make the following remarks:

1. Whereas Albrektson had attacked the unique role, generally attributed to history in the faith of Israel and the Old Testament, by showing that history was of general importance in the whole ANE, Tesfai is more concerned with showing that history is not that important at all in the Old Testament, but that space and related concepts, such as presence, are just as important.

2. In his investigation of the role of time, he puts much emphasis on the things that happen, on the events. In fact, time is not important as such, but what is experienced in the time.

3. The 'spatial view' of time which he develops, occasionally gives rise to questions. For example, he writes: "Such an understanding of time, namely, an understanding which allows for the interpenetration of the past and the present, which is viewed spatially, and which does not draw a sharp line of demarcation

---

1   o.c. , p. 82.
2   o.c. , p. 83.
3   o.c. , p. 94.
4   o.c. , p. 95 - 96.

between what is past and what is present, exhibits itself especially in relation to the era of David."[1] According to the usual view of space, one of its characteristics is that two things cannot occupy the same place at the same time. So what does the author mean by "interpenetration of the past and present, which is viewed spatially"?

4. Of particular interest to our investigation is the attempt undertaken by Tesfai to underline the importance of space, and concepts with spatial overtones in the faith and life of ancient Israel.

2.4. S.L.Terrien: The presence of God as the center of biblical faith.

Although the subtitle of his book refers to biblical theology, seven out of its ten chapters deal with the Old Testament only. Its main concern is with "the reality of the presence of God" which "stands at the center of biblical faith."[2]

A second basic theme is that "Old Testament religion differed from the religions of classical Egypt, Asia Anterior, and the Mediterranean world precisely because it manifested itself through a unique complex of interaction between cultus and faith."[3]

In an introductory discussion of recent developments in the science of the Old Testament, the author opposes in particular the view that the concept of the covenant is the fundament of Israel's faith, and he concludes: "It is the Hebraic theology of presence, not the covenant ceremonial, that constitutes the field of forces which links - across the biblical centuries - the fathers of Israel, the reforming prophets, the priests of Jerusalem, the psalmists of Zion, the Jobian poet, and the bearers of the gospel. The history of biblical religion hinges upon the growth and transformation of the Hebraic theology of presence."[4] His general idea of this concept he outlines as follows: "Because it brings together the divine asserverations, 'I am Yahweh,' of the Hebraic theophany, and 'I am the Lord,' of the Christian faith in the resurrection of Jesus, the motif of presence induces a magnetic field of forces which maintains a dynamic tension, in the whole of Scripture, between divine self-disclosure and self-concealment. The proximity of God creates a memory and an anticipation of certitude, but it always defies human appropriation. The presence remains elusive."[5]

Subsequently, Terrien investigates the ways in which the presence of God is described in the various traditions of the Old Testament. The titles of his chapters are informative about his ideas of the characteristic features of each tradition. We will present brief summaries of each chapter.

---

1   o.c. , p. 56.
2   Terrien, 1978, p. XXVII.
3   o.c. , p. 2.
4   o.c. , p. 31.
5   o.c. , p. 43.

a. Epiphanic visitations to the patriarchs.

The author prefers this special expression for the experience of the presence of God attributed to the patriarchs by the Old Testament in order to underline its differences from theophanies described elsewhere: "In a Hebrew 'theophany,' Yahweh is not really 'seen' by man, but only 'heard,' although there are visible signs of his presence . .... they are free from the display of natural mirabilia; and they are couched in the style of simple meetings, naively and concretely described as the sudden encounter of two strangers who were going their separate ways."[1] After a survey of what happened during these 'visitations,' and in particular of what was said during them, Terrien summarizes: "The various epiphanic speeches are consequently linked together, not by the requirement of cultus, sacerdotal college, or ritual act related to sacred space, but by the principle of continuity in historical time. The God who manifests his presence to Abraham, Isaac, and Jacob is the same God who summons Moses at Sinai."[2]

b. The Sinai theophanies.

According to Terrien these are different from the patriarchal stories in several aspects:

- they are ascribed to one single place;
- at the same time there is no reference to a single shrine: "The stories of the Mosaic theophanies became the literary anchor for the clustering of most of the legislation of Israel, so much so that the final form of the Pentateuch came to be known as the Torah, or 'Law,' and its entire composition became ascribed to Moses by fundamentalist Jews and Christians."[3]
- they contain clear references to natural wonder.
- they are concerned with the theologoumenon of the name.

In the remaining part of the chapter Terrien discusses the various aspects of the theology of the name, especially its relation to another motif of the Sinai theophanies, the glory of God. He summarizes his results as follows: "While many studies have been devoted to the motif of divine glory in Hebrew religion, it is not generally pointed out that the ancient traditions of Israel practically ignored the notion. The northern narratives and the Deuteronomists stress other symbols, such as the name. Because the southerners and the majority of the psalmists have evolved in the shadow of the Davidic monarchy and around the mythology of Zion, it was they who emphasized the significance of the term. The Jerusalem priests and their descendants saw no conflict between the theologoumenon of presence through the name and the theologoumenon of presence through the glory. The two terms became interchangeable in nascent Judaism during the Babylonian exile and the Persian period." At the same time Terrien sees that in the third theophany on Mt. Horeb, "which has been

---

1   o.c. , p. 69, 70.
2   o.c. , p. 94.
3   o.c. , p. 108.

preserved chiefly according to the northern tradition, glory is made dramatically distinct from name, for it remains, as the inner characteristic of the transcendent Godhead, beyond the reach of even a man of God like Moses."[1]

c. The presence in the temple.

In this context Terrien sees the difference embedded in a wider distinction: "Here again it will be useful to distinguish between a theologoumenon of presence through space and a theologoumenon of presence through time. Such a distinction is supported by documentary evidence. It will lead to a more accurate representation of the difference, already observed in the ancient traditions, between a theology of the name and a theology of glory."[2]

Both differences play an important role in his presentation of the development in which he discusses the ark of Yahweh, the tent of meeting and the temple of Solomon. Repeatedly the tensions between the two sides are pointed to, for example in his discussion of the temple: "Once again, we witness a profound tension between two opposite views of presence: the story of the introit of the ark objectifies the psychological awareness of presence and localizes it in a man-made structure. It seeks religious certainty by attempting to revitalize the neolithic and Bronze Age myth of sacred space. Solomon's long prayer, on the contrary, attempts to safeguard a theology of spatial transcendence: it even demythicizes 'heaven' as the spatial container of divinity. At the same time it accommodates to the needs of man the belief in the elusiveness of presence and recognizes within the sacred edifice a reality which justifies its construction."[3]

d. The prophetic vision.

According to Terrien, "the tradition of Elijah on Mt. Horeb (1 Kings 19) offers a dramatic turning point in the Hebraic theology of presence, for it closed the era of theophany and relegated it to the realm of an unrepeatable past. At the same time, it opened the era of prophetic vision, where miracles of nature became miracles of character."[4] In a further comment on the same pericope he writes: "The story of Elijah on Mt. Horeb presents itself chronologically and thematically as a transition between the legenda of the presence in historical events and the historical sobriety of the records of the great prophets, for whom presence is individualized, interiorized, and often curtailed or adumbrated. Three points of theological significance arise:

1. The nature of the encounter between God and the prophet is that of a passing by or an approach. .....

2. The God who is coming is altogether different from the one that man expects. He is not the God whom memory, reason, or imagination anticipates....

3. The encounter between God and man does not operate in a historical vacuum.

---

1   o.c. , p. 145 - 46.
2   o.c. , p. 162.
3   o.c. , p. 197 - 98.
4   o.c. , p. 229.

In the presence of the Hebraic God, man is not separated from his cultural context."[1]

While reviewing the visions of the various prophets, the author considers in particular the 'hiddenness' of God: "The passive latinity of the expression Deus absconditus, the 'hidden God,' may fail to convey the meaning of active and sustained determination which the Hebrew original carries. For the prophet, there is no doubt that the God who hides his face is very much alive. During the eclipse of God, the man of faith formulates a theology of hope, and he is able to wait creatively, for he remembers the power of his prophetic vision. The presence which conceals itself is not an absence."[2] By this faith prophets like Jeremiah and Ezekiel could live, even when the presence left the temple: "They extolled the presence in its mode of prophetic vision, but they could survive the awareness of absence for they knew how to wait for the final epiphany. .... Once again, the ear prevailed over the eye, since the survivor's faith could renounce space for the sake of time."[3]

e. The psalmody of presence.

After having noticed the wide diversity of styles and attitudes in the Psalter, Terrien remarks describes their common characteristics as follows: "By sensing the relativity of cultic ceremonial and by experiencing spiritual alienation, they affirmed in effect the freedom of Yahweh from the techniques of ritual and the resources of institutionalized religion. Even the Royal Psalms, composed by kings or for their use, revealed the religious paradox which characterizes, par excellence, the ancient Hebrews: intimacy with the Godhead tempered by the dread of divine abandon."[4] He gives short comments on a large number of psalms and subsequently mentions another trait of the psalmists: "The professional artists of the Zion ceremonies were authentic theologians, for they refused to separate the sense of wonder from their intellectual reflection. They adored their God with the aesthetics of the rational and the emotion of the mind."[5]

f. The play of Wisdom.

According to Terrien, "the word hokmah, 'wisdom' escapes precise definition, for it covers a wide range of usages. ..... As a personified figure, wisdom belongs to the realm of divinity. ..... In comparing wisdom to a woman, (the wise) expressed in their own way their theology of presence."[6]

In a discussion of the books of Job, Proverbs and Ecclesiastes he emphasizes that in their way they underlined the "theocentricity of all life."[7] The sages

---

1   o.c. , p. 234.
2   o.c. , p. 251.
3   o.c. , p. 268.
4   o.c. , p. 280.
5   o.c. , p. 337.
6   o.c. , p. 351, 352.
7   o.c. , p. 375.

"shifted their attention from history - a stage now empty of God - to the theater of the universe, where they detected his presence."[1]

g. The final epiphany.

In this chapter, Terrien reviews how Judaism evolved from the kingdom of Judah, which disappeared in 587 B.C. "Hebraism had been founded on divine presence. Judaism arose from divine absence. .... Deprived of sacred space, they discovered the sacrality of time."[2] In line with this development, he discusses the day of the Sabbath and the day of Atonement, and the "Day of the Lord". He notices that in particular with this 'latter day' spatially coloured themes like that of the new temple and the heavenly Jerusalem occupied a central place. Another feature he mentions is that apocalyptics like the sectarians of Qumran "transferred the symbolism of the temple to their own community, which they called 'a sanctuary' and 'the holy of holies.'"[3]

After having referred to the word Shekinah, he writes: "For more than a thousand years, the religion of Israel was dominated by the experience, the memory, or the hope of divine presence. .... The abstract word 'omnipresence,' however, is inadequate to describe their awareness of communion. The entire literature now preserved in the Hebrew Bible referred to specific 'events' of divine manifestation in terms of time and space. ..... At the dawn of the Roman Empire, a handful of Jews hailed from their own ranks a new prophet through whom they discerned a radically new mode of divine nearness. A man became for them the bearer of the presence."[4] This remark provides the entry to the final chapters of the book, which deal with the New Testament, and which fall outside the scope of our subject.

As usual we end our discussion with a few general remarks:

1. The word 'presence' stands for a wide concept with both temporal and spatial connotations. The relation between these two requires clarification. In particular it would be useful if it were possible to make some clear form of connection between 'presence in time' and 'presence in space,' and theological concepts such as the Name and the Glory.

2. It also would be interesting to know more about the way in which this broad concept, the presence of God, was experienced in detail in the various literary layers of the Old Testament.

3. In any case the study of Terrien shows that it is possible to use this concept to present the theological ideas within the Old Testament in a coherent way.

---

1   o.c. , p. 380.
2   o.c. , p. 390.
3   o.c. , p. 403, 404.
4   o.c. , p. 404, 405.

2.5. J.D.Levenson: Sinai and Zion, the route over two mountains as entry to the Jewish Bible.

In the introduction to his book, Levenson discusses a few aspects of the development of the theology of the Old Testament: "One of the distinctive aspects of the modern study of the Bible, as it has developed in the past century and a half, has been the effort to delineate a theology of the Old Testament alone, with minimal or negligible reference to the New Testament...... The sad fact, however, is that the endeavor known as 'Old Testament theology' has been, as its name suggests, an almost exclusively Gentile affair. ..... The two major institutions of the religion of ancient Israel in which Christians, especially Protestant, stereotypes continue to dominate are also, it can be argued, the two major foci of ancient Israelite religion itself: law (Torah) and Temple."[1]

After having given a few examples of the 'negative views' of Torah and Temple still prevailing in the theology of the Old Testament, Levenson states that the goal of his book is "to present these two foci of the religion of ancient Israel, Torah and temple, from a perspective which is different from that of the consensus."[2] He wants to use the "immense discoveries in archaeology, epigraphy, and history," and the "post-biblical Jewish tradition."

What makes his study particularly relevant for our subject is that Levenson arranges his discussion of the two themes, Law and Temple, around the traditions of two mountains: Sinai and Zion. It will be of interest to see if spatial characteristics of these locations play a role in his presentations of the topics concerned.

In his chapter on Sinai, Levenson starts by emphasizing the "sense of mystery that pervades the account of the theophany, the apparition of God, that was believed to have occurred on Mount Sinai. ..... What really happened on Mount Sinai? The honest historian must answer that we can say almost nothing in reply to this question. We do not know even the location of the mountain. ..... We know nothing about Sinai, but an immense amount of traditions concerning Sinai."[3] According to him the failure to locate the site of the great mountain of Mosaic revelation "is not simply one of the modern science of topography. Rather, there is a mysterious extraterrestial quality to the mountain in the most developed and least allusive biblical references to it. Sinai/Horeb seem(s) to exist in no man's land."[4]

He considers the covenant, as exemplified by treaties between a suzerain and a vassal, as "a central image, perhaps the central image, for the relationship of

---

1   Levenson, 1985, p. 1, 2.
2   o.c. , p. 3.
3   o.c. , p. 16, 17.
4   o.c. , p. 21.

Israel to her God."[1] and explains how he sees various features of this image operating in practice, viz. in history. And he concludes: "This preference for historical terms over cosmic-primordial symbols sets the Sinai traditions off markedly from those of Zion."[2]

In the remaining part of this chapter Levenson discusses a number of these 'historical issues,' such as the role of the commandments and ethics, the kingship of God and the kingship of man, and the recitation of the Shma as the "rabbinic covenantal renewal ceremony. It is the portal to continuing life in covenant."[3]

Right at the beginning of his chapter on Zion, Levenson makes clear what is one of the differences between the two mountains: "Zion, unlike Sinai, was a known site in Israel. The transfer of the divine home from Sinai to Zion meant that God was no longer seen as dwelling in an extraterritorial no man's land, but within the borders of the Israelite community."[4] Another difference is the emphasis on the visual aspect of the revelation, which is connected with the temple: ".. this concept of the Temple as a primarily visual (as opposed to auditory) vehicle for the knowledge of God is central to the very idea of the shrine on Zion."[5]

As with Sinai Levenson sees a form of covenant which can serve as a kind of model for the relationship between God and his people, but in this case it is the 'covenant of grant,' as identified and described by Weinfeld, which leads to a difference in emphasis: "Rather, the Davidic covenant, a covenant of grant, looks beyond the vicissitudes of history, since they cease to be critical. This covenant fixes attention to that which is constant beneath - or perhaps I should say, above - the flux of history. .... And since the focus is upon the constancy of God rather than the changeability of man, it brings to light what is secure and inviolable, whereas the Sinaitic texts tend to emphasize the precariousness of life and the consequent need for a continuously reinvigorated obedience."[6]

Levenson subsequently argues in favour of the 'vitality of myth in Biblical Israel,' and explains the concept of the 'cosmic mountain,' and how, in the context of Israel, this role is fulfilled by Zion. As far as spatial categories is concerned, it is worth while to point to the following aspects:
- the difference between 'spiritual' and 'physical' nearness in geography: "The point is that we must not understand biblical geography as a statement of a scientific nature. Rather .... geography is simply a visible form of theology."[7]
- the most central aspect of the cosmic mountain is the presence of God or the gods. On Zion this presence is strongly connected with the Temple, which is not

---

1   o.c. , p. 37.
2   o.c. , p. 41.
3   o.c. , p. 86.
4   o.c. , p. 91.
5   o.c. , p. 95.
6   o.c. , p. 101.
7   o.c. , p. 116.

so much a place in the world, but "the epitome of the world, a concentrated form of its essence, a miniature of the cosmos."[1]

- the fact that the Temple is not a place of the earth, also means that it assumes heavenly characteristics, it is "the earthly manifestation of the heavenly Temple, which is beyond localization. The Temple on Zion is the antitype to the cosmic archetype. The real Temple is the one to which it points, the one in 'heaven,' which cannot be distinguished sharply from its earthly manifestation."[2]

- as the Temple is considered to be the essence of the world, its construction, and the construction "of its predecessor, the Tabernacle, should mirror the creation of the world."[3]

After having discussed the meaning of the cosmic mountain in Israel, Levenson, in his final paragraph on Zion, points to a remarkable contradiction: "No people ever placed greater importance upon their land than did the Jews of ancient times, and yet no ancient people other than they has survived the loss of their land. The reason is that the land and the Temple, which are really one, always possessed a significance beyond what one sees if he examines only their mundane reality - in a word, a cosmic significance. Since the land was more than a territory, and since the Temple was more than a building, the loss of both did not mean death. The land was no longer available, but the covenant whose observance grounded Israel's tenure in it remained in force. .... The destruction of the Temple did not close the gates of heaven to those who walk the path of Sinai up to the world of which Zion is the symbol."[4]

In his concluding chapter, in which Levenson discusses the 'manifold relationships between Sinai and Zion,' the following topics are mentioned: the relation between the North and the South in Israel, the role of the kingship, the relation between Moses and David, and the covenants of which they were the central figures. In this discussion he argues that Christianity replaced the Mosaic covenant by the Davidic, whereas despite apparent contradictions the Hebrew Bible and Jewish life maintained both covenants together.

As a preliminary reaction to this review of Levenson's book, we should like to make two remarks:

1. To what extent could the relation between time and space be used to describe the relation between Sinai and Zion?

2. There seems to be an unexpected reversion: Sinai, the mountain of theophany, mystery, impressive natural phenomena, seems to be related more closely with history, whereas Zion, the mountain of the temple, of human ritual and visual phenomena, seems to acquire more extra-terrestrial qualities.

---

1   o.c. , p. 138.
2   o.c. , p. 140.
3   o.c. , p. 142.
4   o.c. , p. 181, 184.

2.6. F. Gorman: Space, time and status in the Priestly theology.

This study is devoted to the ritual system of P in order to obtain an entry into its theology. It takes its starting-point in earlier work by J. Milgrom, B. Levine, M. Haran and G.J. Wenham, who "sought to uncover and explicate a larger conceptual framework for understanding Priestly ritual. These scholars have attempted to address the question not only of the operation of the Priestly rituals, but also the meaning of those rituals. ..... The present study takes these works as its starting point and seeks to develop more fully the precise nature of the conceptual, ideological, and theological framework that informs specific Priestly rituals and which is, in turn, constructed, in part, by those rituals. It is argued that the Priestly ritual system is best understood as the meaningful enactment of world in the context of Priestly creation theology. The theoretical and methodological framework for this study has been drawn primarily from cultural anthropology."[1]

The term 'status' as used in this study "moves in two directions. First, it refers to a person's standing within society. This may be understood in institutional terms, e.g. , the priesthood, but ... also .... in terms of the categories of purity and pollution. .... Secondly ... the priests are concerned with the status of objects and space. At the center of this concern is the tabernacle structure and the holy of holies. The state of this holy area, set apart from all other areas, must be carefully maintained."[2]

Gorman recognizes "that ritual is a social act which takes place in a specific socio-cultural context." The latter refers "primarily to the context of meaning which gives rise to and is embedded in the rituals. It is a world of meaning that gives shape to and is shaped by the rituals. Thus, Priestly rituals must be understood in the context of the world of meaning operative in and through the rituals. The interpreter must seek to discover the world view that stands behind the rituals, that gives rise to the rituals, that is enacted and made real in the rituals. The 'world' of ritual is a world of meaning, a world of symbols; it is the world of meaning and significance within which the ritual is conceptualized, constructed, and enacted."[3]

Regarding time and place, these are "two of the most fundamental elements of cultural situations. ..... Quite often there is a convergence of time and place that produces a matrix calling for specified ritual action. A certain type of behavior that is appropriate at one place may not be appropriate at another place. The same is true of time. The reason for this is that space and time are both creations of culture and, thereby, receive symbolic meanings. Both space and time are 'interpreted' and 'conventionalized.' Thus, culture supplies 'meanings' to

---

1   Gorman, 1990, p. 9.
2   o.c. , p. 10 - 11.
3   o.c. , p. 14, 15.

space and time, which then converge to create situations for ritual."[1]

As already said above, Gorman considers the tabernacle to be the key spatial category of Priestly ritual. Another important spatial distinction is "that between 'inside the camp' and 'outside the camp.' ..... Such categorical distinctions between types of space are examples of a socially defined order constructed by means of divisions and separations. It is appropriate to speak of the establishing of boundaries, lines of demarcation, between basic categories of space."[2]

According to Gorman, the importance of divisions and separations has to do with the Priestly concern for order: "Indeed, at the heart of Priestly theology is the belief that Yahweh brought into being an ordered world and that at the heart of that created order is a ritual order. For the priestly writers, creation and cult cannot be separated; they are dynamically interelated aspects of the Priestly world view."[3] Now this order is in a state of permanent threat: "In the Priestly writings the two most significant threats to order are sin and defilement. It thus becomes necessary for a means to be established by which the created order may be maintained and, when necessary, restored. The thesis is that the Priestly cult is the means by which this is accomplished. ..... The Priestly traditionists see a properly structured cultic order as a central element of cosmic order."[4] A third form of order is the structure of Israelite society, and, according to the author "these various orders are not independent of one another but are intricately connected. ..... The conceptual element that holds these three orders together is that of order through separation. ..... The separation of conceptual categories focusses on three areas in the Priestly ritual material - space, time, and status - and Priestly ritual functions within the context of clearly defined and demarcated categories of space, time, and status."[5]

Gorman argues that the Priestly redaction of the Sinai material (Ex. 24: 15 - Lev. 16: 32) "reflects a theological concern for sacred space," at the heart of which stands the tabernacle. "Thus, the tabernacle structure joins together the two ideas of Yahweh's presence in the midst of Israel and Israel's presence before Yahweh in the sacrified cult."[6]

In order to underline that spatial categories play a crucial role in the enactment of the Priestly rituals, Gorman presents "graphically the basic map of the tabernacle cult. This map is operative throughout Priestly rituals. It will be clear that space is understood as more than just a series of places, but takes on specific qualities with specific meanings in the Priestly ritual system."[7]

Subsequently Gorman investigates a number of Priestly rituals, especially as far

---

1   o.c. , p. 27 - 28.
2   o.c. , p. 32.
3   o.c. , p. 39.
4   o.c. , p. 42.
5   o.c. , p. 44 - 45.
6   o.c. , p. 46, p. 49.
7   o.c. , p. 55.

as the role of space, time and status is concerned, and indeed finds that in all cases these factors are shaping and meaningful categories of the rituals.

He concludes his study as follows: "Thus, Priestly ritual must be seen as a complex, interactive system of three distinct elements: the world view in which the created order is seen to be made up of cosmos, society, and cult; a concern for the categories of order/chaos, holy/profane, clean/unclean, and life/death; and, finally, the categories of space, time, and status. It is as these three elements of meaning and concern interact in ritual that the theology of the priests can be seen and understood. Ritual was not only a way of acting, it was also a way of thinking, speaking, and creating."[1]

After reviewing his book a few comments seem to be appropriate:

1. In the series of publications included in this chapter, Gorman's book provides a more or less detailed study of a particular aspect of the theological world of the Old Testament. He proves that for this area space is one of the important categories.

2. It is not always clear what is the 'status' of certain statements which he announces as 'thesis.' For example, the thesis that the Priestly cult is "the means .... by which the created order may be maintained and, when necessary, restored,"[2] is it a result from the previous line of reasoning, or a working hypothesis which needs confirmation by further research?

3. The point of view, that "space and time are both creations of culture and, thereby, receive symbolic meanings"[3] is one-sided, to say the least.

2.7. Summary.

This chapter has been written with the objective of obtaining some idea of the role of space and of concepts with a 'spatial connotation' in the presentation of the theology of the Old Testament.

In the publication of Heschel space more or less plays the role of the contrast, the opponent to time, while the latter receives the dominant place. Tesfai is more concerned with questioning and criticizing existing time-dominated approaches within the theology of the Old Testament. But Terrien, Levenson and Gorman, each in his particular way, show that space and 'space-related concepts' can be used in a positive sense to obtain a coherent view of Old Testament theology as a whole, or of the theology of one of its tradition layers.

It can even be said that their appoaches shed new light on a number of phenomena, such as the concept of the presence of God, and the role of the cult in Israel.

In all publications reviewed in this chapter, space becomes 'loaded' with experience, or 'translated' into tangible manifestations such as land, temple or

---

1   o.c. , p. 234.
2   o.c. , p. 42.
3   o.c. , p. 28.

tabernacle. This is understandable, since we cannot expect to find in the Old Testament statements on the characteristics of space as a more or less independent category. From our survey of paragraph 1.2., we know that the idea of time and space as separate categories is a development within Western science and philosophy.

But the question arises whether space has features or properties, which are characteristic, especially compared to those of time, and which 'prohibit' loading space with every possible experience. This leads to the question of the relationship and difference between time and space. And ultimately we arrive at the question of the fundamental characteristics of both.

A complete coverage of these questions falls outside the scope of our investigation. But they should not be forgotten entirely. For in the publications reviewed in this chapter we have found a few instances of space being considered in a way which seems questionable (see our remark 3 on Tesfai and remark 3 on Gorman). In both cases it does not seem to be a matter of wording alone, but rather of conceptualizing.

In addition both Heschel and Tesfai ascribe to the Old Testament a way of experiencing time, which is, according to their own saying, completely different from ours. But they do not provide extensive data to support their ideas in this respect.

It is also remarkable that in the theology of the Old Testament the concept of history seems to be connected in particular with time and time experience, whereas we would expect space to be important as well, since (historical) events occur in time and space both.

Summarizing, we can say that our brief survey shows that space and spatial concepts are used in current reflection on the theology of the Old Testament. It also indicates that apart from terminological issues, some more fundamental problems on the basic characteristics of space (and time) ask for attention.

We hope that our investigation of the perception of space in the Old Testament will contribute to a better understanding of some of the issues involved.

3. THE INVESTIGATION OF THE PERCEPTION OF SPACE
IN THE OLD TESTAMENT:
A SURVEY OF THE LITERATURE.

3.1. Introduction.

In this chapter we try to obtain an idea of what is known about the perception of space in the Old Testament. In order to ensure that as much relevant material as possible is included, the subject area of our literature search has been wider, covering general aspects of the experience of space as well.

The publications thought to be relevant will be reviewed in paragraph 3.2. The final section of this paragraph will contain our first reaction to these publications. It appears that in this relatively limited area of research there exist a number of methodological problems, which require further investigation. Thus, the rest of this chapter is used for an exploration of these issues, which demanded a more extensive literature search covering the field of the application of linguistics in the study of the Old Testament.

In view of its scope and importance, the critical approach to the use of linguistic data in biblical research by Barr is reviewed separately in paragraph 3.3.

Following Barr's publication a lengthy debate developed among Old Testament scholars covering the methodological issues involved. In the early stages of the debate, much attention was paid to the so-called Linguistic Relativity Hypothesis (abbreviated: LRH), so this is the keyword in our survey of those aspects of that debate which are relevant for our topic. It is reported in paragraph 3.4.

Although it had been recognized from the beginning that the area of the controversy formed part of the broader subject of the general relation between language and cognition, only gradually did scholars start to consider it within the wider perspectives of linguistics and its use in Old Testament science. We also surveyed the recent literature of this field of study with the aim of finding information relevant to the methodological issues in our target area. A review is given in paragraph 3.5.

The final paragraph 3.6. summarizes the results of our investigation of the literature of the science of the Old Testament and explains why we decided to continue our study by exploring the literature of other disciplines.

3.2. The perception of space in the Old Testament.

3.2.1. Introduction.

In our literature search, we found four publications which discuss certain aspects of the perception of space in the Old Testament. These will be reviewed separately in the subsequent sections. Section 3.2.6. summarizes a few studies of Hebrew words relating to space, whereas the final section contains our first reaction to the literature reviewed in this paragraph.

3.2.2. The comparison of Hebrew and Greek thought; Boman.
In 1952 Boman published a study entitled "Das hebräische Denken im Vergleich mit dem griechischen,"[1] in which he wrote a separate chapter on space.
But before investigating this chapter in detail, it is worth while to pay attention to the general objective of the book, and the method used by the author to achieve it. His subject area is the difference between the Hebrew environment of the Old Testament and the Greek world of the New Testament and (early) Christianity: "Nun sind nicht nur die beiden Sprachen wesentlich verschieden, sondern auch die damit verbundene Vorstellungs- und Denkart."[2] In line with the idea of the difference in thought, Boman sees the objective of his study as follows: "Es ist denn zweifellos eine wichtige Aufgabe, den formalen Unterschied zwischen dem griechischen und dem hebräischen Denken allseitig zu analysieren und zu beleuchten. Erst dann ist es möglich, zu sehen und zu beurteilen, ob und wie weit auch der Inhalt des Christentums von dem Umdenken berührt worden ist. Wir haben deshalb die Untersuchung auf einen Vergleich der Gedankenwelt des Alten Testaments mit der Gedankenwelt der Griechen, und zwar hauptsächlich der Philosophen, insbesondere Platons, beschränkt."[3]
Regarding methodology, the following quotation is illustrative: "Eine einzelne Methode ist in der Abhandlung nicht durchgeführt. Ihr Zweck war ja, die Eigenart des hebräischen Denkens im Vergleich mit dem griechischen darzustellen, und zu diesem Zweck mußte jedesmal die Methode benutzt werden, die für den betreffenden Stoff am geeignetsten schien. Dem Verfasser war aber besonders daran gelegen, dem Vorwurf der Spekulation zu entgehen. Er führte daher überall eine solide und vielleicht gelegentlich - vor allem zu Anfang - zu umfassende empirische Grundlage seiner Anschauungen aus der hebräischen (alttestamentlichen) und griechischen Sprache und Literatur an und berief sich möglichst viel auf anerkannte wissenschaftliche Autoritäten."[4] Apparently Boman wants to base his results on facts, for as he wrote in an additional note to the quotation above, he did not consider a philosophical-deductive method to be suitable for his purpose.
We will now examine to what results this empirical method leads as far as the Hebrew experience of space is concerned. The first paragraph of the chapter on space deals with 'Die Form,' and starts with an explanation of the difference between form and contents: "Ein Gegenstand besteht nach griechischer und überhaupt nach europäischer Auffassung aus Form (Gestalt) und Inhalt (Masse, Materie). Wenn wir von dem Gegenstande die Form des Gegenstandes abstrahieren könnten, bliebe die formlose Masse übrig. Die Form des

---

1   Boman, 1977.
2   o.c. , p. 11.
3   o.c. , p. 13.
4   o.c. , p. 16.

Gegenstandes stellen wir uns weiter als seinen Umriß oder seine Konturen vor. Wenn wir bei den Gegenständen von allem Erfahrungsinhalt absehen, bleiben nach Kant die leeren Formen übrig, die den Raum anschaulich darstellen."[1] Boman points to a few differences between Kant and Plato, as examples of European and Greek thought, but for him the similarity between them is very clear: for both, forms are of utmost importance.

At this point Boman signals an important difference with the Hebrew thought: "Es ist bezeichnend für die Hebräer, daß ihnen die Form dermaßen gleichgültig ist, daß sie überhaupt kein Wort für Form und für Synonyme wie Umriß, Konturen (Gestalt) gebildet haben. Zwar hat man eine Menge Wörter, die wir mit unserem Wort 'Gestalt' wiedergeben können, aber keines, das die Form des Gegenstandes bezeichnet. Die Israeliten interessieren sich nur für die Gestalt als Erscheinung, oder etwas unzutreffend ausgedrückt: für den Inhalt der Gestalt. Der Ausdruck ist insofern unzutreffend, als er eine Unterscheidung, zwischen Form und Inhalt voraussetzt, eine Unterscheidung, die die Israeliten nicht machen. Sofern er aber aussagt, daß die Israeliten sich am wenigsten für die Form interessieren, ist er zutreffend."[2]

On about half a page Boman subsequently discusses the following Hebrew words: דמות, צורה, קצב, תמונה and מראה. In his opinion none of them has the meaning 'form,' and he concludes: "Die hebräische Sprache hat demnach keine eigenen Ausdrücke gebildet zur Bezeichnung des Umrisses oder der Konturen eines Gegenstandes und bedarf ihrer auch nicht."[3]

At the end of the paragraph Boman attempts to describe how the Hebrews managed to experience the world visually without using concepts like perimeter, form or contour. According to Boman, Europeans, who believe that they can actually see contours etc. , are wrong; in fact these are only imaginary lines which they 'put in' in order to obtain a proper image of the visual impression. "Form und Gestalt in der Bedeutung von Umriß und Konturen gibt es also auf unseren Zeichnungen, nicht aber in der Wirklichkeit. Nach einiger Übung können wir unsere natürliche Neigung zurückdrängen und die Gegenstände ohne Konturen sehen, zeichnen und malen. Das ist eben, was die Israeliten von Natur aus tun. Sie sehen die Gegenstände so, wie sie mit ihren Farben und Schatten sind, sie empfinden ihren Härtegrad und ihre Temperatur mit ihren Händen. Konturen sehen sie aber nicht, deshalb brauchen sie auch keine Wörter dafür zu bilden."[4]

In the next paragraph on space, Boman discusses the concept of 'boundary,' which according to him is perhaps the most important line in the European way of thinking. He describes as its characteristic feature that it lies between two

---

1   o.c. , p. 134.
2   o.c. , p. 135.
3   o.c. , p. 136.
4   o.c. , p. 136.

areas having no width of its own. He subsequently investigates the Hebrew words גבול and גבולה, and concludes from their use in a number of texts of the Old Testament, that they never refer to a mathematical line, but always to a thing: a mountain or mountain range, a river or some other natural boundary. And according to him these boundaries have a wider meaning than just demarcating an area. "Wie die Israeliten die natürlichen Zeiteinheiten durch Angaben ihrer Enden feststellen, so auch die Natürlichen Gebietseinheiten, die Länder, die Inseln, die Welt. ..... Wenn ein Israelit den Zustand auf der ganzen Erde beschreiben will, braucht er nur die Verhältnisse in den äußersten Gegenden zu erwähnen."[1] As a consequence of this opinion Boman suggests that the word איים, which is usually translated by 'islands, shores,' should be translated as 'world,' and the word גבול ('boundary') as 'country.'

At the end of this paragraph he writes: "Von entscheidender Bedeutung ist, daß גבול mit Synonymen nie eine Scheidelinie zwischen zwei Gebieten bedeutet und deshalb prinzipiell nicht dasselbe wie unser Begriff Grenze ist. Das ist kein Mangel in der Sprache und Vorstellungswelt der Hebräer, denn die Grenzlinie ist nicht in der Natur oder in der sinnlichen Welt gegeben. Sie ist ein reines Produkt unseres (europäischen) Geistes, eine Hilfslinie, die wir nötig haben, um von unseren Voraussetzungen aus die Welt praktisch und theoretisch zu beherrschen. ..... Eine Hilfslinie sollte man aber nach verrichtetem Dienst auswischen, d.h. sich bewußt werden, daß die Grenze eine Hilfslinie ist, die in der Wirklichkeit nicht vorkommt, und von der man also in seinen Vorstellungen und in seinem Denken zuletzt absehen kann und soll. Dazu sind aber die wenigsten imstande. Die Israeliten müssen die Vorteile unserer Denkweise entbehren, sind aber auch von den Nachteilen befreit."[2]

The final paragraph of the chapter on space bears the title: "Das Grenzenlose oder das Unendliche." Boman tries to demonstrate the characteristic differences between Hebrew and Greek-European thought by exploring the concept "grenzenlose Größe." To European standards this appears to be a contradictio in adjecto, and Boman discusses a number of solutions suggested by European thinkers. Kant, in his considerations on infinite time (= eternity) and infinite space (= cosmos), simply rejected the problem of infinity, since he thought all experience to be finite, hence declaring that infinity does not belong to the realm of empirical data. The attempts by others who try to explain the concept of infinity by means of the idea of movement are not acceptable to Boman either.

He thinks that the most simple solution can be obtained when we start from the concept of infinity itself: "Jede Gesichtswahrnehmung ist ja buchstäblich grenzenlos. .... Von einer das Blickfeld umgebenden Grenze, etwa einem Kreise, ist gar nichts zu spüren. Das Grenzenlose ist also nicht das Schwierige und

---

1   o.c. , p. 136, 137.
2   o.c. , p. 138.

Problematische, sondern das Natürliche, Ursprüngliche und immer aufs neue Gegebene. Die Grenzen, die von uns gebildet und in die Wahrnehmungen hineingelegt worden sind, um als Konturen um die Gegenstände zu dienen, können, wie die Semiten es beweisen, entbehrt werden."[1]

Boman concludes this paragraph by pointing to the relevance of infinity for religion: "Der geborene religiöse Mensch lebt in der unendlichen und ewigen Welt wie in seiner wahren Heimat (Fil. 3, 20). Es ist deshalb keine Zufälligkeit, daß die Semiten, die ohne Grenzen auskommen können, Schöpfer von drei Weltreligionen geworden sind. Für sie ist Unendlichkeit oder Grenzenlosigkeit kein Problem."[2]

Except in the chapter on space, Boman discusses spatial aspects in other parts of his book. For example, in the chapter on "Größe und Zahl" he emphasizes the importance of the mathematical ideas of the Greek: "Weil die Raumanschauung die gegebene Denkform der Griechen war und die sichtbare Form der Dinge ihre Aufmerksamkeit auf sich lenkte, mußte für sie die Geometrie der wichtigste Zweig der Mathematik werden. ...... So war ihnen der Begriff groß, Größe in erster Reihe etwas Räumliches. Die hebräische Sprache hat keine Ausdrücke für die einfachsten geometrischen Figuren, wie Dreieck, Viereck, Quadrat usw. oder für die entsprechenden Adjektive. Die Passivpartizipien רבוע und מרבע, von dem Verbalstamm רבע gebildet, übersetzen wir zwar mit viereckig, doch haben sie mit Ecken und visuellen Vorstellungen nichts zu tun. Sie bedeuten einfach: das, was zu einer Vierheit gemacht worden ist."[3]

He further examines briefly a number of other Hebrew words which usually are translated by geometrical or quantitative terms, but which according to him have nothing to do with visual or abstract concepts, but are dominated by the verbal root from which they derive. Hence he concludes: "Der Begriff der Größe ist also im Alten Testament nicht durch räumliche Anschauung, sondern durch dynamische Vorstellungen und Handlungen entstanden."[4]

This same 'dynamic approach' to reality is described by Boman in an earlier part of his book, when he discusses the impression which buildings make on the Israelite mind. He remarks that as a rule the Old Testament does not describe what a building or object looks like, but how it has been constructed. As examples Boman refers to Genesis 6 (the ark), Exodus 25 - 28 (the tabernacle) and 1 Kings : 6 - 7 (the temple). This phenomenon is explained by Boman in the following way: "Wenn ein Israelit ein Gebäude sieht, beschäftigt sich sein Bewußtsein sofort mit dem Gedanken, wie es nun errichtet worden ist, etwa wie eine Hausfrau, die sich nicht mit dem Geschmack eines Kuchens begnügen kann, sondern sich besonders dafür interessiert, welche Ingredienzen er hat und

---

1   o.c. , p. 139.
2   o.c. , p. 140.
3   o.c. , p. 142 - 43.
4   o.c. , p. 143.

wie er gemacht worden ist. Das Gebäude ist also nicht eine ruhende harmonische Ganzheit, an deren schönen Linien seine Augen Freude haben, sondern etwas Dynamisches und Lebendiges, eine menschliche Tat; ihr nachzugehen und zu bewundern, ist seine Freude und sein Verlangen."[1]

The results of Boman concerning the Hebrew experience of space can briefly be summarized as follows:

a. Space is not the main parameter of the Hebrew mind; in comparison with the Greek the Hebrews adopt a more dynamic approach to reality, for which time is the dominating factor.

b. The Hebrews do not have an abstract concept of space. They see objects (and in fact reality as a whole) as they are, without auxiliary lines such as contours and boundaries. Therefore infinite space does not present a problem to them.

c. Objects, even as large as a whole country or the whole world, are considered to be homogeneous. This implies that a description of the situation at the outer ends is sufficient for knowing the whole object.

d. The Hebrews are not interested in an accurate description of what things look like, but in the way they have been constructed.

It cannot be denied that these results provide a more or less coherent and detailed picture of a way of experiencing space. However, the method used by Boman to arrive at these results is very problematic indeed. As early as 1961, Barr has severely criticized the use of linguistic data by Boman. His criticism is of such fundamental importance, also for our own investigation, that we will discuss it separately in the next paragraph. At this moment we mention only the very limited amount of linguistic evidence, brought forward by Boman, and his awkward way of considering the meaning of words.

In addition, a critical comment should be made regarding the general foundation of his method. His objective is to analyze the difference between Hebrew and Greek thought, so it is understandable that at the start of his investigation he describes this difference in a few statements. In his study, he subsequently tries to support these statements by enumerating linguistic data and by giving quotations of opinions, comments, analyses, etc. from other scholars. A balanced approach, however, also requires a critical examination of one's own pre-suppositions. As far as we can see, this is completely absent in Boman's book, and this makes his results, how appealing they may seem to be, of very questionable quality.

3.2.3. Mythical space in the Old Testament; Childs.

In his study on the problem of myth in the Old Testament Childs includes a separate paragraph on the influence of the mythical concept of space on the Old

---

1   o.c. , p. 61.

Testament.[1]

The general thesis developed in his book is "that myth and the Old Testament have as their ultimate concern an understanding of reality; however their concepts are at variance with one another."[2] The author uses the following definition of myth: "Myth is a form by which the existing structure of reality is understood and maintained. It concerns itself with showing how an action of a deity, conceived of as occurring in the primeval age, determines a phase of contemporary world order. Existing world order is maintained through the actualization of the myth in the cult."[3]

In an exegetical study of a number of texts from the Old Testament, Childs tries to demonstrate that the concept of reality of the Old Testament shows varying degrees of conflict with the mythical concept. In the next chapter he provides a further analysis of this conflict by contrasting "the unique elements of Biblical thinking" with "the thought patterns underlying myth in general."[4] Within the framework of this analysis he investigates the categories of time and space. For our investigation the latter concept is of course the most interesting and we will look in particular at what Childs writes about this category.

He starts his paragraph on this subject with an analysis of mythical space, in which he gives three characteristics of it as compared to those of space in Euclidean geometry:

a. "Mythical space is non-homogeneous in character. ..... As with the mythical understanding of time, space cannot be abstracted from its content. This content is afforded to mythical space by the immediate contact of the individual with spatial reality. His sensuous experience fills that particular space with its unique character. By attaching his experience to certain limited areas, he makes the qualitative distinctions within space of sacred and profane, each bearing its emotional character."[5]

b. "Mythical space is conceived of as a copy of the primeval world structure which shares the same sacred reality. What once came into being is what now exists. ..... It is characteristic of myth that creation corresponds to the various parts of the body. ..... This establishes an ontological correspondence between the world structure and the life of man."[6]

c. "Mythical space conceives of every sign of similarity in the world of reality as an indication of an identity in essence. No matter how separated in space these forms appear the fact that they evidence kinship is cause for their identification."[7]

---

1   Childs, 1962.
2   o.c. , p. 7.
3   o.c. , p. 29 - 30.
4   o.c. , p. 73.
5   o.c. , p. 84.
6   o.c. , p. 85.
7   o.c. , p. 85.

Childs subsequently examines the Old Testament traditions concerning Jerusalem in order to "see if there is any evidence that a mythical concept of space is present."[1] As a result of this investigation which also covers utterances on Zion and Eden, he concludes that "the main characteristics of mythical thinking about space are clearly present."[2] It appears that "Jerusalem possesses a quality which sets it apart from all other spaces within the world. Zion is a holy place because she belongs to God. ... He dwells in her midst." It "is conceived as a copy of a heavenly reality. ..... Jerusalem as the navel of the earth is also the heavenly city come to earth. ..... Finally, there is evidence of the mythical understanding of space in the identification of Zion with Eden."[3]

At the same time, however, Childs also found "evidence to show that in important places within the Old Testament the mythical pattern has been altered."[4] He mentions the following points:

a. "Zion is not a holy place established in the Urzeit as part of God's initial creation. Rather, it only became a holy place in the course of Israel's history." So, "the establishing of Zion is an historical, not a mythical event."[5]

b. "While Zion is pictured as a manifestation of Eden, there is never a simple identification between the two as in the myth. ... Instead, the content of Zion has been filled with new elements not present in the Urzeit. ..... The processes of history are viewed as producing something new over and above the sacred space of the primeval age."[6]

c. "The mythical understanding of sacred space as possessing an unchangeable quality of holiness was emphatically rejected by the Hebrew prophets. ..... A place is never holy apart from its relation to Yahweh. It can possess no permanent quality of holiness. The content of space is determined by its relationship to Yahweh rather than an inherent quality of the sacred."[7]

After having demonstrated in this way that "the Old Testament makes use of a mythical concept of space - but in a form which has been altered at decisive points," Childs subsequently addresses himself to the question: "Did the Biblical writers find in the altered mythical pattern a compatible vehicle by which to bear witness to a new reality?"[8] In this respect he gives the following suggestions as a kind of reply:

- ".... in the first place, that the mythical concept of space was useful to the Biblical writers in emphasizing the quality of space rather than the location."[9]

---

1   o.c. , p. 85 - 86.
2   o.c. , p. 89.
3   o.c. , p. 86, 87.
4   o.c. , p. 90.
5   o.c. , p. 90.
6   0.c. , p. 91.
7   o.c. , p. 92.
8   o.c. , p. 92.
9   o.c. , p. 92.

According to the author this is in line with the Old Testament's main interest in the kind of space.

- "Secondly, the mythical concept of space in its Biblical form offers testimony to a spatial reality which appeared at the beginning of history and which continued to manifest itself throughout Israel's history. ..... The continuity of God's redemptive acts as participating in the spatial reality of the same new creation is given clear expression in the broken myth. However, the mythical form was altered in the Old Testament, since it did not do justice in its unbroken state to the acts of God in history as the revelation of his new creation. The new elements found in the description of Zion but not present in Eden indicate the further historical manifestation of God's new creation in space."[1]

Childs concludes his discussion of the role of mythical space in the Old Testament by indicating the differences between the myth and the Old Testament. "The myth attempts to understand spatial reality in terms of the present world order which is conceived of as occurring in a primeval act, overcoming the world of non-being. ... This mythical category of space reflects a world view which conceives of reality as a static unchangeable substance, indeed fluctuating in a rhythmic pattern, but always having for its goal a return to the past. .... In contrast, the Old Testament category of space, while adopting a quasi-mythical form, was used basically to express a different concept of reality. The Old Testament understood spatial reality in terms of a new creation which was not to be identified with either the present world order or the world of non-being. God in history was bringing into existence a new spatial reality, analogous to the new temporal reality. It was not divorced from the present world of space but differed in the quality of its space. ..... The Old Testament's understanding of space was eschatological, not mythical. It looked to the future, not to the past."[2]

It is clear that Childs pays attention to other elements of space experience than Boman. Whereas the latter seems to be more interested in space perception, the former rather describes the role of space in the world view of the Old Testament, as compared with the 'unbroken myth.' There is also a difference in methodology: Boman bases himself mainly on a discussion of lexical meanings of words, but Childs investigates the contents of relevant statements.

In his investigation Childs restricts himself to the Old Testament traditions concerning Jerusalem, whereas, from our review in chapter 2, we know that other concepts, like 'the land,' 'the cult,' etc. , are important as well.

But summarizing, we can say that the publication of Childs provides a useful contribution to the subject area of our investigation. He applies a method which has an open eye for the context in which the words are being used. He seems to

---

1   o.c. , p. 93.
2   o.c. , p. 93, 94.

confirm Boman's idea that in the Old Testament space was perceived as 'qualified,' whereas the continuity of the new spatial reality which he supposes, suggests that it has some form of 'independent existence.'

3.2.4. Spaciousness; the study of a semantic field; Sawyer.

In the introduction to his publication Sawyer remarks that "the use of a number of Hebrew words for 'enlarge,' 'give room to,' etc. in Old Testament language about salvation .... is well attested ..."[1] He gives a few quotations from lexicographical and theological writings which, by means of etymology and root-meaning, try to connect the concept of salvation with that of 'width, spaciousness'. He himself, however, has no intention of using these "faulty linguistics", but wishes to give "simply a description of this feature of OT Hebrew, together with some suggestions concerning its origin and development in Biblical tradition."[2]

The method he uses is the study, "not of one word, but of a 'semantic field,' or more precisely of a lexical group within a wider 'associative field.'"[3] This lexical group which corresponds to English 'wide, broad, enlarge, etc.,' contains in Hebrew a number of verbal and nominal forms which are related to the consonant-combinations רחב, רוח and פתה. He is particularly interested in "metaphorical usage which concerns only part of the field."[4] So he does not discuss all passages exhaustively, but rather those showing this type of use. The term 'passage' "is used to denote immediate linguistic environment," whereas 'context' "is reserved for the wider situational framework in which the words in question are applied."[5]

The passages are divided into three groups, namely those in which the words under investigation are used:

a. to denote literally physical dimensions;
b. metaphorically, in a context of physical danger or distress;
c. metaphorically, in a context of psychological or spiritual distress.

For each group of passages the author presents first the essential characteristics and then quotes one example, while other references are listed in a footnote. His final statement regarding the method to be followed deserves particular attention: "No conclusions are put forward either on the relation between the 'Hebrew mind' or Weltbild and the Hebrew language, or on the 'concept of spaciousness in the OT.' It is hoped that this will prove that a number of valuable semantic and theological statements can be made concerning OT

---

1   Sawyer, 1967 - 68, p. 20.
2   o.c. , p. 20.
3   o.c. , p. 20.
4   o.c. , p. 21.
5   o.c. , p. 21.

Hebrew, without raising either of these thorny questions."[1]

From the analysis of the first group of passages, which cover "territorial spaciousness" Sawyer concludes "that spaciousness was a prominent feature ... of the language of God's promise of land from an early time."[2] The boundaries of the promised land are a theme that figures quite frequently in the Old Testament, as is the idea of its enlargement. Regarding the latter, Sawyer distinguishes "between God's territorial expansion on behalf of Israel, and man's imperialism," the ultimate aim of the former being "the establishment of a rule of righteousness in which the whole world would share."[3]

Investigation of the metaphorical use showed that for words like רָוַח and רְוַח this usage is much more frequent than for words like רָחַב and הִרְחִיב. In the context of spiritual freedom the form רְוַח even takes the main place, although a few other forms have psychological application. Sawyer points to Psalm 119: 45 where בָרְחָבָה is to be translated as 'at liberty.' According to him "in Ps. 119 the language of spaciousness is applied in a striking way to the spiritual freedom of a man who knows 'die heilschaffenden lebenerneuernden Kräfte der Torah.'"[4] This freedom is described in two ways:
- intellectual breadth of vision;
- escape from false ways.

In his concluding remark Sawyer writes: "In the light of the evidence for this development from ideas of territorial freedom, with its concomitant jubilation in the time of David and Solomon, to the colourful, poignant expressions for liberation from all kinds of restricting danger and distress, it would be unwise to reject these last spiritualizing interpretations as late or spurious. An important feature of OT tradition is the remarkable applicability of ideas like the spaciousness of salvation to an infinite variety of human situations."[5]

This publication by Sawyer also contributes in two ways to the subject of our investigation.

Regarding methodology it uses an approach which is rather restricted as far as objective is concerned: no conclusions on concepts such as the Hebrew mind or Hebrew conception of the world are aimed at, but only a number of semantic and theological statements concerning Old Testament Hebrew. In this connection the author refers to the ideas of Barr which we will discuss in paragraph 3.3. He uses the method of investigating a lexical group within an associative field, which gives the possibility of looking at the meaning of a word, as compared with those of other words of adjacent meanings, and as compared with the context in which the word(s) occur(s). So he restricts himself to noticing that

---

1   o.c. , p. 21.
2   o.c. , p. 22.
3   o.c. , p. 24, p. 25.
4   o.c. , p. 30.
5   o.c. , p. 31.

certain words are being used in certain situations, without speculating about the reasons why people do that.

As far as the subject area is concerned, Sawyer's publication pays special attention to the experience of space in a metaphorical sense, an aspect which we did not find explicitly in both publications reviewed so far in this chapter.

3.2.5. The Hebrew conception of the world; Stadelmann.

In the preface to his book the author points to "the Hebrews' unique contribution to man's knowledge and understanding of the cosmos. .... Through their awareness of Yahweh's dealings with his people and of cosmic realities the ancient Hebrews gradually came to discover the attributes of God. .... In order to appreciate the Hebrews' unique world view we shall investigate the creation narratives against the wider background of the ancient Near Eastern literature."[1]

The following quotation illustrates his method of investigation: "Since the world view of the ancient Hebrews cannot be comprehended from a mere study of notions and themes, we shall examine the meaning of the relevant terms by determining their etymology and we shall gather all biblical material which bears on the subject. By this method we shall endeavor to study the ancient Hebrew's vision of the whole universe."[2]

In line with this objective Stadelmann's interest for space is mainly directed towards 'cosmological space', on which he makes a number of remarks which are spread over various parts of his book. The following examples are of importance for our investigation:

a. After an initial analysis of the terms and expressions for 'world,' Stadelmann concludes "that the spatial complex of the universe was conceived as a structure of strata separated from but related to each other. .... Since the concept of an external world seems to be a Greek abstraction, unknown, at all events, to the Semites, it is not surprising that the Bible does not distinguish container from contents, or, conversely, the living from its environment. Thus, for example, space never appears as an inert, lifeless receptacle; it is the sea where fish swim, the ground on which beasts tread, the land belonging to such and such people, the heavens where the winds are stored, the snow and hail are kept."[3] In connection with the notion of "'world' as an event" the author writes: "The system of location in space, called a frame of space, is only part of a fuller system of location of beings in space and time."[4]

b. In connection with his analysis of the terms for earth and their context, Stadelmann makes a few further comments on the experience of space by the Hebrews: "As seen above, the term אֶרֶץ denotes either the whole area of the

---

1   Stadelmann, 1970, p. VII.
2   o.c. , p. VII.
3   o.c. , p. 2.
4   o.c. , p. 3.

earth or the entire region of a country. Thus, it would seem that the ancient Hebrews never succeeded in abstracting a sector from the world. .... It might be too much, however, to advance an explanation for this specific usage of ארץ in terms of a unique thought pattern of the Hebrews who understood distinct items in the universe as component elements of the whole."[1]

c. Whereas in the initial analysis of terms for earth he dealt with words with an exclusive spatial extension, in a subsequent part Stadelmann describes the interaction of spatial and temporal aspects: "In the term חלד however, we find an oscillation between the spatial and the temporal significance. Between the two there is actually no sharp differentiation, and by virtue of this relationship the term חלד denotes both 'era, age, lifetime' and 'space of the world.'"[2]

d. "The interchange of temporal and spatial relations is partly retained in the designation of the directions of the horizon,"[3] which Stadelmann reviews on the pages to follow. He distinguishes between "three different systems of names, each resting on a separate principle.

The first system is based upon the functional relation between the position of the observer facing one direction (i.e. east); the determination of the other three are related to the direction toward east. The directions are defined in relation to him facing קדם 'that which is before,' which corresponds to the east. .... In addition to the spatial meaning 'front, east,' קדם denotes also the temporal idea of 'past, ancient time.' The opposite of קדם is אחור or אחרון 'behind,' corresponding to the west. .... Another aspect of the word אחרון is the temporal notion denoting 'latter, last, future time.' .... The direction to the north is defined in relation to the left-hand side of the observer facing east.(שמאל) Similarly, ימין 'the right hand,' and תימן 'what is on the right-hand side' denote the south. ....

The second system of names .... is associated with the sun's daily course. Thus east is called מזרח 'place of sunrise' .... and מוצא 'place of going forth' .... Likewise, the setting of the sun is identified with the west, for which there are two expressions: מבוא השמש 'the entrance (i.e. place of setting) of the sun,' and מערב .... 'the place of sunset, the west,' derived from the root ערב 'to enter.' On the other hand, the north is known as צפון .... דרום designates the south quarter.

The third system, which takes in to account the topographical features of Palestine, indicates directions by means of descriptive terms corresponding to the local panorama. .... The south is frequently designated by the name נגב, derived from the root נגב 'to be dry, parched,' denoting 'south country, south.' There is also a great number of biblical references to the west described by the name ים 'sea,' i.e. , the Mediterranean, which forms the western boundary of

---

1   o.c. , p. 127 - 28.
2   o.c. , p. 130.
3   o.c. , p. 131.

Palestine. Parallel topological allusions to the two other cardinal points, the east and the north .... do not appear to have been used."[1]

After having described these three systems, Stadelmann concludes: "The very fact of the division of the world into four sections is consistent with the conception of space held by the ancient Hebrews. As appeared in the analysis of the cardinal points, they were never conceived as mere functional realities, devoid of all content, mere expressions of ideal relations. But the cardinal points were associated either with the position of an observer or with the sun's daily course or with topographical features. Hence, the ancient Hebrews could not conceive of those four directions in terms of purely functional relations, and likewise they did not realize the concept of infinity; from the very outset the extension of the world is confined within certain spatial limits imposed by their sense perception. As the different countries were in some way distributed among the diverse cardinal points and were differentiated accordingly, so the whole world was permeated by this form of classification. Thus, the spatial world was intelligible to them to the degree that they were able to describe it in terms of concrete images."[2]

In fact these sentences, which Stadelmann partly repeats in his final conclusion, form his main result as far as the experience of space by the ancient Hebrews is concerned.

Although the objective of Stadelmann's study is different from that of Boman - he aims to describe the Hebrew conception of the world, whereas Boman wants to compare Hebrew and Greek thought - there is a lot of similarity as far as methodology is concerned: both rely heavily on the study of word meanings and etymology and use the results of these studies to devise a coherent picture of the Hebrew way of experiencing space. So Barr's criticism of Boman also applies to Stadelmann and his results should be considered with caution.

His review of the three systems for denoting the geographical directions in Old Testament Hebrew adds a new element to what we found so far on the perception of space in the Old Testament.

3.2.6. Studies of words relating to space.

In addition to the investigation of the semantic field of spaciousness by Sawyer (see above section 3.2.4.), a number of studies of particular words relating to space and spatial aspects has been published. We will summarize a few of them in this section.

In his series of investigations of the 'valence' of Hebrew verbs, Richter so far

---

1   o.c. , p. 132 - 33.
2   o.c. , p. 133 - 34.

has published two volumes, which describe his explorations of אֶרֶךְ [1] and גֹבַהּ, עֵמֶק, and קְצַר II.[2] His analyses are mainly directed towards syntactic aspects and show that it is possible to describe all Hebrew verb sentences with a restricted number of structural patterns. At the same time, different structural patterns can be assigned to separate verbs which requires an analysis of their contents resulting in semantic characteristics.[3]

The main part of his publications consists of an analysis of the various passages of the Old Testament containing the verbs concerned. Although all verbs include spatial connotations, Richter does not specifically refer to the perception of space. Recently published volumes of TWAT contain surveys on a few words which are relevant in relation to space. In his article on קוּם, Gamberoni refers to substantives such as מָקוֹם and קוֹמָה. Regarding the latter, he reports that it is used 45 times in the Old Testament, "meist als Angabe der Höhe von Bauten und Gegenständen der Einrichtung des Wüstenheiligtums und des Tempels, gelegentlich (dichterisch) vom Wuchs von Pflanzen .... und Menschen ...., nie in einem sicher alten Text."[4]

Bartelmus reviews the root רחב, to which he assigns the general meaning 'to be wide.' He points to the fact that the number of occurrences of nominal derivatives greatly exceeds the number of occurrences of verbs derived from this root, a phenomenon which can be found with more 'verba stativa.'[5] The most frequent nominal form is רֹחַב (101 times), which occurs in particular in the following pericopes: Exodus 25 to 40 (22 times), Ezechiel 40 - 48 (55 times) and 1 Kings 6 -7 / 2 Chron. 3 - 6 (16 times). Bartelmus comments: "Es handelt sich dabei durchwegs um Texte, in denen im Rahmen von Maßangaben für Bauwerke bzw. Werkstücke Länge, Breite und Höhe des jeweiligen Gegenstands verhandelt werden, so daß die Verwendung des terminus technicus rohab 'Breite' unumgänglich ist."[6] In connection with Ezechiel 40 ff, he writes: "Die extreme Häufung des Terminus in diesen Kapiteln hat zweifellos etwas damit zu tun, daß es um verbindliche himmlische Maszangaben geht, bei denen Verwechslungen - etwa von Längen- und Breitenangaben - unbedingt vermieden werden müssen."[7]

Within the framework of this dictionary, these articles put most emphasis on the theological significance of the words concerned and we were unable to find any reference to the perception of space.

3.2.7. A first reaction.

In this initial discussion of the literature, we restrict ourselves to the four

---

1   Richter, 1985.
2   Richter, 1986.
3   Richter, 1985, p. 4.
4   Gamberoni, 1989, p. 1256.
5   Bartelmus, 1990, p. 450.
6   o.c. , p. 451.
7   o.c. , p. 455.

publications reviewed in sections 3.2.2. to 3.2.5. The articles included in section 3.2.6. do not contain direct reference to the perception of space, but may be of help in a further stage of our study.

Having reviewed the literature, naturally the next steps would be to compare its results and assess their value and try to fit them together into a coherent picture of the present state-of-the-art on the perception of space in the Old Testament. There are a few reasons, however, which make it desirable for us to postpone our final summary and limit ourselves at this point to giving a first reaction only.

The main reasons are the differences, and sometimes unclarities, as far as both method and scope of investigation are concerned. These are illustrated by the following points:

a. Boman and Stadelmann try to cover the whole Old Testament, and use quotations on space from all of its parts. Sawyer also covers the whole Old Testament, but limits himself to the semantic field of spaciousness, which only contains a limited number of words. In his study of the relation of space and myth in the Old Testament, Childs restricts himself to the Jerusalem traditions. These occur in many parts of the Old Testament, but nevertheless there is a strong limitation due to his choice of this theme. It is clear that there are great differences as far as 'data-collecting' is concerned.

b. In their 'handling' of the data, Boman and (to a lesser extent) Stadelmann mainly investigate the lexical meaning and etymological background of a number of words and pay very little attention to the context in which they are used and to the role which the statements containing them play in the broader outline of topics presented by the text. The latter aspect receives a lot of attention in the study of Childs, whereas Sawyer apparently attempts to maintain a balanced approach between lexical and contextual meaning.

c. The results of their handling of the data are used by Boman and Stadelmann as the basis for the construction of a more or less complete and coherent model of the space perception and experience in the Old Testament. Their models contain clear and assertive statements concerning the thought world of its people. Sawyer, on the contrary, does not seem to include any 'model-building' at all, but restricts his conclusions to "linguistic and theological statements." The results of his investigation of the data are used by Childs only for devising a picture of the role of mythical thinking in the Old Testament.

This brings us to an additional reason why our present comment can only be considered as a first reaction. In all publications reviewed, the investigation of the experience and perception of space in the Old Testament is not the only or main target, but it is incorporated in a study of wider or at least different scope:

Boman: the comparison of Hebrew and Greek thought;

Childs: the role of myth in the Old Testament;

Sawyer: spaciousness as feature of language about salvation;

Stadelmann: the Hebrew conception of the world.

This raises the question of the influence of this wider objective on the investigation of the role of space, both in relation to methods used and results formulated.

In addition, a clear distinction between the perception of space on one hand, and its further role in (expressing) thought on the other, is not made in any of the publications reviewed. Boman makes many statements on the perception of space, but these are not clearly delineated from statements on the further role of space. This makes it difficult to identify their scope and to assess them properly.

As already stated in chapter 1, methodological questions figure heavily in our subject field. Our initial review of these four relevant publications enables us to get a clearer idea of the problems concerned and it seems wise to investigate them more extensively, since that may help us in a proper evaluation of the present state-of-the-art and in the preparation of possible further research into this area.

In this connection, at this stage of our study, we can formulate some questions, the answers of which would greatly facilitate the clarification of the methodological problems:

1. Is there a relation between language and thought in general and, in particular, between language and perception, way of thinking and the formation of concepts?

2. What is the nature of this relation?

3. To what extent and in what way can this relation be used to obtain a model of the thought patterns (perception, way of thinking, etc.) of people on the basis of their (use of) language only?

It is with these questions in mind that we continue our survey of the literature, in particular on the use of linguistics in the study of the Old Testament.

3.3. The methodological criticism of Barr.

James Barr was one of the first scholars who recognized the importance of developments in modern linguistics for biblical research. In 1961 he published his book titled "The Semantics of Biblical Language,"[1] to which we referred above when discussing the work of Boman.(see section 3.2.2.)

The purpose of his book is "to criticize certain methods in the handling of linguistic evidence in theological discussion."[2] He does this within the framework of the "current contrast of Greek and Hebrew thought," a contrast which Barr thinks is not the correct one to make: "But for the understanding of the Old Testament what we need to know is how its ideas differ from those of

---

1   Barr, 1961.
2   o.c. , p. 6.

56

'in particular' not the Greeks but the Canaanites, the Arabs and the Babylonians."[1] Barr extensively reviews much work on the linguistic aspects of both the Old and New Testaments, and the relating of them to theological concepts, and pays attention in particular to the methods used in these studies. His general judgment is quite negative: "In this modern theological attempt to relate theological thought to biblical language I shall argue that the most characteristic feature is its unsystematic and haphazard nature. For this lack of system I think there are two reasons - firstly the failure to examine the relevant languages, Greek and Hebrew, as a whole; and secondly the failure to relate what is said about either to a general semantic method related to general linguistics."[2]

A few quotations will illustrate this critical attitude: "We see here how much the theological viewpoint is dominated by theory. You know how distinctive the Hebrew mind is, and surely all this distinctiveness in concepts and in thought must somehow be manifested in the linguistic phenomena. .... It is this starting from the theoretical end, from the assurance of understanding the Hebrew mind, and working from there to its linguistic form, that causes the haphazardness of modern theological treatments of linguistic evidence. .... Thus, since a systematic examination or description of the language is not being done, a few phenomena which illustrate the theory seem to be striking confirmation of it, and what were occasional and possible illustrative examples come to appear as a total system corresponding to the realities of Hebrew thought. The theory thus becomes presumptive evidence for the interpretation of facts that are doubtful."[3]

In his discussion Barr does not restrict himself to criticism alone, but also gives conditions which should be fulfilled in order to achieve a proper use of linguistic evidence:

".. firstly, a strict and systematic method of discussing the relation between grammatical structures and lexical phenomena on the one hand and the Hebrew or Greek mind or any other national or cultural mind on the other.

Secondly, a systematic examination of the relevant language as a whole, not purely motivated by the interest in correlating the Hebrew mind with the Greek, so as to display the structure of the language as such and not to emphasize unduly those elements which can be specially fitted into the contrast between the Hebrew and the Greek minds.

Thirdly, a semantic method which is used for Greek or Hebrew must be integrated with general linguistics as a whole, and must therefore be open to relevant data for semantics of any language, since otherwise the languages specially relevant in this case, namely Hebrew and Greek, receive a distorted

---

1   o.c. , p. 20.
2   o.c. , p. 21.
3   o.c. , p. 22, p. 23.

image from their isolation."[1]

The author does not "suggest that these requisites can be readily supplied in a form applicable to the needs of theological study." His aim is to show how difficult it is to establish a relation between mental patterns and linguistic structure and "how impossible it is to by-pass the discussion of it in philosophy, psychology and linguistics."[2]

He subsequently considers a number of, in particular methodological, difficulties in the current handling of the Hebrew-Greek contrast in language and thinking within the science of the Old Testament. At the end of this discussion, he concludes: "All this can be summarized by saying that where linguistic evidence has been used in the Greek-Hebrew contrast it has not been adequately protected against, or indeed has positively presupposed, the idea of a logico-grammatical parallelism, a doctrine, which can be traced from Aristotle through scholasticism, and which gained some of its plausibility from the predominant position of Latin and the corresponding attempt to force the forms of other languages into the moulds of Latin grammar."[3] In this respect he refers to a few publications which give a negative judgment on this logico-grammatical parallelism.

It is clear that Barr himself also takes a very critical attitude towards this idea which has been described in particular in the publications of Sapir and Whorf and hence also is known as the Sapir-Whorf hypothesis. It is also known as the 'Linguistic Relativity Hypothesis'. We will use this name and its abbreviation LRH.

Based on this critical attitude, both of the use of the Hebrew-Greek contrast and of the LRH, Barr criticizes in his book a considerable number of publications in the field of the study of the Old Testament, which according to him use linguistic facts in a wrong way. One of his victims is Boman, whose work he quotes as an example "to show how an accepted contrast of Hebrew and European thought is applied as a presupposition in the selection and evaluation of linguistic data."[4] In addition he repeatedly attacks him because of improperly relating elements of language with elements of thought.[5]

The value of Barr's publication for our investigation is obvious. He gives a clear-cut answer to the first question which we formulated at the end of the previous paragraph in section 3.2.5. According to him the relation between language and thought is of such a nature that it can only be used in scientific work, when certain methodological conditions are observed. So in order to achieve our objective it would be wise to consider these conditions when

---

1   o.c. , p. 24 - 25.
2   o.c. , p. 25.
3   o.c. , p. 43.
4   o.c. , p. 98.
5   e.g. , see p. 61, 65, 77.

choosing the method to be used for our investigation.

At the same time, it is clear that the LRH, in some form or another, has a long history and that, also in modern times, it has many supporters. In his book Barr considers it, and the work of those scholars who, consciously or unconsciously, base themselves on it, from one philosophical point of view only. So it is fair to listen to 'the other side' as well, and we will now discuss the reactions to Barr's publication in the literature of Old Testament science.

3.4. The role of the Linguistic Relativity Hypothesis in the study of the Old Testament; the reactions to the publication of Barr.

The sharp criticism of Barr on the improper use of linguistic methods in the study of the Old Testament prompted many scholars to give their opinion on this issue. In this paragraph we do not aim at a complete survey of all these reactions, but restrict ourselves to a few publications which discuss in particular the relation between language and thought, as suggested in the LRH and as relevant in connection with the questions formulated above in section 3.2.7.

In view of his work on the experience of space in the Old Testament, we start with the reaction of Boman. His comments on Barr's criticism can be found in a final paragraph which he added to the main text of his book in editions appearing after the publication of Barr's "The Semantics of Biblical Language". This paragraph, titled "Language and Thought" clearly shows the point of departure of Boman, which is completely different from that of Barr. The following quotations, all from the same page, illustrate Boman's approach:

"Das Thema meines Buches ist also das Denken der Hebräer und nicht ihre Sprache. Ich gebrauche nur die Sprache als ein Mittel um zu ihrem Denken vorzudringen. Ich gebrauche allerdings auch andere Mittel dazu, aber hauptsächlich die Sprache, weil dieses mich zuerst auf die Eigentümlichkeit des Hebräischen Denkens aufmerksam gemacht und mich gezwungen hatte, über diese eigentümliche Denkweise zu reflektieren. ..... Barr aber argumentiert die ganze Zeit, als ob ich eine formal-linguistische Abhandlung geschrieben hätte. Er transformiert konsequent meine sprachphilosophischen Argumente und Ausagen zu linguistischen. ..... Seine Handlungsweise ist nur unter einer Voraussetzung psychologisch verständlich und moralisch verantwortlich, nämlich, wenn seine Semantik es verbietet oder ausschließt, daß man philosophische Schlüsse aus linguistischen Tatsachen ziehen kann. Dies ist offenbar seine unausgesprochene Grundanschauung."[1]

A further illustration of Boman's idea about the approach by Barr is the following: "Hinter allen seinen Argumenten steht sein falscher Grundgedanke, daß es nicht möglich ist, aus linguistischen Tatsachen zu schließen, welche Art des Denkens diese Tatsachen widerspiegeln, da er meint, man solle Sprache und

---

1   Boman, 1977, p. 200.

Denken streng auseinanderhalten."[1]
Although this conclusion goes too far, Boman clearly indicates that he is operating from a philosophical tradition which is very different from that of Barr. His guides are W.von Humboldt, Sapir and Whorf, and with approval he quotes Kronasser's statement: "Der Grundgedanke, die Mentalität und das Weltbild einer Gemeinschaft sei durch das Medium der Sprache zu ertasten, ist gewiß richtig."[2]
The big difference in philosophical tradition prevents Boman from discussing Barr's objections against his results in a fruitful way. In most cases he only shows that the arguments of Barr originate from an approach which he rejects, and that is the end of the matter.
It looks as if Boman believes that Barr's view on the application of linguistic evidence in the investigation of the Old Testament is based on an attitude towards the relation between thought and language, which is completely outside the main stream of thinking on this topic. Hence, according to him, Barr's criticism should not be taken too seriously.
A similar attitude we find in an article by G. Friedrich, one of the editors of Kittel's Dictionary, so heavily criticized by Barr.[3] He gives a survey of recent developments in semantics in which he does not only pay attention to German scholars, but also refers to Anglo-Saxon authors, at the end of which he concludes: "Wenn man von diesen Fragestellungen der modernen Semantik her gespannt das Buch von Barr aufschlägt, um zu erfahren, wie er sich zur 'modernen Semantik' stellt, was er bei der vielfalt der Meinungen unter Semantik versteht und wie man die von ihm charakterisierte Semantik sinnvoll für die Bibelexgese anwenden kann, dann ist man enttäuscht."[4]
According to Friedrich, Barr criticizes many exegetes on the basis of a very one-sided approach: "Aber er vertritt mit seinen Anschauungen, daß es nicht auf das Wort, sondern auf den Satz ankomme, daß es nicht darum gehe zu fragen, was der Sprecher denkt und ob mit dem Wort die Sache getroffen sei, daß die Sprache ein willkürlich gesetztes System semantischer Zeichen sei, die Thesen einer anderen Philosophie, nämlich die des Positivismus. Er ersetzt in seiner Semantik eine Philosophisch geprägte Sprachlehre durch eine andere. Aber ist sie wirklich die bessere und sachgemäßere? Diese Antwort ist mit seinem Buch nicht gegeben."[5]
The title which N.H.Ridderbos gave to his reaction on Barr indicates in what direction his ideas move: "Is Hebrew one of the sources of the revelation?"[6]
Although he agrees that Barr is making many 'correct and useful remarks' and

---

1   o.c. , p. 209.
2   o.c. , p. 201.
3   Friedrich, 1970.
4   o.c. , p. 57.
5   o.c. , p. 57.
6   Ridderbos, 1964.

is completely right on a number of details, he believes him to be wrong on the main line of his argument. Ridderbos supports this statement with the following points:

1. Barr errs in suggesting that authors like Pedersen, Boman, Bultmann, etc. are basing themselves on an attitude towards language that is completely obsolete.
2. He also distinguishes insufficiently between religious structure and linguistic structure. Ridderbos thinks it to be certain that there is a connection between the thought structure of Israel and the structure of the Hebrew language. But he agrees that it will be much more difficult to demonstrate a connection between the structure of its religion and its language.[1]

In order to support his first statement Ridderbos gives a few extensive quotations from recent publications of Stephen Ullmann, whom he considers to be a generally accepted expert in linguistics. These show that "one does not need to be considered an adherent of an obsolete view of language, when one believes that there is a correlation between linguistic structures on one side and thought structures, 'mental patterns,' 'mentality' on the other. This can strengthen us in our opinion that it makes sense to ask: is there a correlation between the structures of Hebrew and the thought-world of Israel, its mentality? In my opinion this question needs to be answered in a confirmative way."[2]

Ridderbos arrives at this positive attitude, which forms the basis for his second statement, after giving a few examples from the study of the Old Testament. In the first one he refers to the concept of the 'corporate personality' as devised by Wheeler Robinson.[3] Ridderbos sees a connection between this concept, which reflects a characteristic feature of Israel's thought, and peculiar and sudden changes from plural to singular, and vice-versa, which occur so frequently in the text of the Old Testament. In another example he uses the inconsistent functioning - at least to our western mind - of some particles in Hebrew, as an illustration of the "Hebrew way of thinking which not always distinguishes sharply between cause and effect, but confines itself to stating that two things are mutually dependent upon each other."[4]

While discussing these examples Ridderbos maintains that they provide sufficient support for the positive correlation between the structure of the Hebrew language and the 'mentality' of Israel.

Regarding the correlation between the structure of the Hebrew language and the religion of Israel, Ridderbos concludes that thanks to the particular revelation which Israel received, all kinds of changes did take place in the structure of Hebrew. These changes, however, do not constitute an 'organic unity,' as is the

---

1   see o.c. , p. 211 - 212.
2   o.c. , p. 215.
3   Wheeler Robinson, 1980; see also De Fraine, 1959.
4   o.c. , p. 218.

case with the features of Hebrew which reflect Israel's mentality.[1]

We conclude our survey of reactions to Barr's approach of the use of linguistics in biblical research by mentioning a few points from the thesis of Wells.[2] The author critically examines the whole work of Barr, in which he sees "an evolution of theological thought from an authority-centred structure to one which is much less concerned with authorising statements by means of a prior norm."[3] Since Wells himself adopts a view of the Bible which emphasizes the analogy between Christ and Scripture, he cannot follow Barr completely in his critical approach of a lot of recent research of the Bible. Nevertheless, he values some aspects of it: "Positively considered, this criticism represents a continued seeking after a freedom in explaining and listening to the message of Scripture."[4] But it appears that Wells does not trust Barr's underlying motivations for this attitude. He asks: "Is it simply for linguistic reasons that Barr rejects the lexical approach to biblical theology suggested in this tradition? I suspect that the reasons for Barr's rejection lie deeper than the linguistic level, although this is obviously a central factor. It is the idea of justifying the distinctiveness of Christian language in the sphere of revelation that Barr rebuts."[5]

So it looks as if Wells is quite positive towards Barr's contribution to the linguistic aspects of biblical exegesis: "Barr's emphasis on the need to direct the search for meaning to the examination of larger units of sense rather than to the atomistic consideration of words as bearers of meaning and on the usefulness of translation were positive propositions. The affirmation that the distinctiveness of biblical thought is on the level of what the writers say, not in the words as individual units, provided a useful corrective to the then current biblical concept theology. The proposition that a fuller examination of the contexts was needed in exegesis could be positive only in terms of biblical interpretation."[6] He also appreciates that Barr "seems to perceive a certain complementarity in interpretation between the linguistic implications of a structuralist method and the historical implications of the intentionalism of historical criticism."[7]

But he deplores "the limitations of Barr's approach to biblical language. His linguistic comments, although having implications for theology, tend to be of a descriptive nature centred upon questions of usage, and for this reason fail to reach a statement of what might be the particular character of biblical language."[8] He believes that Barr does not fully exploit the special character of

---

1   see o.c. , p. 227.
2   Wells, 1980.
3   o.c. , p. 2 - 3.
4   o.c. , p. 9.
5   o.c. , p. 85.
6   o.c. , p. 326.
7   o.c. , p. 327.
8   o.c. , p. 329.

the Bible as a 'religious tradition' in his linguistic and semantic considerations: "Barr's positive contribution to biblical semantics might have been greater had he sought an integration of the linguistic patterns of the text with the field of religious behaviour which provides the context in which the texts have their meaning."[1] He quotes Lyons who, as a linguist, also asks for attention to the 'situation' in which the text arises, which he even calls fundamental for a semantic consideration.

Apparently Wells is afraid that Barr sees the Bible too much with the eyes of a neutral, twentieth-century observer, who restricts himself to the human aspect of the text alone, instead of giving full credit to its religious importance: "Once again, Barr's considering the Scripture in 'one element' human terms produces a duality between the text as expressive of the human mind of the writers and the reality of God. Language in the Bible has no special status owing to a connection with revelation. Theologians who do not accept Barr's view of the Bible may well doubt that Barr's semantics can really attain the correlation with the situation he seeks because of the elimination of situations in which God makes himself known in history."[2]

The reactions to Barr's publication, reviewed in this paragraph, lead us to make two remarks:

1. Boman and Friedrich, and to a lesser extent Ridderbos, emphasize that Barr's criticism is grounded in a language-philosophical tradition, which is different from the one they operate from. Whereas the approach followed by Barr is very reluctant in drawing firm conclusions on the thought structure of people on the basis of their language, the other approach seems to allow more possibilities in this respect.

2. Both Ridderbos and Wells believe that Barr is neglecting the special character of the language of the Bible which is due to its being used in divine revelation. Ridderbos limits himself to wondering whether it is possible to make positive statements on the correlation of the structure of religion and the structure of language, but Wells seems to be more certain in this respect.

The second remark, although very interesting, touches a topic which falls outside the 'technical scope' of our investigation. But it should be taken into account when we consider its wider implications. The first one, however, indicates that in linguistics and in the philosophy of language several different approaches are possible, and the question arises to what extent all these have been used in the study of the Old Testament. In particular it is important to find out in what way these different approaches influence both the fundamental ideas and the methods of investigation in subject areas like ours where the relation between language and thought figures heavily.

Summarizing, we have to conclude that the publication of Barr and the reactions

---

1   o.c. , p. 329.
2   o.c. , p. 332.

it provoked do not provide enough information for a proper answer to the questions formulated at the end of section 3.2.7. So we will continue our search by investigating the literature on the application of linguistics as a whole in the study of the Old Testament.

3.5. The relation between language and cognition as applied in Old Testament research.

In the previous paragraph, we looked in particular into the debate on the role of the LRH following the critical publication of Barr in 1961. We now take a somewhat broader view: the relation between language and cognition in general will be considered and we intend to cover the whole literature on the application of the results of modern linguistics to the study of the Old Testament. Regarding the latter, although it has been attempted to read as many publications as possible, no claim of completeness can be made, because of their high number and because not all of them could be obtained for consultation. In this report of our literature search we will discuss only those publications which provide a main contribution to answering our questions. We start by reviewing four publications from the last two decades which consider the general application of linguistics or semantics in biblical research.

In 1972 Nida published an article on the "Implications of Contemporary Linguistics for Biblical Scholarship."[1] In his discussion of the relation between the semantic level and the syntactic structure of texts, he writes: "One of the severe handicaps to objective analysis of grammatical structures has been the mistaken concept that there is something so uniquely individual about the grammatical structure of each language and so intimately connected with the entire thought processes of the speakers of such a language, that one cannot really comprehend the meaning of a message without being immersed in the syntactic formulations. Moreover, the grammar of a language has been regarded by some as being a model of people's world view. This is simply not true."[2] After having discussed a number of aspects of the relation between grammar and thought, he concludes: "Attempts to link grammatical structures and national characteristics or world views are doomed to failure, largely because grammatical features are all arbitrary, 'fossilized' structures. They may have represented alternative choices some thousands of years ago, but they must be arbitrary and conventional if they are to function satisfactorily in providing a structure which is sufficiently redundant to be usable and sufficiently supple to make it possible for people to say something which they have never heard before. The requirement that language provide for novelty means that

---

1   Nida , 1972.
2   o.c. , p. 83.

conceptual determinism based on syntactic forms is basically false."[1] From these quotations it is clear that Nida completely rejects the LRH.

In agreement with his attitude in his earlier publication on "Spaciousness,"[2] which we reviewed in section 3.2.3 above, Sawyer, in his book on Semantics in Biblical Research,[3] takes a more careful position. He again uses the method of the investigation of a semantic field in order to elucidate the meaning of a number of words. In his review of the concept of semantic fields, he remarks: "The relation between language and culture is a well worn problem and one which this is not the place to tackle. It is obviously dangerous to base any conclusion concerning the cultural or religious conditions of a people on the presence or absence of one word in their language ...." At the same time he agrees: "Few would dispute the claim of the field-theorists, however, that the size and structure of a field reflect to a very large extent the conditions of its historical context. The language of the OT, as we have seen, originated in various distinct contexts, and therefore no field which takes in the whole of OT Hebrew, could satisfactorily be used as a guide to any one historical situation. But there are some general historical observations that can be made on the size and structure of the הוֹשִׁיעַ-field. They can conveniently be grouped under three headings: (1) 'Sperber's law,' (2) cultic origins, and (3) the distinctiveness of OT Hebrew."[4]

According to Sawyer, 'Sperber's law' says that "if at a certain time a complex of ideas is strongly charged with feeling, this will affect semantic development. In the OT, ideas connected with divine intervention are clearly a case in point, and the size and richness of the הוֹשִׁיעַ-field provide an obvious example of the influence of thought on language."[5] Under the second heading Sawyer mentions the importance of the cult as a formative influence on Hebrew idiom, whereas under the third heading he considers "a distinctive combination of both the factors already discussed, not only the overwhelming preoccupation of OT writers with the subject of God's intervention on behalf of his people (cf. Sperber's theory), but also the persistent and formative influence on their language of ancient Near Eastern cultic practice. .... While Israel undoubtedly shared many beliefs and much cultic practice with their neighbours, the degree to which their language about divine intervention was developed (by metaphorical transference, extension of meaning, semantic borrowing, and the like), is a measure of the distinctiveness of the religion of Israel. It is the highly developed language in which historical events are represented as acts of divine intervention that is distinctive, whether or not this language originally reflected

---

1   o.c. , p. 84.
2   Sawyer, 1967-68.
3   Sawyer, 1972.
4   o.c. , p. 40, 41.
5   o.c. , p. 41.

cultural practice."[1]

So it seems that Sawyer is more involved with the influence of thought on language, and does not refer to the opposite influence of language on thought, as postulated in the LRH.

In a monograph which attempts to introduce the basic principles of semantics to those readers of the Bible who are not familiar with them, Kedar shows more interest: "Es wäre eine lockende Aufgabe, die strukturellen Besonderheiten des Lexikons auf eine Charakterisierung der betreffenden Sprachgemeinschaft hin zu interpretieren, doch ließe diese sich bei der Überfülle der Daten gar nicht bewältigen. Aber auch Einzelbeobachtungen, wenngleich sie keine Folgerungen erlauben, sind nicht uninteressant."[2] At the same time he takes a critical attitude towards "das bemühen protestantischer Theologen, zu den Aussageintentionen des NT auf einem Umweg zu gelangen, nämlich aufgrund eines genaueren Verständnisses der hebr. Denkweise, wie sie sich in der Sprachstruktur manifestiert. Diese Methode stützt sich auf die von manchen Linguisten vertretene Auffassung von der engen Verknüpfung der Sprachstruktur mit dem Weltbild der betreffenden Sprachgemeinschaft. Die Theologen dieser Schule haben manch wertvollen Beitrag zur Wortforschung geleistet, doch sind ihre Arbeitshypothesen und -methoden vom linguistischen Standpunkt unzulässig in einem Maße, daß sie damit die biblische Semantik als solche in Mißkredit gebracht haben."[3] On the basis of this statement it is clear why Kedar himself does not undertake any attempt to develop a picture of the world view of Old Testament Hebrew or of the people who used that language.

The last publication of these four is a recent book by Cotterell and Turner which "introduces the interested student in a non-technical way to some aspects of linguistics which are relevant to biblical exegesis." It concentrates "on three main areas: first, the concept of meaning (semantics), and especially on the vexed question of lexical semantics, the meaning of words; second, the particular significance to be assigned to author, text, and reader in the search for the meaning of any particular part of the Bible; and third, the significance of the recognition of the role of the discourse as a whole (a conversation, a parable, an anecdote, an epistle) in determining meaning."[4]

In the chapter on "Dimensions of the Meaning of a Discourse" the authors make two observations: "First, significance is a relation of meaning between the sense of an utterance and some person's world, or at least some aspect of that world. We may thus appropriately talk both of the significance of the discourse for the speaker/writer (involving the premises and consequences he considered immediately relevant, and focused by it) and of the (possibly quite different)

---

1   o.c. , p. 44.
2   Kedar, 1981, p. 30.
3   o.c. , p. 49.
4   Cotterell & Turner, 1989, p. 9 - 10.

significance for his hearers or readers. As Hirsch put, significance is always meaning-for-someone. .... Second, the significance an utterance has for any hearer depends not only on the sense of what is spoken, and on the shared presupposition pool, but also on presuppositions held by the hearer that he does not share with the speaker."[1] By outlining these aspects the authors attempted "to indicate some of the kinds of clarification we may require in order to be sure we have discovered the discourse meaning of a text."[2]

With consent the authors discuss, in a separate chapter, Barr's criticism of word studies and, in the remaining part of their book, investigate the various aspects of meaning (of words, sentences, and discourses), but they do not seem to refer to any relation of it to the world or to the world-view of persons.

This last publication illustrates recent developments in the application of linguistics in biblical research. It appears that the field is broadening: whereas in the beginning mainly the meaning of words was investigated, now, sentences, discourses, and even whole texts are being considered. But for the relation between linguistic characteristics, such as grammar or lexicon on one hand, and world, world view or thought on the other, there seems to be little attention. So for the answering of the questions which formed the basis for our enquiry, these more recent general publications provide little help. In the remaining part of this chapter we will discuss a few publications which deal with more detailed aspects of the application of linguistics to the study of the Old Testament.

In the first place, we pay attention to the addendum which Koch wrote in 1974 to his well-known introduction to the exegetical method of the 'Formgeschichte.' For our purpose the most interesting section is the one entitled: "Besitzt das Hebräische eine besondere Weltansicht?"[3] After having emphasized the unique and characteristic features of each individual language, he asks: "Ist dann denkbar, daß eine anders gebaute Sprache, welcher andere Ausdrucksweisen und Vorstellungsinhalte eignen, den gleichen Verweisungszusammenhang und damit dieselben Unterscheidungsmöglichkeiten exakt anbieten kann? Das wäre nur der Fall, wenn Ausdrucksseite und Inhaltsseite so voneinander lösbar wären, daß jede Vorstellung durch einen beliebigen anderssprachlichen Ausdruck oder eine Ausdruckskombination völlig anderer Zusammensetzung bedeutungsidentisch wiederzugeben wäre. Das ist zwar in der Tat die Überzeugung mancher Linguisten, die mehr an sprachlichen Universalien als an Einzelsprachen interessiert sind. Aber es beruht auf eine Überzeugung axiomatischer Art, die aus dem unablässigen Austausch moderner europäischer Sprachen gewonnen sein mag, aber selbst hier nur für sondersprachliche Bereiche (Wissenschaft!) angesichts der alltäglichen Erfahrung wahrscheinlich ist. Zwar liegt auf der Hand, daß ein Wortlexem aus einer Sprache in einer anderen, wo ein

---

1   o.c. , p. 93, 94.
2   o.c. , p. 102.
3   Koch, 1974, p. 333 - 336.

entsprechendes Lexem nicht zur Verfügung steht, durch eine Umschreibung, also ein Syntagma, ebenso bedeutet werden kann. Aber eine Umschreibung birgt vermutlich jedesmal Konnotationen in sich, die dem Einzelwort abgehen. Ist eine Sprache ein Zeichen- und Bedeutungssystem, so wird der Gesamtstruktur ebenfalls eine charakteristische Bedeutung als Weltdeutung eignen, die sie von anderen Sprachsystemen unterscheidet. Ein Nachweis ist synchron kaum zu führen, da der Untersuchende die andere Sprache immer schon durch die Brille der eigenen sieht. Um so mehr drängt er sich bei diachronischer Betrachtung auf."[1] Koch realizes that this situation puts severe limitations to the possibilities of translating, but "Wo die Übersetzung aufhört, kann Interpretation weiterführen."[2]

It is noteworthy that Koch sees the 'Weltdeutung' of a language in connection with its total structure and not mainly with its lexicon, such as is apparent from the work of Boman.[3]

A similar broader view, which even includes the use of language, is described by Thiselton in the chapter on "Hermeneutics and Language" in his study of New Testament hermeneutics and philosophical description with special reference to Heidegger, Bultmann, Gadamer, and Wittgenstein: "The classification achieved by Wittgenstein, however, is to show that the influence of language on thought is not merely a matter of vocabulary-stock and surface-grammar, but of how language is used. The arguments of Boman, Whorf and others, that accidents of lexicology and surface-grammar condition thought, remains entirely open to question and doubt. We can now see why it is possible to claim that, on the one hand, Barr is right and Boman is wrong about the role of vocabulary in shaping thought; but that, on the other hand, Barr has not said the last word about the relationship between thought and language. .... To investigate this issue further, we need to inquire not about 'grammar' in the morphological sense of surface-grammar, but about 'grammar' in the conceptual or logical sense employed by Wittgenstein."[4]

Of the author's review of the work of the four scholars mentioned above, only a few remarks on Gadamer are directly relevant to our questions: "If every language represents a view of the world, it is this primarily not as a particular type of language (in the way that philologists see it) but because of what is said or handed down in this language."[5]

At the end of his investigation Thiselton arrives at the following conclusion: "The relation between hermeneutics and language introduces the questions about language and thought. Two sides have to be held together. On the one hand,

---

1   o.c. , p. 335 - 336.
2   o.c. , p. 336.
3   see also Koch, 1968 and Koch, 1991.
4   Thiselton, 1980, p. 138.
5   o.c. , p. 311.

accidents of surface-grammar and vocabulary stock do not usually determine thought in a decisive way. In this respect the claims of Saussure and his successors in linguistics are correct. Similarly Barr's attack on Boman, which is based on them, is also valid. But this is only half of the problem. On the other side, language-uses, as language habits, can and do influence thought in the way suggested by Gadamer and Wittgenstein. There is a half-truth in the Whorf hypothesis, which is significant for hermeneutics, especially for the problem of pre-understanding."[1]

In 1985 Thiselton contributed, together with Lundin and Walhout, to a monograph on "The Responsibility of Hermeneutics"[2] in which the authors try "to explore new models for interpretation, and have been drawn especially to those built upon concepts of action and responsibilty."[3] In this work they use ideas from literature theory in the development of a method of interpreting biblical texts. In his contribution, Walhout discusses the question of the reference of texts. After having reviewed a number of possibilities, he opts for the concept of self-reference. "On this view the referent is available in language itself: words have meaning because their referential power is contained within them or in their relationships to other words within a language system."[4] In this way he avoids all the problems which have to do with the relation of language/text with world/reality. In a similar way he eliminates nearly all problems connected with the relation of language/text to thought/cognition by following Iser who is "equally wary of a subjective and psychological view of reference and speaks of the text as representing to the reader not just signs or a set of directives but also a 'world' that is given in and through the language: 'We may assume that every literary text in one way or another represents a perspective view of the world put together by (though not necessarily typical of) the author. As such, the work is in no way a mere copy of the given world - it constructs a world of its own out of the material available to it. It is the way in which this world is constructed that brings about the perspective of the author.'"[5]

In line with his interest in interpretation, he subsequently pays much attention to the role of the reader. A remark he makes in connection with this aspect of the concept of reference, seems also of interest to the relation with the author: "All language has reference, though in case of fiction the language refers descriptively to fictional states of affairs, not to ones in the actual world. In a novel the language of the text refers to the fictionally projected states of affairs which constitute the fictional world of the novel. Because this is the case, the world of the text is designated by the language of the text and does not depend

---

1   o.c. , p. 440.
2   Lundin, Thiselton, Walhout, 1985.
3   o.c. , p. IX.
4   o.c. , p. 50 - 51.
5   o.c. , p. 53.

on the interaction of text and reader. In reading the novel the reader does not bring the world of the text into existence; rather the reader encounters it or witnesses it via the text's language. This is made possible by the text's descriptive references."[1] So it seems that all emphasis is put on language and text, which is also illustrated when Walhout writes that "our interest .... is not so much the author's deployment of the language as it is the descriptive references of language, the states of affairs it presents."[2]

It is true, that in Thiselton's contribution the reader and his world receive much attention, but too strong an emphasis on the 'reader-response hermeneutics' as developed recently by some literary critics is avoided, as will be clear from the following sentences both taken from the final page of his chapter: "This does not mean however, that the Bible becomes the nose of wax about which Luther warned, as if it could be pushed into any shape that the reader may fancy. .... No theoretical model provided by hermeneutical theory can obviate the need first and foremost to look at the text itself in its linguistic and historical particularity."[3]

In this application of modern linguistics for hermeneutical purposes, a number of interesting approaches of the relation of language and its use are brought forward. But for answering our specific questions it provides little new information.

The final publication which we wish to consider in this review of literature is a study of "Biblical Semantic Logic" by Gibson, in which he introduces "insights in mathematical logic and logic theory of meaning to biblical studies.[4] In his paragraph on "Reference and Intention," he critically examines a number of publications in the field of Old and New Testament, whereby his beginning words characterize the whole of his approach: "It is not uncommon to discover linguistic phenomena unguardedly psychologized ...."[5] His opinion on the relation of language and cognition is very clear: "It is a subtle task to make true statements about people's intentions because mental states and causality are more remote from public view than the functions of a text's values; thus it is easier to determine the function and effect of a text than to measure intention and intended effects. .... No linguist or philosopher has yet produced a theory presenting authoritative criteria for fixing a means of defining the relation of language and mind especially in the role of predicting the content of intention via linguistic expression."[6]

Gibson's approach provides support for the critical attitude of Barr and in particular underlines his first condition for a proper use of linguistic evidence

---

1   o.c. , p. 55 - 56.
2   o.c. , p. 63.
3   o.c. , p. 113.
4   Gibson, 1981.
5   o.c. , p. 87.
6   o.c. , p. 90, p. 91.

(see above paragraph 3.3.).

3.6. Summary.
We started this chapter with a literature search on what is known of the perception of space in the Old Testament. The initial assessment of the result of that search led us to an additional search into some more fundamental issues of language and thought as they play a role in the study of the Old Testament. Since the area is very broad, we formulated a few questions as a guideline for this search hoping to keep it within reasonable limits. Although we cannot claim complete coverage of the whole literature on the application of linguistics in the study of the OT, we feel confident that we have collected the most essential evidence available for answering the questions as formulated in section 3.2.7.
This evidence can be summarized as follows:
Question 1. Is there a relation between language and thought in general, and in particular between language and perception, way of thinking and formation of concepts?
To the general part of this question we obtained a clear answer: yes. Even critical authors, like Barr and Gibson, agree that there is a relation between language and thought, although they believe it to be very complicated. The complex character of this relation seems to be connected with the complex nature of the two phenomena involved, as emphasized regarding language in particular by Barr, and regarding thought by Gibson. According to both scholars, this relation is not easily available for (scientific) description, and can only be used adequately when certain conditions have been met.
Question 2. What is the nature of this relation?
Contrary to the critical approach described above, other scholars, in agreement with the LRH, adopt a more positive attitude. According to them, the relation is very simple, and consists of a more or less clear parallelism between thought and language. Most of them also emphasize that it operates mainly in one direction: the lexicon and grammar of a language influence in a decisive way the thought of the people who use that language. However, there are others like Sawyer who seem to emphasize the other direction of the relation: the emotional feeling, the interest and the situation of the people have a great influence on the language they use.
Question 3. To what extent can this relation be used to obtain a model of the thought patterns (perception, way of thinking, etc.) of people on the basis of their (use of) language only?
Those who believe in a clear parallelism between thought and language simply use data of the lexicon and grammar of a particular language for devising a model of the thought patterns and world-view of the people speaking that language. Examples are Boman and Stadelmann, whose descriptions of the ideas and conceptual approaches of the people of the Old Testament suggest that they had direct access to their minds.
Those who believe the relation between thought and language to be very

71

complicated either consider it to be of no use in scientific research (some authors as quoted by Barr), or provide strict conditions for such an investigation (Barr himself and Gibson).

Others seem to take a position between these extremes. Sawyer restricts the results of his investigation to a few 'linguistic and theological statements,' which describe the use of certain linguistic features for expressing certain theological ideas. However, he does not indicate any cause or motive why the connection between these particular features and these particular ideas has been made.

Koch assumes that each language possesses a characteristic world-view. According to him, this implies that the user of that language can express his thoughts only in a particular way. From his considerations, however, it is not clear whether and in what way we can move the other way round: decide on features of the world-view of the speakers on the basis of the world-view of their language.

The same concept is used by Walhout and Thiselton, but in most cases they connect it with the text, and speak of the world-view of the text. It is not clear what the contribution of the language used by the text is to its world-view. On one or two occasions they refer to the world-view of the language.

The idea that texts, in particular narratives, 'project' or 'call into being' an imagined world or reality, is not new as far as the study of the Old Testament is concerned.[1] Even the spatial characteristics of this process and its product have been discussed, but only in a very general way, which pays no attention to the influence of the perception of space, either by the author or by the reader.[2] Nevertheless, the use of this idea for obtaining a well-founded picture of the perception of space in the Old Testament looks promising. If it were possible to describe more or less exactly the spatial characteristics of the world or reality projected by the Old Testament, we could try to relate these to 'ways of perceiving' and subsequently arrive at a picture of the perception of space in the Old Testament.

From this discussion of what we have found in the light of the three questions which guided our literature search in the field of the study of the Old Testament, it is obvious that it provided us with much useful information. At the same time, it will be clear that a number of problems remain.

1. The position of the LRH.

It is remarkable that as far as the literature on the Old Testament is concerned no new evidence on the LRH has been brought forward since about 1970. More recent publications seem to repeat only the older arguments. Is this due to the fact that no further discussion has taken place in the fields of linguistics and other disciplines? As long as the position and scope of the LRH remain unclear, a satisfactory assessment, both of the methodological aspects and of the results

---

1   see for example Licht, 1978, p. 10.
2   Crites, 1987.

72

of the publications reviewed in paragraph 3.2., is not possible.

2. The concept of world-view.

It looks as if this concept can be used in connection with persons, languages and texts. In the first case, it is directly related to the contents and patterns of human thought. In the second and third case, it seems that language and text receive a more independent position, and the concept of world or reality connected with them is of a more descriptive, or even 'objective,' nature. This raises the question of the influence of the world-view of the reader on this description. Thiselton rejects an important role for such an influence, but he refers to some literary critics who assign it a dominating position. There seem to be conflicting ideas on this concept. A similar question exists as far as the influence of the world-view of the author on that of the text is concerned, but the publications of Lundin and Thiselton are silent on this point. Before using the concept of world-view ourselves, it seems wise to explore its merits in linguistics and related fields.

3. The structure of thought.

Our study is concerned with the perception of space in the Old Testament. The perception (and experience) of space, however, often is accessible to us only through the way people think or express their thoughts on other subjects, rather than directly through the contents of their texts. In ancient texts, authors do not write on their perception of space as a separate topic. Thus, we will have to obtain a picture of it by 'reading between the lines' of texts of the Old Testament in which the authors write on other subjects. In this connection, it would be helpful to have a better idea of the structure of thought, and in particular, in what way its various levels are interrelated. Do perception, 'way of thinking' or 'thinking pattern,' and the contents of the thought(s) influence each other? As might be expected, the literature of the study of the Old Testament does not provide much information in this respect.

Since we consider these three points to be very important for achieving the objective of our study, we decided to continue our literature search.

All three points have to do with the broad concepts of language and thought, and the relation between them. Disciplines which might be relevant for information on these concepts and their relation are linguistics and psychology, but also cultural anthropology.

On the basis of the Old Testament literature which we have reviewed so far, we also know that at the basis of the methodological problems involved, philosophical issues play an important role, so it will be necessary to cover these as well.

Hence, our study will continue with a 'reconnaissance survey' especially directed towards the three points mentioned above and covering linguistics, psychology, cultural anthropology and philosophy.

4. THE LINGUISTIC RELATIVITY HYPOTHESIS AND THE CONTRIBUTION OF LINGUISTICS, PSYCHOLOGY AND ANTHROPOLOGY.

4.1. Introduction.

The literature of these disciplines (and of philosophy which is covered in chapter 5), is of so extensive that we need to discriminate carefully in order to keep the amount of publications retrieved by our search (see above paragraph 3.6.) at a reasonable size.

Initially we used the following key-words: linguistic relativity; Whorf-Sapir hypothesis; language, and thought or cognition or reality or world. While searching, we soon discovered that in a number of publications on linguistic relativity, space and spatial aspects in language and culture in general played an important role. This led us to including the words space and spatial in our search scheme in order to find more publications covering space and language, which might be relevant for our own investigation of the perception of space in the Old Testament.

By applying this set of words to the literature of the last ten years, and in addition consulting relevant quotations in publications retrieved, we were able to select a collection of literature which we will use for obtaining a better picture of the situation of the LRH, and the other two points mentioned in 3.6.

Of course, this literature search cannot claim total coverage, but we hope that it will serve our aim to carry out a reconnaissance survey only. In this chapter we will concentrate on the contribution of the disciplines mentioned in its title. More fundamental and philosophical issues will be covered in chapter 5.

Since our main reason for making this search is the unclear position of the LRH in the science of the Old Testament, we will present the material to be reviewed in this chapter around this topic. In paragraph 4.2. we will concentrate in particular on questions of formulation and scope of the LRH. Paragraph 4.3. contains reviews of a number of publications which deal with particular aspects of the LRH. A review of the literature on space and spatial aspects, considered to be relevant in connection with our study of the perception of space in the Old Testament, is given in paragraph 4.4. A preliminary summary, only covering this part of the literature search is given in paragraph 4.5.

4.2. Formulation and scope of the Linguistic Relativity Hypothesis.

Unfortunately there exists no generally accepted or authoritative formulation of the LRH. In order to illustrate the problems to which this situation leads, we start by giving two quotations, one from each of the scientists whose names are closely connected with the LRH. The first one is from a paper by Sapir from 1929, as cited by Stam:

"Language is a guide to 'social reality' .... It powerfully conditions all our thinking about social problems and processes. Human beings do not live in the objective world alone, nor alone in the world of social activity as ordinarily understood, but are very much at the mercy of the particular language which has become the medium of expression for their society. It is quite an illusion to imagine that one adjusts to reality essentially without the use of language and that language is merely an incidental means of solving specific problems of communication or reflection. The fact of the matter is that the 'real world' is to a large extent unconsciously built up on the language habits of the group. No two languages are ever sufficiently similar to be considered as representing the same social reality. The worlds in which different societies live are distinct worlds, not merely the same world with different labels attached."[1]

The second quotation is from the other proponent of the LRH, Whorf:

"When linguists became able to examine critically and scientifically a large number of languages of widely diverging patterns, their base of reference was expanded; they experienced an interruption of phenomena hitherto held universal, and a whole new order of significances came into their ken. It was found that the background linguistic system (in other words, the grammar) of each language is not merely a reproducing instrument for voicing ideas but rather is itself the shaper of ideas, the program and guide for the individual's mental activity, for his analysis of impressions, for his synthesis of his mental stock in trade. Formulation of ideas is not an independent process, strictly rational in the old sense, but is part of a particular grammar, and differs, from slightly to greatly, between different grammars. We dissect nature along lines laid down by our native languages. The categories and types that we isolate from the world of phenomena we do not find there because they stare every observer in the face; on the contrary, the world is presented in a kaleidoscopic flux of impressions which has to be organized by our minds - and this means largely by the linguistic systems in our minds. We cut nature up, organize it into concepts, and ascribe significances as we do, largely because we are parties to an agreement to organize it in this way - an agreement that holds throughout our speech community and is codified in the patterns of our language. The agreement is, of course, an implicit and unstated one, but its terms are absolutely obligatory; we cannot talk at all except by subscribing to the organization and classification of data which the agreement decrees.

This fact is very significant for modern science, for it means that no individual is free to describe nature with absolute impartiality but is constrained to certain modes of interpretation even while he thinks himself most free. The person most nearly free in such respect would be a linguist familiar with very many widely different linguistic systems. As yet no linguist is in any such position. We are thus introduced to a new principle of relativity, which holds that all

---

1   Stam, 1980, p. 240.

observers are not led by the same physical evidence to the same picture of the universe, unless their linguistic backgrounds are similar, or can in some way be calibrated."[1]

These quotations certainly provide us with an idea of what the LRH is about, but at the same time they prompt us to consider a few questions:

1. What exactly is the influence of language on thought? Is it only restrictive, as expressed by Sapir: "It powerfully conditions ....", or by Whorf: ".... no individual is free to describe ...."? Or is there a positive influence as well, as suggested by expressions as ".... the 'real world' is .... built up on the language habits of the group" (Sapir), or ".... shaper of ideas ...." (Whorf)?

2. What areas of thought are covered by the LRH? Is it restricted to human ideas about 'nature' (Whorf), or does it include 'social reality' as well (Sapir)?

3. What aspect of language is involved in its influencing thought? Whorf seems to put emphasis on the grammar, whereas Sapir uses a more general term: 'language habits of the group.'

As a result of these 'open aspects' of the LRH, scholars writing on it have distinguished between various forms of linguistic relativity and the LRH.

In her study of the origins of the LRH in German thought, Penn suggests that it "might better be regarded as two hypotheses, an extreme one asserting the dependence of thought on language and a mild one suggesting some influence of linguistic categories on cognition. The extreme hypothesis will be shown to be the one that Whorf, Sapir, Humboldt and Herder each asserted at some time."[2] The addition of the words 'at some time' to the last sentence points to an additional unclarity in the study of the LRH: the scholars involved with it seem sometimes to be in favour of the extreme version and sometimes to support the less extreme form. Since we are not interested in the historical development of the LRH, this problem does not need to bother us too much. The important point is that these various forms of the LRH exist. In connection with the scope of the LRH the following conclusion of Penn is worth noting: "The extreme relativity hypothesis was propounded first by Hamann and Herder. Both were interested in asserting the ineffable, magical individuality of each separate people. Therefore, both were interested in countering Kant's rationalist doctrine of innate ideas (which assumed all people are alike in certain ways, regardless of their nationality)."[3] So her study reveals the early connection between the LRH and ethnology and the more fundamental controversy between universalism and particularism.

By using a 'two-way classification' Slobin arrives at four forms of the LRH. Similar to Penn he recognizes a 'strong' version, which holds "that the language determines thought and behavior patterns; that the language is a sort of mold

---

1   Whorf, 1956, p. 212 - 214.
2   Penn, 1972, p. 10.
3   o.c. , p. 53.

for thought and philosophy", and a 'weak' form, which "merely asserts that certain aspects of language can predispose people to think or act in one way rather than another, but that there is no rigid determinism: One is not fully a prisoner of one's language; it is just a guide to thought and other sorts of behavior."[1] Regarding the linguistic side he distinguishes between the stock of words as included in the lexicon of the language involved, and the grammatical processes used in it.

By combining the two distinctions he notices four forms of the LRH:

		Linguistic Variables	
		Lexical	Grammatical
Form of	Strong		
Determinism	Weak		

At the beginning of his review of the LRH, Steinfatt writes: "I believe linguistic relativity implies that there is a set of independent variables (a), based on differences between languages in phonology, grammar, or semantics which must be the basis for the proposed difference, which must influence a dependent variable set (b), composed of logic (LR-LO), or cognitive structure and world-view (LR-GCS), or perception, individual cognitions, or areas of cognition (LR-CA), each manifested in observable behavior. This has the effect of proposing three linguistic relativity hypotheses corresponding to LR-LO, LR-GCS, and LR-CA, where at least one of these areas must be influenced by one or more of the independent variable areas for linguistic relativity to be said to occur."[2] So Steinfatt, whose review we will discuss in more detail in section 4.3.7., arrives at a diversification of the LRH by distinguishing several levels at the thought side of the relationship.

Fishman initially distinguishes between "two theories commonly associated with Whorf (the linguistic relativity hypothesis .... and the linguistic determinism hypothesis ....),"[3] which have received widespread attention. He points to a third aspect of the scientific activity of Whorf: "It is Whorf's abiding faith in the benefits of linguistic diversity that attracted many of us to him and to the language-related disciplines and that may well continue to do so for others regardless the fate of (the two theories)."[4] It is this 'value-related aspect' of Whorf's work which is at the root of the current "revival of Whorfianism in

---

1   Slobin, 1971, p. 122.
2   Steinfatt, 1989, p. 35 - 36.
3   Fishman, 1989, p. 565.
4   o.c. , p. 574.

linguistics and anthropology."[1]

Others have also pointed to the social issues connected with the LRH.[2] In line with this approach these publications tend to pay more attention to the use of language than to its structure.

In an attempt to connect linguistic relativism with poetic indeterminacy, Friedrich argues "that the most interesting and surely the most complex differences between natural languages are centered in the relatively poetic levels of sound and meaning, be this poetry strictly speaking or a poetic stratum in other kinds of discourse."[3] In the final chapter of his book Friedrich indicates a few problems for the future development of linguistic relativism, the second of which reads: "A theory of linguistic relativism, if it is to be realistic and contemporary, must be conceptualized at once vaguely and precisely so that it transcends the partly terminological paradoxes and dilemmas of structure/content, structure/process, structure/variation, and for that matter, subjective/objective and rational/irrational."[4]

From this review of a few more general publications on the LRH it will be clear that its formulation, investigation and consequences cause a lot of problems. In addition they show that the debate on its merits and role has by no means ended. Recently, general and historical surveys of the idea of linguistic relativity have been published by De Pater[5] and Werlen.[6]

In the following paragraph we will discuss a number of publications which deal with those particular aspects of the LRH, which seem to be important in view of the questions formulated in paragraph 3.6.

4.3. Investigations of the Linguistic Relativity Hypothesis.

4.3.1. Introduction.

In this paragraph we will review a number of publications of the last two decades which have the LRH as their main topic, and consider it from a particular point of view. Publications which are directed to more fundamental issues of the relation between language and thought will be included in chapter 5. At the end of each section we give a short, initial comment on the publication concerned. Our summary of the results will be included in paragraph 4.5., after reviewing the publications on language and space.

4.3.2. Is there a linguistic relativity principle? Gipper.

The most extensive investigation of the LRH which we have been able to find

---

1   o.c. , p. 565.
2   see e.g. Hickmann, 1987.
3   Friedrich, 1986, p. 3.
4   o.c. , p. 157 - 58.
5   De Pater, 1986.
6   Werlen, 1989.

is the study of Gipper published in 1972. We will also refer to the text of a lecture which the same author held at a Colloquium on the Sapir-Whorf Hypotheses in 1973, and which was published in the proceedings of that meeting in 1976.

The empirical basis of his study is an attempt to verify the linguistic evidence which led Whorf to devise his hypothesis, viz. the conception of time and space of the Hopi, a tribe of Indians who live in the state of Arizona, USA. In addition he gives a thorough introduction to the underlying ideas, the historical setting and the scientific disputes concerning the LRH. It seems wise to start our review of his work with a lengthy quotation which illustrates his own attitude towards the whole field concerned:

"To explore the fundamentals of the linguistic relativity principle, we must distinguish among three concepts, which are clearly delineated in the German philosophical tradition: (1) Weltbild, (2) Weltanschauung, and (3) sprachliche Weltansicht (Humboldt) or sprachliches Weltbild (Weisgerber).

1. By Weltbild is meant the scientific view of the interconnections of the world or cosmos, i.e. a cosmography. Thus we speak of a Ptolemean Weltbild, of a Galilean or a Einsteinian Weltbild. In this sense Weltbild is the product of scientific thought of an era.

2. Weltanschauung refers to the structure of human belief concerning the nature of the world and human affairs. It is an ideological concept with religious or political implications. We speak thus of a Christian, a Marxist, or materialistic Weltanschauung.

3. With the term sprachliche Weltansicht or sprachliches Weltbild we imply that our experience of the world is construed not only by our senses but also by the categories of the language we have learned. The vocabulary we use construes a specific view of things, of facts, and of events. Sprachliches Weltbild is an a priori condition making specific thought and speech possible.

Following G. Frege we may say that sprachliches Weltbild has to do with the 'Art des Gegebenseins von Welt in den Kategorien und semantischen Gliederungen einer natürlichen Sprache' (the nature of the representation of the world in the categories and semantic structures of a natural language). The concept is devoid of ideological speculation; it points to the condition of human existence.

There are, of course, relations between (scientific) Weltbild, (ideological) Weltanschauung, and (linguistic) Weltansicht or Weltbild. The first two are impossible without the mediation of the last concept. They are founded and expressed by means of a particular language and hence are colored by its semantic categories and structures. We must, therefore, at the same time keep in mind that different, even contradictory, views of the world may be expressed in the same language. A competent speaker of German or English may be an adherent of different Weltbilder and Weltanschauungen: He may become a partisan of Kopernicus or Einstein, of Christ or Marx.

Nevertheless, whatever he may think or believe, he owes to the means his

79

language places at his disposal. This undeniable fact must be accounted for in our discussion of the linguistic relativity principle. If we hold these distinctions in mind and if we take care not to lose sight of them in the translation of relevant contexts from one language to another we shall avoid tedious, unproductive discussions. We might add that by comparison with other languages and discovering the relationships between words and things we can gain insight into the specific world view of our language. We are not hopelessly bound by the limits of our mother tongue."[1]

His attempt to verify the ideas of Whorf concerning the different space-time-conception of the Hopi as compared to the one adopted by Western Europeans has been directed mainly towards the time component. He mentions the following reason for this decision: "Das Raumproblem ist, wenigstens soweit es sprachwissenschaftlich relevant wird, wesentlich unkomplizierter, weil es sich hier um die mehr materiale Seite der Wirklichkeitserfahrung handelt, die wesentlich leichter sprachlich objektiviert werden kann."[2]

On the basis of an investigation of the available literature on the Hopi language, and two visits to their living area and further personal contacts Gipper was able to compile a list of expressions for spatial and temporal relations in Hopi.[3]

This list and the results of his discussions with Hopi Indians themselves enabled him to draw a number of conclusions, including a few corrections to the views of Whorf. Below, we cite those thought to be important, either in general or in connection with our own investigation:

"2. There is evidence for time intervals which can be said to belong, contrary to Whorf's view, to the category of nouns, and at least some of these nouns can be pluralized. ....

4. Contrary to Whorf's opinion, expressions for spatial relations are used metaphorically in a temporal sense, in other words, there are space-time metaphors as in Indo-European languages. ....

7. There are grammatical means in Hopi to express present, past, and future, though the Hopi thinking seems to be governed by a bipartition of time ('present + past' and 'future') instead of the tripartion of time ('past' - 'present' - 'future') we are accustomed to. ....

11. I was not able to verify Whorf's statement that the Hopi world view is dominated by the distinction of 'two aspects of one reality,' the 'objective or manifested' and the 'subjective or manifesting (or unmanifested)' or that this dualism is expressed by use of special linguistic forms.

We may thus conclude that although Whorf's exaggerated statements require some correction, there remains evidence for the fact that Hopi time is, in various aspects, different from ours.

1   Gipper, 1976, p. 219 - 220; see also Gipper, 1972; p. 15 - 42.
2   Gipper, 1972, p. 173.
3   o.c. , p. 253 - 296.

As to the conception of space, the difference between Hopi views and ours is far less evident. There are many expressions for spatial relations and for dimensions of things. They are in part comparable to the spatial prepositions and adverbs in Indo-European languages. ....

The four cardinal directions are very important. We have to add to these the two vertical directions (up to the sky and down to the 'hadir'), These six dimensions are often referred to during ceremonies.

Whorf seems to be right in stating that there are no special words for the different rooms of a Hopi house (such as kitchen, bedroom, etc.). But the word 'kiva' is certainly the expression for the underground ceremonial chamber.

To date it has not been possible for me to verify Whorf's statement concerning the operational character of time-space expressions (an event which has happened far away is said to have happened in the past since the report of it can only come when the event is past)."[1]

Following the discussion of his results, Gipper considers the question, what remains of Whorf's statements. Again, we give a number of quotations from his reaction:

"Our analysis seems to imply a negative answer, but in reality the problem is more complicated. First, we must not forget that fundamental conceptions of human life such as space and time are not exclusively bound to language but are dependent - as language itself - on the whole 'context of culture' of the given society. Language can not express all the details; language is always abstractive and the meaning of words has to be supported by the thing meant. We must take into account the whole of Hopi life, the beliefs of the people as well as their remarkable geographical location. ....

Here we find evidence for the predominance of a cyclic conception of time combined with a dual conception of human life on earth and the 'life of the dead' in the underworld. ....

The Hopi are still completely integrated in their environment. They have not yet reached that detachment from events which is one of the prerequisites for our Western concept of physical time. Their conception of time corresponds to that of old peasant societies. ....

In a 'primitive' or original culture like that of the Hopis a scientific Weltbild has not yet been developed. The Hopi cosmography - if there is any - closely linked with the Hopi Weltanschauung, that is their religious beliefs. Hopi thinking has not yet reached a critical distance towards language. The confidence in the 'truth values,' so to speak, of the mother tongue is therefore greater than in our societies. Thus the Hopi language can be said to be an authentic key to the understanding of the Hopi Weltanschauung. In other words, the sprachliche Weltansicht of the Hopi language is a more adequate expression of Hopi thought than this is nowadays the case with the Indo-European

---

1   Gipper, 1976, p. 221 - 225.

languages. Therefore a careful study of the Hopi language and that of the other Indian languages is important for the problem of the linguistic relativity principle. ....

.... linguistic research cannot be undertaken in isolation from the speakers and the world they refer to.

Human thought is, to be sure, relative to the possibilities of the languages in which it is expressed, but it is not determined by language. Each natural language represents an open system and therefore it is open to be changed by the speakers."[1]

From these quotations it will be clear that Gipper's work provides an important contribution to the study of the LRH. He pays attention to a number of more fundamental issues and his publications contain a number of interesting suggestions regarding our questions. In particular his remarks on the concept of world-view, and on the 'distance' between this concept and language in 'primitive' cultures deserve careful attention.

4.3.3. Epistemic Universals. Pinxten.

At the same colloquium at which Gipper lectured on his study of the LRH, Pinxten presented the result of his work in this field. As the title of his paper already suggests, his starting-point is completely different from that of Gipper, and this is corroborated by the following quotations: "It seems most improbable to me that the systems of man's knowledge profoundly differ, relative to the linguistic system he uses. This incredulity rests upon two intuitions:
- the hierarchical structure of knowledge systems. ....
- the identity of a whole set of fundamental physical and biological determinants for all human beings. ....

This set of invariants in a highly variable surrounding defines two interacting systems: man (self, body) and environment. Language and mind - two human subsystems - are the results as well as the instruments of this interaction. The problem, then, is to determine which one is primary to the other; which one is subject/object of the other, the latter being a direct instrument of the interaction with environmental phenomena. ....

Since concrete grammars seem to differ quite largely, but since, on the other hand, the environment as well as the initial biophysiological equipment of man are universally comparable and to some degree uniform, I conclude that it may be interesting to try to search for universal elements in the semantic (cognitive or representational) subsystem. ....

It is my intuition that these epistemic phenomena are indeed universal up to a strictly definable degree, and thus form a universal subsystem of human interaction with the environment. If this intuition should be validated, then at least the hypothesis of the absolute primacy of language upon thought

---

1   o.c. , p. 225 - 227.

(synchronically and diachronically) can be rejected; at most the reverse could be taken into consideration."[1]

The implications of these intuitions with regard to the problems put forward by Whorf, are described by Pinxten as follows: "Attacking the problems involved in the study of the language-thought relation, two positions remain possible: the relativistic and the universalistic. A choice must be made.

Complementing this choice, another decision is required: shall we be concerned with the analysis of linguistic or of epistemic (cognitive) phenomena?"[2]

For various, mainly pragmatical, reasons, Pinxten decided to investigate whether "the most fundamental cognitive (epistemic) concepts are universal," and he chose space as an example.[3]

As regards the investigation itself, the author mentions four requisites, which he describes as follows:

"The material to be analyzed consists of descriptions of knowledge systems and cultural habits of a few non-Western civilizations. ....:

Chinese civilization before Christ ....;

Liberian and Dogo civilizations, and two studies on Sub-Saharan African cultures ....;

Some Indian world views, complemented with two works on Ancient Aztecs;

two works on pre-Socratic thought.

I understand that these choices will be subject to much criticism.

Moreover, the material is entirely secondhand, since I had to draw completely on experiences and descriptions of others. I think it nevertheless important that a first approach in this direction should be attempted."[4]

The analytical tool used by Pinxten is "an elaborate model of space by the psychologist Jean Piaget, worked out through many observations and experiments on children of different age classes."[5] In a separate paragraph he gives an extensive description of this model of space: Piaget distinguishes during the development of a child three phases of space perception: topological, projective, and euclidian. Each of these phases represents a certain way of experiencing space and spatial relations, and can be characterized by typical behaviour and utterances. A detailed survey of the Piaget-model falls beyond the scope of our survey; what is important for us is the way in which it is used by Pinxten in his investigation. He sees it as a "hierarchic system representing the constitution of psychological spatial features," and wants to use it for the comparison of the space concepts of our and other civilizations: "It is thus out of the question to take into consideration the genetic aspects of Piaget's model,

---

1   Pinxten, 1976, p. 117 - 119.
2   o.c. , p. 119.
3   o.c. , p. 122.
4   o.c. , p. 126.
5   o.c. , p. 126.

which could imply that non-Western man is, by definition, comparable to the Western child of some specific age, rather than to Western adults."[1]

The method used in the investigation is described by Pinxten as "processes of matching and recognition." Each level of the Piaget-model "is constituted by a spatial characteristic that is neatly distinguished from, but in itself fully implies, the concept of the previous, lower level. The method to be followed consists of the systematic matching of the subsequent spatial characteristics of the (with regard to the research) a priori framework with the spatial concepts of each non-Western civilization."[2] In this way the author wants to find out what levels of the Piaget-model can be recognized in the other cultures. Together these common levels might form a/the universal concept of space.

By this investigation Pinxten hopes to solve the problem, which he formulates in the following hypothesis: "There exists a universal concept of space that is independent of cultural and/or linguistic differences. Specifically, the fundamental features of the hierarchical space concepts are universal; the more complicated and higher features are particular for each culture."[3]

The empirical part of his investigation consists of an attempt to find in all the descriptions of non-Western civilizations the equivalent of each component of the model of Piaget.

Before presenting his conclusions Pinxten makes the rather enigmatic remark: "Since it is my opinion that not the actual results of the analysis on the preceding pages, but rather the analysis itself and its underlying epistomological principles are the most important, I shall stress only these latter aspects of my article."[4]

From his conclusions we give the following quotations:

"First, it appears that a few, and namely the most basic features of spatial representation - according to Piaget's model, of course - turn out to be universal; that is, all topological notions can be recognized with ease in the spatial constitution of all civilizations. ....

Second, some higher level constitutions appear in nearly all non-European civilizations. ....

Third, a set of Piagetian spatial features appears as culture specific, with a high probability of their specificness. ....

Finally, ... [i]t is clear that universals are to be found mainly in the more fundamental regions of representation - the topological notions and some of the projective notions. .... I would ... claim to have produced evidence for the

---

1   o.c. , p. 141.
2   o.c. , p. 126
3   o.c. , p. 127.
4   o.c. , p. 165.

universality - the cultural independence - of the more fundamental features."[1]
Considering the implications of his work for the LRH, Pinxten writes: "It would thus be pointed out that universal cognitive features exist, and that the conditioning influence (there can be no more question about determining influence) of language would be restricted to the higher level constructs. The Whorfian hypothesis in its weakest form is then pushed up (or aside?) to the level of less fundamental, more differentiated representations of space. It most probably remains relevant (cf. the impossibility of reognizing spatial features on the higher levels inall civilizations), though perhaps on less 'vital,' fundamental topics than Whorf had hoped. Instead of determining one's outlook on the world as such, it would serve as a modifying instrument in the perception and conceptualization of more specific differenciations of segmentations or structurings of the world.

A further consequence of this analysis, and - I gather - the most crucial aspect of my contribution, is the denial of absolute linguistic primacy, both synchronic and diachronic, to be replaced by either cognitive or epistemic primacy (as Piaget advocates), or by some sort of coexistence of fundamental cognitive and linguistic characteristics."[2]

Pinxten's investigation covers many languages, and shows methodological clarity, but unfortunately it does not go into much detail. This implies a number of limitations of which the author seems to be well aware. The most important drawback is that his 'raw material' (the descriptions of the non-Western cultures) has been written by Westerners, people who are not original to the cultures and languages concerned. It is interesting that he uses the experience of space as the area for assessing the LRH. As compared to Gipper, he pays more attention to its cognitive side; whereas in this publication he uses the Piaget-model of space-experience as an analytical tool, in a later book on space experience which we will discuss in paragraph 4.4., he applies a more general 'universal frame of reference.'

4.3.4. Linguistic relativity and linguistic structure. Robins and Langacker.
At the same colloquium at which Gipper and Pinxten reported on their investigations of the LRH, Robins reviewed the changes in linguistics since the time Sapir and Whorf formulated the LRH: "The important changes in linguistics since 1960, after the impact of transformational-generative theories, are, as far as the Sapir-Whorf hypothesis is concerned, the present emphasis on the underlying sameness, or at least the similarity, of languages, the renewed emphasis on linguistic universals as evidence of the unity of the structure of the human mind as species-specific to man (e.g. Chomsky), and the recognition, in one or another form, of two levels of syntactic structure - deep structure and

---

1   o.c. , p. 165 - 66.
2   o.c. , p. 167.

surface structure. One could say that in Whorf's time the structures of the structuralists and of Whorf's linguistic writings were surface structures."[1]

After having noticed that most adherents of the transformational-generative theory of linguistics assume universality in the deep structures, and diversity in the surface structures, Robins continues: "Any reexamination of the Sapir-Whorf hypothesis today must take into account the concepts of deep structure and surface structure. It would seem that linguistic relativity would most readily be locatable in the effects of surface structure patterns, which are the syntactic structures of sentences as they are produced and as they are heard and read. .... Do different surface structures make certain conceptualizations easier or more natural, though not, of course, obligatory? Perhaps we should test the Sapir-Whorf hypothesis in this form by reference to various typologically diverse languages, comparing the ways in which their habitual overt pattern of surface syntactic relations differ from the underlying, probably universal, relations between entities of thought and the elements of deep structure syntax."[2]

This suggestion gives rise to questions on the nature of these deep structures: Do they belong to the syntactic or semantic side of language? What is their precise relation to thought?

From the point of view of generative semantics, these questions have been discussed by Langacker. He starts by stating that no rigid division can be made between syntax and semantics, and continues: "I agree with the notion that the underlying representations posited to account for syntactic structure have semantic motivation, and I agree further that the most abstract underlying representation that can be syntactically motivated is itself of such a nature that it is not improperly characterized as a semantic representation. Thus I reject the idea of a significant level of representation, called deep structure, intermediate between surface and semantic representations and dividing grammar into separate syntactic and semantic components."[3]

So Langacker accepts the generative semantic claim that the concepts and constructs needed for the characterization of syntactic structure are also appropriate for the characterization of at least certain aspects of semantic representations. But he believes that two other notions, "transformational grammarians, and generative semanticists in particular, have flirted with," are incorrect, namely:

"(1) semantic representations are universal, i.e. there are no language-specific differences at the level of semantic structure; and

(2) semantic structure can, in some unclear but hopefully straightforward way, be related directly to thought and cognition, i.e. the structures manipulated in cognition are essentially the same as the semantic structures underlying

---

1   Robins, 1976, p. 103.
2   o.c. , p. 103 -104.
3   Langacker, 1976, p. 315.

sentences. ....

These two ideas are closely tied to a third notion entertained by many generative grammarians (one to which I subscribe):
(3) cognition is essentially the same for speakers of all languages. (3) is basically denial of the LRH."[1]

In the remainder of his paper, Langacker tries to demonstrate that both (1) and (2) are false, despite the validity of (3). Against (2) Langacker maintains that the coding transition, i.e. the translation of a current conceptual structure into a linguistic form, specifically into a semantic representation, is not a vacuous operation, but "involves two aspects, 'selection' and 'reformulation,'" in which "linguistic factors, at both the lexical and sentential level, play a significant role. .... Even when we have a fairly precise idea of what we want to say, we must submit our conceptualization for coding to the exigencies of language structure, which impose significant constraints on its content (and possibly also its form)."[2]

After having noticed that the formal or configurational properties of semantic representations are still very much a matter of debate in linguistics, Langacker summarizes his arguments against (2) as follows: "I have argued that coding is a non-vacuous and probably significant step in the linguistic manifestation of conceptual structures, even if we construe it narrowly to include only linguistic factors, and regardless of the specific claims we might make about the formal properties of semantic representations and conceptual structures. While we can hardly talk of proof in the present context, I hope at least to have established the plausibility, if not the probable truth, of the claim that conceptual structures and semantic representations cannot be equated. We must cast our thoughts in an appropriate, linguistically-determined form before we can proceed to express them.

This conclusion has the following important implication: there is no necessary reason to suppose that semantic representations are universal. .... I believe that (1) is in fact false, that semantic representations are not universal in all respects."[3]

In subsequent paragraphs of his paper, Langacker illustrates this statement with a number of examples, both at the lexical level, and from the grammar. During the discussion of the latter, he underlines that "[v]irtually all language is figurative to some degree." He explains why he has been careful to use the terms 'figurative' and 'image' rather than the term 'metaphor,' as follows: "Though usage of course varies enormously, the term 'metaphor' is generally applied to cases where the literal meaning of an expression is used to convey - by analogy, parable, or gross exaggeration - a sense that is largely or totally different from the literal one, as when we say 'She blossomed into an attractive young woman.' The term 'image' as I use it here includes metaphor as a special

---

1   o.c. , p. 317.
2   o.c. , p. 326 - 27.
3   o.c. , p. 330.

case, but it also includes instances where alternate means are available for construing or visualizing a conceived situation for purposes of coding, none of which is necessarily metaphorical in the strong sense of the term."[1]

At the end of his paper Langacker gives a number of implications of his presentation and support of a "fairly elaborate conception of the relation between language and thought in the context of modern linguistic theory. ....

First, linguistic theory cannot continue to ignore the figurative aspects of language. These are not restricted to idioms and special uses of certain lexical items, but rather pervade lexical and grammatical structure. Linguistic imagery lies at the heart of synchronic language structure and figures importantly in language change.

Second, identity of semantic representations for equivalent sentences cannot be taken for granted. Semantic representations are not universal in all respects, but vary with the lexical, grammatical, and figurative resources off the language.

Third, the nature of the coding transition needs more careful study. How, for example, should the figurative patterns of a language be represented in a grammar? .... What type of grammatical model will handle imagery in a natural way and capture the relationship between the synchronic state of a language and its diachronical evolution?

Finally, the view of semantic representations I have advanced casts doubt on their viability as the formal objects in terms of which logical relations can be defined and logical deductions carried out. The figurative aspect of language is the main spoiler."[2]

In Langacker's publication we meet emphasis on broader aspects of language than in the one of Gipper. In particular his attention to its figurative use deserves careful consideration, in particular in the light of what has been suggested by Friedrich (see above paragraph 4.2.). The list of implications of his presentation for the relation between language and thought underlines the importance of this publication for our study.

4.3.5. Man, language, and world. Van Liere.

Although the subject of Van Liere's book is wider than the LRH, we include a review in this paragraph, because his publication forms one of the most recent contributions from the field of anthropology that we have been able to find.

Central to the first part of his book is the thesis: "Language is a necessary condition for becoming aware of thought, and for making the world into an object; and a 'being without language' would not be able to achieve such a 'distancing operation.' The reverse is true as well: that this awareness is a necessary condition for the ability of speaking a language. But that is a truth

---

1   o.c. , p. 343.
2   o.c. , p. 355.

which is less interesting."[1]
For his conception of language Van Liere refers to Bühler (see also below section 5.2.1.), considering the possibility of 'creating distance,' as belonging to the essence of language. He realizes that this entails the idea that language implies thought.[2]

He subsequently provides for 'anthropological support' of his thesis, mainly basing himself on Plessner, for whom the concepts of distance' and 'distancing' are central ideas in his developing the framework of anthropology.[3]

His next step is to consider the question whether there are 'conditions/facts' which refute his thesis. Prior to addressing this issue, he writes: "Our thesis is not a psychological thesis, which might be falsifiable; it is an anthropological thesis, which attempts to put together into a sensible, comprehensive structure all kinds of data about man, which are known to us, either on the basis of scientific investigation or on the basis of intuition. Such a thesis will only be abandoned if too much becomes evident which speaks against it. It can also be corroborated, because there is much that speaks in favour of it. It cannot be proved, nor can it be refuted unambiguously at one time."[4]

As a review of Van Liere's discussion of the evidence found, we give an extensive quotation from his own summary in English at the end of the book: "[t]he question is raised of the influence of the structures of language on human thought. That such an influence exists is generally recognised. More interesting, however, is the question of the influence of the structures of language on the perception of reality (as formulated, for example, in the Sapir-Whorf-hypothesis). What to think of that?

Language, in this connection, cannot be separated from culture in its entirety. It is found that it is in the field of socially defined reality which is maximally exposed to the suggestion that reality must correspond with the structures of a given language. Examples are taken from the names that are given to human sentiments and emotions.

A deeper structure is the subject-predicate form of our sentences. It is my suggestion that the conscious philosophy of western civilisation, especially its ontology, has been strongly influenced by this linguistic structure, and especially by its suggestion that what 'really' exists must be a timeless and unchanging substance. Other languages, with a different basic structure, do not carry this suggestion.

The opinion has been sometimes voiced that people with a different language would have, by virtue of that fact, a different logic. This suggestion is rejected. Language and logic are interdependent, in so far as logic is identical with the

---

1   Van Liere, 1985, p. 25.
2   see o.c. , p. 34.
3   see Plessner, 1971.
4   o.c. , p. 61.

language in which we choose to exercise it; that is trivial. But in different cultures it is not logic as such, it is the facts (the premisses) that are different.

Lastly, we conclude that if our thought may be said to be imprisoned in language, it is a strange prison: its walls recede when we push against them."[1]

In the next part of his book, Van Liere investigates in more detail the nature of the cognitive process. He makes a distinction between "a dominative aspect (cognition is a form of subjecting reality to our interests, making things serve us); and a receptive aspect (learning to know things as they are, independent of us)."[2]

Finally, he examines the relation between language and world-view. Again, we quote from the English summary of the author himself: "It is rather self-evident, that there must be a relation between the language of a people, and its culture and world-view. More interesting is the question: can we illustrate that fact, by establishing a direct relation between the world-view prevailing in a particular culture, and certain linguistic structures to be found in its language?

In the first part of this dissertation, we formulated some conclusions regarding the relations between the thoughts of an individual, and the language of the community. What about the world-view of a community, taken in its entirety? It is impossible to establish a priority, either of language with regard to any culture, or the reverse. The question, however is sensible and relevant, when we ask: what happens, when thoughts are taken over from one culture into another? Do they change in any way; and if so, what is the role of language in that process?

To find an answer, we would have to find concepts capable of describing the differences between the world-views of two cultures; concepts, capable of describing the differences between their linguistic structures; and these two kinds of concepts should be comparable, that is: broad enough to embrace both fields, not so broad as to be capable of embracing everything.

.... Methodological considerations alone should warn us not to expect too much from such an undertaking. One of the difficulties is the vagueness of the concept 'world-view' or whatever we may substitute for it."[3]

In the final part of his book, Van Liere discusses the following problem: "In view of the theological importance of the contact between Hebrew and Greek language and culture, we ask if the concepts 'dominative' and 'receptive' would serve to describe important differences, between the two languages, as well as between the two cultures.

.... We see that it is impossible to compare concrete linguistic patterns with concepts or ideas prevailing in a culture (for instance, the tense system of the verb in both languages, with supposed differences in the concept of time). There

---

1   o.c. , p. 235 - 236.
2   o.c. , p. 236.
3   o.c. , p. 237 - 238.

is no basis for comparison.

It is possible to say, that Greek culture approaches reality more dominatively than Hebrew thought; it is possible to find this same difference in the comparison between the two languages; but it is impossible, to do more than strengthen an already established intuition. Such an undertaking is not entirely worthless; but we have not yet learned to pose the problem in such a way that we can come to empirically verifiable or falsifiable hypotheses. What changes ideas will undergo that are passed on from one culture to another cannot be deduced from any differences in their language. It must be established by historical research, and by nothing else."[1]

The main thesis of Van Liere's publication involves a close link between language, and thought or culture. On one hand this leads him to make rather strong statements on the influence of language on thought, for example in the case of the relation between language and ontology in Western civilization. But at the same time he seems to be reluctant to go that far in his comparison of Greek and Hebrew thought. Perhaps the reason for this discrepancy can be found in the rather unclear status of his thesis, which he considers not amenable to empirical testing. In fact, the whole of his approach does not seem to include extensive investigation of linguistic evidence, which makes it difficult to assess its value for our study.

4.3.6. Testing the Linguistic Relativity Hypothesis. Rosch.

In contrast to the attitude demonstrated by Van Liere, many authors describe their attempts to test and verify the LRH. A detailed survey of all investigations aiming at this purpose would be too big a task in view of the limited objective of our literature search. Extensive reviews have been written by Cooper,[2] Leech,[3] and Werlen.[4] Whereas in the next section we will discuss a more recent general review in this field, we consider in this section in some detail a publication of E.R.Rosch (who also published under the name E.R.Heider), because her work provides a good illustration of the possibilities and difficulties involved.

At the beginning of the publication in which she reviews her involvement with the LRH, she writes: "In summary: the most dramatic form of the Whorfian hypothesis - the assertion that each language embodies and imposes upon the culture an implicit metaphysics - does not, in that form, appear to be an empirical statement. If it must be interpreted as meaning only that languages differ, then it is true but trivial. If it is to mean more than that, we find that we have no idea what the state of the world would 'look like' if the hypothesis were true, or, correspondingly, if it were false. The rest of this paper discusses

---

1   o.c. , p. 238.
2   Cooper, 1973, p. 94 - 123.
3   Leech, 1981, p. 231 - 254.
4   Werlen, 1989, p. 158 - 179.

successive attempts to reinterpret the Whorfian view into claims which are sufficiently specific that we can understand their meaning and test whether they are true or false."[1]

The first linguistic phenomenon which she considers as a possible area for testing the LRH, are the grammatical form classes, which obviously are not the same in all languages. She comments: "As long as form classes are considered only 'structural' (defined only by position of occurrence in sentences), they do not suggest important cognitive differences between speakers of different languages. However, Whorf and others have stressed that form classes also have semantic (meaning) correlates. .... Whorf speaks of the semantic correlates of form classes (he calls them 'cryptotypes') as the 'covert categories,' the 'underlying concepts' of the language. In fact, it is the pervasive, covert influence of cryptotypes on thought which may be one relatively concrete interpretation of what it might mean for grammar to influence metaphysics."[2]

But Rosch notes that the "semantic interpretation of form class has not gone unchallenged. Descriptive linguistics considers the relation between structurally defined form classes and their semantic correlates highly dubious."[3] In addition, the results of a number of investigations which attempted to demonstrate the influence of these grammatical categories on cognitive processes, are not very convincing. After having concluded: "So, at least in these memory tasks, grammatical class seems to be more like a dead metaphor than like a psychologically real classification of reality,"[4] she moves to another area where languages are different as far as classification is concerned: the vocabulary.

Before addressing herself to investigations in this field, she discusses the factors which "are necessary in order to have a real test of the effect of a natural language lexicon on thought:

(a) We must have at least two natural languages whose lexicons differ with respect to some domain of discourse - if languages are not different, there is no point in the investigation.

(b) The domain must be one which can be measured by the investigator independently of the way it is encoded by the languages of concern (for example, colour may be measuered in independent physical units such as wavelength) - if that is not the case (as, for example, in such domains as feelings or values), there is no objective way of describing how it is that the two languages differ.

(c) The domain must not itself differ grossly between the cultures whose languages differ - if it does, then it may be differences in experience with the domain, and not language, which are affecting thought.

---

1   Rosch, 1977, p. 502.
2   o.c. , p. 503.
3   o.c. , p. 503.
4   o.c. , p. 507.

(d) We must be able to obtain measures of specific aspects of cognition - such as perception, memory, or classification - having to do with the domain which are independent of, rather than simply assumed from, the language.

(e) We must have a cross-culturally meaningful measure of differences in the selected aspects of cognition - preferably we should be able to state the hypotheses in terms of interaction between the linguistic and cognitive variables, rather than in terms of overall differences between speakers of the languages."[1]

It appears that in particular the domain of colours has been used for the testing of the LRH. In the remainder of her paper the author traces the history of language-cognitive research in this area, and considers her own contribution to it. The first publication she reviews is that of Brown and Lenneberg[2] who "reasoned that cultures, perhaps because of differing colour 'ecologies' should differ with respect to the areas of the colour space to which they paid the most attention. 'Culturally important' colours should tend to be referred to often in speech and, thus, their names should become highly 'available' to members of the culture. 'Availability' of a name should have three measurable attributes: .... words used frequently tend to evolve into shorter words; .... thus, the length of colour words should be an index of their availability. Secondly, a more available word should be one which a speaker can produce rapidly when asked to name the thing to which the word refers. Finally, words frequently used in communication should come to have meanings widely agreed upon by speakers of the language. These three indices of availability are linguistic measures; for a measure of cognition, Brown and Lenneberg chose the recognition memory, the ability of subjects to recognize a previously viewed colour from among an array of colours. The hypothesis relating the linguistic and cognitive variables was ....: names which are more available should be more efficient codes for colours (you can hang on to them better in memory) - thus, people should be able to retain them longer."[3]

The experiments carried out by Brown and Lenneberg confirmed their hypothesis, and, according to Rosch their study "is the classic demonstration of an effect of language on memory."[4]

Subsequently, she discusses the work of Berlin and Kay, published in 1969.[5] Contrary to Brown and Lenneberg, who had studied speakers of a single language only, these investigators "looked at the reported diversity of colour names linguistically, and claimed that there were actually a very limited number of basic - as opposed to secondary - colour terms in any language. 'Basic' was defined by a list of linguistic criteria: for example, that a term be composed of

---

1   o.c. , p. 508.
2   see Brown, Lenneberg, 1954.
3   Rosch, 1977, p. 509.
4   o.c. , p. 510.
5   see Berlin and Kay, 1969.

only a simple unit of meaning ('red' as opposed to 'dark red'), and that it name only colour and not objects ('purple' as opposed to 'wine'). Using these criteria, Berlin and Kay reported that no language contained more than eleven basic colour names."[1] In their experiment, Berlin and Kay asked speakers of different languages to identify the colours to which the basic colour names in their language referred. Using a set of coloured chips the participants performed two tasks: "(a) they traced the boundaries of each of their native language's basic colour terms, and (b) they pointed to the chip which was the best example of each basic term. As might have been expected from the anthropological literature, there was a great deal of variation in the placement of boundaries of the terms. .... Surprisingly, in spite of this variation, the choice of best examples of the terms was quite similar for the speakers of the twenty different languages. Berlin and Kay called the points in the colour space where choices of best examples of basic terms clustered 'focal points,' and argued that the previous anthropological emphasis on cross-cultural differences in colour names was derived from looking at boundaries of colour names rather than at colour-name focal points."[2]

This result of Berlin and Kay prompted Rosch to consider an alternative explanation of the results of Brown and Lenneberg: "Suppose that there are areas of the colour space which are perceptually more 'salient' to all peoples and that these areas both become more codable and can be better remembered as the direct result of their salience?"[3] In an attempt to verify this hypothesis she first investigated the codability of focal colours in different languages. "The results of the study were clear: the focal colours were given shorter names and named more rapidly than were the nonfocal colours. Thus, in twenty-three languages, drawn from seven of the major language families of the world, it was the same colours that were most codable."[4]

She also investigated a second aspect to the hypothesis: "If memory were the direct result of salience rather than of codability focal colours should be better remembered than nonfocal, even by speakers of a language in which these colours were not more codable."[5] To verify this statement Rosch administered a colour memory test very similar to the one used by Brown and Lenneberg to a sample of Dani, a Stone Age agricultural people of West Irian, whose language has basically two terms for colours, and to a sample of Americans. Although the Dani memory performance as a whole proved to be poorer than that of the Americans, both were similar as far as the pattern of recognition of colours was concerned: "Dani, as well as Americans, recognized the focal colours better than

---

1   Rosch, 1977, p. 510.
2   o.c. , p. 511.
3   o.c. , p. 511.
4   o.c. , p. 511 - 12.
5   o.c. , p. 512.

the nonfocal."[1]

At the end of her discussion of the use of colour terminology in the testing of the LRH, Rosch writes: "We began with the idea of colours as the ideal domain in which to demonstrate the effects of the lexicon of a language on cognition, thereby supporting a position of linguistic determinism. Instead, we have found that basic colour terminology appears to be universal and that perceptually salient focal colours appear to form natural prototypes for the development of colour terms. Contrary to initial ideas, the colour space appears to be a prime example of the influence of underlying perceptual-cognitive factors on linguistic categories."[2]

A brief discussion of the possibility of using other 'natural categories,' such as geometric forms and human emotions, for testing the LRH, leads Rosch to the conviction that they also provide evidence for the opposite position, namely, the effect of the human perceptual system in determining linguistic categories. So her final judgment on the LRH is very clear: "At present, the Whorfian hypothesis not only does not appear to be empirically true in any major respect, but it no longer even seems profoundly and ineffably true."[3]

It must be said that the approach by Rosch makes a reliable impression, and hence her results should be given a high value. At the same time it should be remembered that her area of investigation is rather limited, so that her final and general repudiation of the LRH seems to go too far. Other authors, however, who mainly base themselves on psychological investigation seem to arrive at a similar conclusion.[4]

4.3.7. An appraisal of the Linguistic Relativity Hypothesis. Steinfatt.

So far, in this paragraph, we reviewed the work of a number of scholars, each of whom approached and investigated the LRH from a different point of view, and sometimes from a different discipline of science. It is clear that their own approach and results strongly influence their opinion of it. Since we want to obtain as wide a picture as possible on the present position of the LRH, we will in the final section of this paragraph summarize the results of Steinfatt in his recent review on the LRH.

As already mentioned in paragraph 4.1. , Steinfatt distinguishes between three forms of the LRH: LR-LO, LR-GCS, and LR-CA. He arranges the evidence which he considers, in a number of subject areas in which we will follow him.

a. Language learning.

This area is very much theory-dominated. Although much experimental work has been carried out, no conclusive empirical evidence in support of one of

---

1   o.c. , p. 512.
2   o.c. , p. 516.
3   o.c. , p. 519.
4   see e.g., Anderson, 1980, p. 386.

those theories has been obtained. The 'innateness-hypothesis' of Chomsky does not favour whatever form of the LRH, the 'development-model' of Piaget allows for LR-GCS, and only the ideas of Vygotsky, a Russian psychologist who was a contemporary of Whorf, support fairly strong and broad formulations of the LRH. According to him "it is an 'indisputable fact of great importance' that 'thought development is determined by language, i.e. , by the linguistic tools of thought and by the sociocultural experience of the child. .... The child's intellectual growth is contingent on his mastering the social means of thought, that is, language.'"[1] In the recent "revival of Whorfianism in linguistics and anthropology"[2] interest in the ideas of Vygotsky is growing, as is clear from a comparison of his approach with that of Whorf by Lucy and Wertsch.[3] This is in particular due to his emphasis on the 'social aspects' of language which we will consider under the next heading.

b. Language differences.

In this connection Steinfatt at first looks into the "interlanguage evidence," the results of the comparison of different languages. This is the area to which most of the work of Whorf himself can be assigned, and also many of the more recent investigations which we discussed in the previous sections of this paragraph, e.g., Gipper, Pinxten, Rosch, and publications cited by them. Steinfatt's comments on Whorf seem to apply to all of them: "Whorf's examples show a clear relationship between the metaphysics of the culture and the structure of its language. They do not establish the causal direction. If one argues that language influences thought, a minimum condition should be independent demonstrations of the existence of a level of language, the existence of a level of thought, and a connection between them that produces a result. Examples can suggest such conditions but cannot demonstrate them."[4]

The next area which Steinfatt considers under this heading is the intralinguistic evidence, which is based on investigating the differences in language structure, semantics, and phonetics which occur within a given language community, and their consequences. In this connection Steinfatt refers to the work of Bernstein who distinguishes between 'elaborated' and 'restricted codes.' The following quotation from Steinfatt's review will illustrate his ideas: "Restricted codes are context bound. Elaborate codes are relatively context free - one does not need the context, publicly observable or phenomenological within the speaker, in order to make sense of the message.

The importance of this distinction to linguistic relativity is made clear by Bernstein's belief that different codes create different orders of relevance and relation. The speaker's experience is affected by the relevance selection

---

1   Vygotsky, as quoted in Steinfatt, 1989, p. 38.
2   Fishman, 1982, p. 564.
3   Lucy, Wertsch, 1987.
4   Steinfatt, 1989, p. 44.

parameters of different speech systems. Children learn their culture's social structure, according to Bernstein, through the social structure embedded in speech, an LR-GCS position. Bernstein (1970) comments: 'Every time the child speaks or listens, the social structure is reinforced in him, and his social identity is shaped. The social structure becomes the child's psychological reality through the shaping of his acts of speech .... Children who have access to different speech systems or codes - that is, children who learn different roles by virtue of their families' class position in a society - may adopt quite different social and intellectual orientations and procedures despite a common development potential.' The similarities to Whorf's LR-GCS views are striking."[1]

In more recent publications, Bernstein's ideas have been used in explaining the influence of language on lower-class people's chances for breaking out of the poverty cycle. They have been used to formulate the 'deficit position' which "argues that both employment and economic disadvantages lead to developmental disadvantages, including a deficit in language development, and that deprived language in turn leads to continued employment and economic disadvantages."[2]

Contrary to this position others have devised the 'difference position,' which argues "that no natural language is any less developed or more primitive than any other .... that all languages are capable of producing thought of equal quality, and that observed differences result from difficulties caused by the second language interfering with the first, not the first alone. .... Thus any performance deficit by poor children must be explained in terms of forcing them to work within a second language."[3]

After an extensive review of the arguments and experiments used to support the positions involved, Steinfatt concludes: "In summary, the difference position seems to account for the available data on intralanguage cases better than the deficit position. LR-GCS-type linguistic relativity is strongly associated with the deficit position and the restricted code notion on which it is based. Little support for either the deficit position or LR-GCS is found when the available evidence is reviewed together with critiques of the evidence. The support for the difference position discussed above does not in itself necessarily imply evidence against LR-GCS, since the difference position is not directly associated with any LR view. While the deficit position clearly implies LR-GCS, LR-GCS does not necessarily imply the deficit position."[4]

The final topic which Steinfatt discusses under the heading 'language differences' is the evidence from bilingualism: "If linguistic relativity is correct, the formation of thinking of bilinguals should be influenced by two different world

---

1   o.c. , p. 46; for the quotation of Bernstein, see Bernstein, 1970.
2   Steinfatt, 1989, p. 47
3   o.c. , p. 47.
4   o.c. , p. 55.

views (LR-GCS). Prior to 1962 it was commonly believed that childhood bilingualism impaired intellectual development, particularly verbal intelligence (LR-LO), with arguments similar to those of the deficit position discussed above."[1] But Steinfatt reports that since then data have been published which contradict these ideas. He also discusses a publication by Bloom of 1981, describing an investigation of Chinese-English bilinguals, which "provides the strongest pro-LR-GCS and LR-CA data since Brown and Lenneberg."[2] But a more recent study of the same category of people did not lead to the same findings, so the evidence cannot be considered to be conclusive.

c. Investigation of aphasics and deaf.

From a brief discussion of a few publications in this area it appears that all of them provide evidence against LR-LO, but do not lead to a clear yes or no as far as the other forms of linguistic relativity are concerned.

In a final paragraph Steinfatt considers the implications of his review, and discusses future research, by commenting on the three forms of the LRH which he distinguishes.

As far as the first one - linguistic relativity-logical operations - is concerned, his conclusion is very clear: "The evidence from the deaf seems so compelling that we can essentially dismiss the LR-LO hypothesis unless and until new evidence is presented in its favor that takes into account the evidence from the deaf."[3]

In connection with the second form - linguistic relativity-general cognitive structure - he comments: "It is almost impossible to read Whorf's work and dismiss it. Hopi, both language and culture, employs a view of the world different from that used by persons nurtured in European languages. The question remains, does the language cause the Weltanschauung or do the culture and Weltanschauung provide a need for language forms to support them?"[4] After having considered the evidence concerned, he answers, contrary to the ideas of Whorf: "If the evidence from the deaf is correct, it must be the case that the correlation between language and Weltanschauung demonstrated by Whorf does not have language in a causal position."[5]

Regarding the third form - linguistic relativity-cognitive areas -, Steinfatt's judgment is more positive: it "has received considerably more empirical support."[6] He believes that the essence of linguistic relativity may be found in what Hockett wrote in 1954: "Languages differ not so much as to what can be said in them, but rather as to what it is relatively easy to say."[7] In addition, he asks attention for the role of cognitive dissonance: "Now cognitive dissonance holds

---

1   o.c. , p. 55.
2   o.c. , p. 57.
3   o.c. , p. 60.
4   o.c. , p. 60 - 61.
5   o.c. , p. 61 - 62.
6   o.c. , p. 62.
7   Hockett, 1954, p. 122.

that beliefs follow behavior, that thought can follow statements. Saying something slightly different from what we mean, because it is easier to do so in our particular language or dialect, and then changing our meaning to conform with our words, away from our original intent, may be where the main truth of the linguistic relativity hypothesis lies. .... In this way, cognitive dissonance interacts with ease or difficulty of expression in a given language to produce differences in thought between languages, or between dialects within a language."[1]

Looking into the future, he writes: "The differences in ease of expression between languages should produce different types of meaning shifts in each language, as meaning moves from intent to statement to adjusted thought. The real question for future research is, of course, can the occurrence of this process be demonstrated and, if so, what are the conditions that foster or inhibit it? To what extent are the speakers, and the listeners, in a given language aware of and/or able to compensate for this process? And to what extent does this process account for Weltanschauung differences between languages?"[2]

We conclude our summary of Steinfatt's review by quoting the following passage from his closing remark: "[I]t needs to be pointed out that where linguistic relativity effects are found in the studies mentioned above, they are seldom in the more interesting grammatical or worldview area, but usually in the less interesting and inherently more limited area of semantic and category boundary differences, which may be overcome by learning new words and categories, though the linguistic relativity - cognitive dissonance process outlined above should make that difficult."[3]

Steinfatt presents an honest and reliable attempt to assess the value of the LRH. Some of his conclusions seem to reflect his personal favour for certain topics: why is the grammatical and world view area more interesting than that of semantic and category boundary differences? It may be that the latter refers to the open and mobile aspects of language, its possibilities to adapt to new developments. These also belong to its characteristic features. But as a whole his results and conclusions should be considered very seriously, as well as his suggestion that cognitive dissonance is the main form of influence of language on thought.

4.4. Language and space.

4.4.1. Introduction.
Among the publications which we found in our literature search on language and cognition, there are a few which pay special attention to the role of space

---

1   Steinfatt, 1989, p. 63 - 64.
2   o.c. , p. 64.
3   o.c. , p. 64.

and spatial relations in connection with the LRH.[1] In addition to them we came across other publications which refer to language and space in general.

For example, many textbooks on the theory of literature contain separate sections on the way in which literary texts - poetry and prose - structure space and spatial relations. Meyer wrote a special article on space and space symbolics in narrative art.[2] In his monograph on the 'Poetics of Space,'[3] Bachelard investigates the role of 'spatial categories,' such as houses, drawers, chests, wardrobes, corners, etc. , in literature, but also pays attention to the 'images' which language uses in this respect. The role of imagination by language has also been discussed by Friedrich in a publication which we mentioned already above (see paragraph 4.2.).[4] In this connection Langacker's emphasis on the 'figurative aspects' of language should also be referred to.[5] It is noteworthy that Lakoff and Johnson conclude that "most of our fundamental concepts are organized in terms of one or more spatialization metaphors."[6]

Other scholars pay more attention to the question in what way language itself structures space and spatial relations. A classical publication in this area is of Cassirer,[7] whereas Scherer should be mentioned as well.[8] To this category can also be reckoned Gipper, who limits himself to giving lists of Hopi expressions for spatial and temporal relations, which should be adequate to provide an impression of the "Reichtum der sprachlichen Möglichkeiten in diesen Bereichen."[9]

Pinxten, who intended to cover in his first publication the whole spectrum of space experience, did not base himself on investigation of the language itself, but on second-hand descriptions (see above section 4.3.3.). But in a later publication he reported on his explorations into the natural philosophy and semantics of the Navajo, who live in Arizona and New Mexico, USA, and in which he included an extensive investigation of their language.[10]

He used a 'Universal Frame Of Reference' (UFOR) which attempts "to present the spatial terminology available in any human language by a single standard, a maximally complete set of spatial discriminations that human beings are capable of making."[11] The entries of the UFOR which were thoroughly discussed with a number of native speakers of Navajo, cover "three different 'spaces' in semantic representations:

---

1   e.g. Gipper, 1972; 1976; Pinxten, 1976.
2   Meyer, 1957.
3   Bachelard, 1969.
4   Friedrich, 1986.
5   Langacker, 1976, p. 355.
6   Lakoff, Johnson, 1980, p. 17.
7   Cassirer, 1985, p. 149 - 169.
8   Scherer, 1957.
9   Gipper, 1972, p. 253; see also Gipper, 1976.
10   Pinxten, Van Dooren, 1983.
11   o.c. , p. IX.

1) The physical space (also termed object space) ranges over all those characteristics of space or of spatial phenomena that human beings can manipulate, handle, look upon as a whole, move in totality, and so on. ....
2) The sociogeographical space is comprised of all those aspects of space that are ascribed to phenomena of larger magnitude than object space. That is, it concerns those spatial phenomena that human beings can only be confronted with or locate themselves in, without being able to genuinely manipulate them. ....
3) The cosmological space is comprised of all phenomena of a still larger range of magnitude, for example, the sun, the universe, and the like."[1]
"In actual use each and every entry of the UFOR are handled as if they were 'primitives' to the native system of differentiation and segmentation: that is, any set of basic spatial characteristics can only be agreed upon by the consultants themselves, and not by the bias or the philosophical or cultural preference of the investigator. It is only through the detailed and painstaking analysis of the relationships between all native differentiations, carried out with the help of native consultants, that the more basic notions will be distinguished from 'derived' ones.[2]
By using the UFOR in this way Pinxten was able to arrive at "a synthetic picture of Navajo spatial semantics," of which he writes: "Fundamental characteristics of such a semantic model were: the determination of meaningful characteristics exclusively on the basis of empirical analysis (a nonaprioristic approach), the combined use of purely linguistic and extralinguistic analyses (the topological test, the reference to behavioral and material culture), and the search for compatibility between the spatial, representational notions and broad, natural philosophical notions."[3]
This approach indeed offers a broad perspective on space perception of people, who speak a certain language, but it cannot be used for our investigation because of its heavy reliance on native consultants. So in our case, it seems better to look for a method which perhaps is less satisfactory as far as comprehension is concerned, but which can be applied in our situation: the investigation of the perception of space of people who lived many centuries ago and spoke a language which is no longer used, at least not in the form as they did. This means that we have to look for approaches which emphasize the investigation of written language in as many aspects as possible, and not limit themselves to providing an inventory of words and expressions. In the following sections of this paragraph, we will briefly summarize three publications which contain such an approach.

---

1   o.c. , p. 188.
2   o.c. , p. 187.
3   o.c. , p. 154.

4.4.2. Space, time, semantics, and the child; Clark.

In his study of "how the child acquires English expressions for space and time," Clark assumes that "the child knows much about space and time before he learns the English terms for space and time, and his acquisition of these terms is built onto his prior cognitive development."[1] In line with this thesis he argues that "[t]he child is born into a flat world with gravity, and he himself is endowed with eyes, ears, an upright posture, and other biological structure. These structures alone lead him to develop a perceptual space, a P-space, with very specific properties. Later on, the child must learn how to apply English spatial terms to this perceptual space, and so the structure of P-space determines in large part what he learns and how quickly he learns it. .... [T]he concept of space underlying the English spatial terms, to be called L-space, should coincide with P-space: any property found in L-space should be also found in P-space."[2]

After discussing the properties of P-space, Clark summarizes these as follows: "When man is in canonical position, P-space consists of three reference planes and three associated directions: (1) ground level is a reference plane and upward is positive; (2) the vertical left-to-right plane through the body is another reference plane and forward from the body is positive; and (3) the vertical front-to-back plane is the third reference plane and leftward and rightward are both positive directions. Only when man is not in canonical position can we define a geological vertical that is separate from the biological vertical. Finally, there is the notion of canonical encounter, which consists of one man confronted face to face by another man a short distance away."[3]

Clark's summary of L-space, given after he has explored it, reads: "English spatial terms, therefore, reveal that L-space has properties that are identical with those of P-space. First, L-space shows the universal use of points, lines, and planes of reference, both in prepositions, where there is one or two, and in adjectives, where there are two. Second, there are three specific primary planes of reference: (1) ground level, with upward positive and downward negative; (2) the vertical left-right plane through the body, with forward positive and backward negative; and (3) the vertical front-back plane of symmetry through the body, with right and left both equally positive. Third, L-space requires the use of canonical position to define uses of vertical expressions for dimensions that do not coincide with gravitational vertical. And fourth, L-space requires the notion of canonical encounter to account for the egocentric uses of terms like front and back. The coincidence of these properties with those of P-space is

---

1   Clark, 1973, p. 28.
2   o.c. , p. 28.
3   o.c. , p. 34.

102

obvious."[1]

The similarities between the description of both spaces are striking indeed, and one may wonder whether close examination of Clark's approach might not reveal some effect of 'investigator's bias' (see the remarks by Pinxten quoted above, section 4.4.1.). Be that as it may, for us the most important feature of his publication is that he is able to describe and to use in a reasonable way the concept of 'linguistic space,' i.e. a space structured according to linguistic terminology and usage.

4.4.3. How language structures space; Talmy.

In this study, which "aims beyond pure description of spatial categories to an account of their common fundamental character and place within larger linguistic-cognitive systems,"[2] Talmy distinguishes between two main levels "how conceptual material is represented in language. .... One of these is the macroscopic expository level. Here, within the scope of a sentence, a paragraph, or a whole discourse if need be, one can convey conceptual content of any sort, including feelings, local gossip, and practical medicine - or indeed, the organization of space, time and causality. The main resource for this level is a language's stock of open-class lexical elements - i.e. , the stems of nouns, verbs, and adjectives.

The second level, which can be characterized as the fine-structural, is that of closed-class 'grammatical' (as distinguished from 'lexical') forms - including grammatical elements and categories, closed-class particles and words, and the syntactic structures of phrases and clauses. These forms also represent conceptual material, but from a much more limited array. They represent only certain categories, such as space, time (hence, also form, location, and motion), perspective-point, distribution of attention, force, causation, knowledge state, reality status, and the current speech event, to name some main ones. And, importantly, they are not free to express just anything within these conceptual domains, but are limited to quite particular aspects and combinations of aspects, ones that can be thought to constitute the 'structure' of those domains. Thus, the closed-class forms of a language taken together represent a skeletal conceptual microcosm. Moreover, this microcosm may have the fundamental role of acting as an organizing structure for further conceptual material (including that expressed by the open-class elements) - as if it were a framework that the further material is shaped around or draped over. More speculatively, this language-based microcosmic selection and organization of notions may further interrelate with - and even to some degree constitute - the structure of thought

---

1   o.c. , p. 48.
2   Talmy, 1983, p. 225.

and conception in general."[1]

In the next part of his publication, Talmy discusses the basic spatial distinctions made by language and it is worthwhile to quote his introduction to the paragraph titled "The primary breakup of a spatial scene.": "One main characteristic of language's spatial system is that it imposes a fixed form of structure on virtually every spatial scene. A scene cannot be represented directly at the fine-structural level in just any way one might wish - say as a complex of many components bearing a particular network of relations to each other. Rather, with its closed-class elements and the very structure of sentences, language's system is to mark out one portion within a scene for primary focus and to characterize its spatial disposition in terms of a second portion ...., and sometimes also a third portion ...., selected from the remainder of the scene. The primary object's 'disposition' here refers to its site when stationary, its path when moving, and often also its orientation during either state."[2]

After having noticed the close relationship between his distinction of 'primary' and 'secondary' object and the 'figure/ground distinction' in Gestalt psychology, Talmy gives a detailed discussion of possible geometric relations for it, and their properties.

At the end of this discussion, he remarks that they are concerned with only the first of the four 'imaging systems,' that he has been able to identify in language, "encoded at the fine-structural level, that characterize different kinds of relationships among entities within space or time," namely the one which "specifies geometries: abstract geometric characterizations of objects and their relationships to each other within different reference frames."[3] The other systems, he describes as follows: "The second imaging system specifies 'perspective point' - the point within a scene at which one conceptually places one's 'mental eyes' to look out over the rest of the scene - and characterizes its location, distance away, and mode of deployment. .... The third imaging system specifies in particular 'distribution of attention' to be given to a referent scene from an indicated perspective point. .... The fourth imaging system indicates 'force dynamics,' i.e. , the ways that objects are conceived to interrelate with respect to the exertion of and resistance to force, the overcoming of such resistance, barriers to the exertion of force and the removal of such barriers, etc."[4] With this list of systems Talmy shows what kind of phenomena an exhaustive treatment of the structuring of space by language has to cover.

In the final part of his publication, he points to the fact that "a fundamental character of the way that space is represented at language's fine-structural level is that it is schematic. That is, only particular selections of all the aspects present

---

1   o.c. , p. 227 - 228.
2   o.c. , p. 229.
3   o.c. , p. 253.
4   o.c. , p. 252, p. 254, p. 256, p. 257.

in spatial scenes are actually referred to by linguistic elements, while all the other aspects are disregarded."[1] As a result of this 'schematization' a speaker may run into trouble when wishing to represent a certain 'spatial scene' in linguistic form. The 'schema' which seems the most appropriate may say 'too much', and the next one available 'too little'.

As compared to Clark, Talmy provides a much more detailed account of the way in which the possibilities of a language influence the expression of spatial relations. His conclusion that the closed-class forms of a language together form a microcosm, which functions as an organizing structure for further conceptual material, seems to be a more specific formulation of the idea of linguistic world-view as mentioned by Gipper and others. It also appears to support the LRH. In addition to these theoretical issues, his approach offers a number of practical suggestions for examining the spatial characteristics of languages, which might be useful for our own investigation.

4.4.4. Semantics of spatial expressions; Jackendoff.

Jackendoff's investigation of this topic is included in his book on <u>Semantics and Cognition</u>,[2] in which he considers many basic issues of these phenomena themselves, and in particular of their interrelationship. To have some idea of his theoretical approach we quote the beginning sentences of his first chapter, which he gave the title "Semantic Structure and Conceptual Structure."

"This book is intended to be read from two complementary perspectives. From the point of view of linguistics and linguistic philosophy, the question is: What is the nature of meaning in human language, such that we can talk about what we perceive and what we do? From the point of view of psychology, the question is: What does the grammatical structure of natural language reveal about the nature of perception and cognition?

My thesis is that these two questions are inseparable: to study semantics of natural language is to study cognitive psychology. I will show that, viewed properly, the grammatical structure of natural language offers an important new source of evidence for the theory of cognition."[3]

Within the framework of this paragraph, we will concentrate on the more 'technical aspects' of his work, and mention his further theoretical assumptions only when necessary.

In his approach, Jackendoff adopts "a theory of metaphysics that embraces four domains: the real world, the projected world, mental information, and linguistic

---

1   o.c. , p. 258.
2   Jackendoff, 1985.
3   o.c. , p. 3.

expressions."[1] The real world he describes as "the source of environmental input," and the projected world is "the world as experienced."[2] According to Jackendoff: "We have conscious access only to the projected world - the world as unconsciously organized by the mind; and we can talk about things only insofar as they have achieved mental representation through these processes of organization. Hence the information conveyed by language must be about the projected world."[3] The domain of mental information has a certain structure; it consists of mental constituents: images, concepts, functions, etc. , and language enables us to 'handle' these and to envisage them in the projected world. So Jackendoff can write: "Hence the information conveyed by language must be about the projected world."[4]

Mental constituents are indicated by a word in capitals, between square brackets, e.g. [DOG], [BOOK]. Jackendoff pays much attention to the process of categorization, which answers the question: when do human persons assign a particular thing to a certain category? When does he judge [A] to be a [DOG]? In this connection he refers "to the representation of the thing being categorized as a [TOKEN] concept and that of the category as a [TYPE] concept. The [TOKEN] .... is a mental construct of potentially elaborate internal structure, which can be projected into awareness as a unified entity (of the projected world). .... A [TYPE] concept is the information that the organism creates and stores when it learns a category."[5] Regarding their role in the projected world there is a difference between the two kinds of concepts, which Jackendoff formulates in his "Referentiality Principle": "Unless there is a linguistic marking to the contrary, all phrases that express [TOKEN] constituents are referential; phrases that express [TYPE] constituents are nonreferential."[6]

Jackendoff starts his chapter on the semantics of spatial expressions with an investigation of spatial prepositional phrases. He distinguishes between places and paths, and accordingly between place-function and path-function. Some words, such as 'here' which Jackendoff calls an 'intransitive preposition,' are able to express a [PLACE] all by themselves; but most prepositions express a place-function and require a "subcategorized object NP" (noun phrase), which has the role of expressing the reference object, the argument of the place-function. "Each place-function imposes conceptual constraints on the nature of the reference object. .... For instance, the place-function IN requires its reference object to be regarded as a bounded area or volume .... A [PLACE] projects into a point or region. .... Within the structure of an event or state, a [PLACE] is

1   o.c. , p. 31.
2   o.c. , p. 28.
3   o.c. , p. 29.
4   o.c. , p. 29.
5   o.c. , p. 78.
6   o.c. , p. 94.

normally occupied by a [THING]."[1]

Regarding paths Jackendoff remarks: "[PATHS] have a more varied structure than [PLACES] and play a wider variety of roles in [EVENTS] and [STATES]. The internal structure of a [PATH] often consists of a path-function and a reference object, as expressed by phrases like 'toward the mountain,' 'around the tree,' and 'to the floor.' Alternatively, the argument of a path-function may be a reference place. This possibility is most transparent in a phrase like 'from under the table,' where 'from' expresses the path-function and 'under the table' expresses the reference place. Prepositions such as 'into' and onto' express both a path-function and the place-function of the reference place, meaning roughly 'to in' and 'to on,' respectively."[2] In his subsequent discussion Jackendoff gives a detailed account of the various possibilities of [PATHS] and their roles.

His next section is devoted to verbs of spatial location and motion. In the class of spatial sentences he distinguishes between "those that express [EVENTS] and those that express [STATES]. A clear linguistic test for the distinction is the possibility of occurring after 'What happened/occurred/took place was that ......'; events happen, while states do not."[3]

Regarding events he distinguishes between things that go a certain path, and things that stay at a certain place. For states he makes a threefold distinction: things can be at a certain place, they can orient 'along' a path, or extend 'along' a path.[4]

A further step involves the role of causation. In this connection Jackendoff introduces a binary function CAUSE which connects a THING with the EVENT which it causes. For example, the event can be described by: 'Sim came into the room,' whereas this event can be included into the 'causative sentence': 'The wind pushed Sim into the room.' After considering the possibilities of this function, Jackendoff not only allows THINGS, but also EVENTS, in the role of 'causative.' In addition to the function CAUSE, he also introduces the concept LET, which means something like 'cease to prevent'; for example: 'Bill released the bird from the cage.'[5]

After having explored ACTIONS as a subcategory of EVENTS, in the final section of the chapter on spatial expressions, Jackendoff addresses the problem of lexicalization, i.e. : "how a conceptual structure can be carved up into lexical items."[6] After comparing the sentences: 'The dog went into the room,' and 'the dog entered the room,' he concludes: "[t]he verb 'enter' itself lexicalizes the path- and place-functions instead of leaving them to be overtly expressed by a

---

1   o.c. , p. 162.
2   o.c. , p. 163.
3   o.c. , p. 170.
4   o.c. , p. 174.
5   o.c. , p. 178.
6   o.c. , p. 183.

preposition."[1] In this connection he develops the "Lexical Variable Principle: A variable in the structure of a lexical item must be capable of being filled by a conceptual constituent."[2] As an example he considers the event represented by the sentence: 'Joe put butter on the bread.' This could also be formulated as 'Joe buttered the bread,' or 'Joe breaded the butter on.' The second possibility violates the lexical variable principle, because the variable of the verb 'to bread' is "not a conceptual constituent, but a path-function, whose argument position has been lexicalized." In addition, 'to bread' subcategorizes "a transitive preposition occurring without its object."[3]

In the following chapter of his book, Jackendoff investigates the idea "that the semantics of motion and location provide the key to a wide range of further semantic fields."[4] It would go too far to include this chapter in this survey, although it seems interesting to compare his approach at 'lexical level,' with the way in which Lakoff and Johnson work at the level of metaphorical usage of language, and consider "spatialization metaphors" as organizing "most of our fundamental concepts."[5]

Jackendoff's approach is to a certain extent similar to that of Talmy, which we discussed in the previous section. Both base themselves on one language and try to describe in what way this language accounts for spatial phenomena. It is true that they differ as far as the detailed treatment of the structural features of language is concerned, and Jackendoff gives a much wider and deeper discussion of the theoretical aspects of his work, but both seem to follow the same approach: by a careful examination of the structure of a language they arrive at a picture of the way it represents space and spatial relations. Both operate with a concept of an 'intermediate world' between the outside world and man and his language. The difference is that Talmy seems to place this world mainly within the structure of the language, whereas Jackendoff locates it in the human mind.

As compared to the approaches of Gipper and Pinxten these two publications and the one by Clark discussed in section 4.4.2. base themselves on the investigation of language alone, without the use of native consultants. So it is possible to use them in the study of extinct languages such as Old Testament Hebrew. Whereas the emphasis in Clark's publication lies on the description of the properties of space, both of L-space and of P-space, Talmy and Jackendoff each present a method for investigating linguistic expressions of space which is at the same time very specific and broad enough for application to other languages.

So both should be taken into account when we need to devise a method for

---

1   o.c. , p. 183 - 84.
2   o.c. , p. 185.
3   o.c. , p. 186.
4   o.c. , p. 188.
5   Lakoff, Johnson, 1980, p. 17.

further study of the perception of space in the Old Testament.

4.5. Summary.

Having completed our report of what we found in our search of the literature of linguistics, psychology and anthropology, it seems useful to include a brief summary of what we have found so far. This summary can be preliminary only, since our search will continue covering the philosophical literature. We will present the results using the three points as formulated in paragraph 3.6. as a guideline.

1. The position of the LRH.

Our literature search revealed that up to now the LRH continues to attract the attention of the related disciplines. Apparently it represents an idea which appeals to many people. But it looks as if it recedes, and withdraws itself from empirical proof, as soon as scholars set themselves to examine its scope by detailed investigation.

As compared to earlier publications, there is a tendency to describe in more detail the structure of the three areas involved in the LRH: language, thought and world. This leads to more elaborate, and sometimes, sharper distinctions between elements of these areas, as the following survey illustrates:

- Language.

Whereas initially only grammar and lexicon had been distinguished, more recent publications pay attention to figurative (Langacker), metaphorical (Lakoff and Johnson), and poetic (Friedrich) aspects of the use of language. In addition, the emphasis on the social function of language can be mentioned.

- Thought.

Perhaps the most extensive distinction in this area has been suggested by Steinfatt, who considers three levels: logic, cognitive structure and world-view, and perception, individual cognitions or areas of cognition. Rosch limits herself clearly to the perception side of thought, whereas Jackendoff tries to cover the whole of conceptual activity.

- World.

In this connection Pinxten can be mentioned with his three-level-model of space, which distinguishes between physical, sociogeographical, and cosmological space. In her investigation, Rosch clearly directs herself to the first level, and also Talmy and Jackendoff start with it, but both indicate, and partly even extend their investigations, to the other areas.

The increased diversity of language, thought and world provides for new possibilities of viewing the value of the LRH. In addition to the position which supports it for of all areas in toto (Whorf), and the one which rejects it completely (Rosch, Pinxten), it is also possible to locate the value of the LRH in certain domains of the areas involved (Steinfatt: individual cognitions or areas of cognition; Friedrich: poetic use of language).

Another way of seeing the scope of the LRH more 'locally,' seems to be involved in Gipper's remarks on the 'distance' between thought and language (see above section 4.3.2.). According to him the thinking of the Hopi, the Indian people whose language he investigated, has not yet reached a critical distance towards language. So he believes the Hopi-language to be an authentic key to their Weltanschauung (= their belief concerning the nature of the world and human affairs).

The result of these developments seems to be that a simple formulation of linguistic relativity is no longer feasible, but that it should specify exactly what relations, and what aspects of language, thought and world are covered by it.

2. The concept of world-view.

The discussion of this concept by Gipper, who distinguishes between scientific Weltbild, ideological Weltanschauung, and linguistic Weltansicht, is certainly helpful. But it is not completely clear to what area they belong. The first two seem to belong to thought completely, but is the latter something which is simply attached to a certain language, or is it also dependent on the way this language is being used? The 'microcosm' which according to Talmy results from the particular fine-structure of a language seems connected with that language. But Jackendoff's 'projected world' to which language refers, appears to be located in the mind.

3. The structure of thought.

Steinfatt clearly distinguishes between the contents of thought, and the way people think (logic). And he rejects any influence of language on the latter. Bearing in mind the fundamental role which generally is assigned to perception, we wonder whether that aspect should not be considered in the same way. The results of Rosch seem to confirm this, at least as far as colour perception is concerned. But the position of the perception of space remains unclear. With regard to the expression of spatial scenes, Talmy has pointed to the restrictions due to the 'spatial schematization' of language. In this connection, it is also relevant to consider the role of cognitive dissonance as suggested by Steinfatt. Does the influence of the availability of a certain scheme to represent spatial characteristics in a particular language go as far as changing the perception of space of its speakers?

In any case, this initial summary of the results of our literature search shows that much useful information on the three points which we formulated at its start has been gathered. At the same time it has become clear that the LRH touches on fundamental aspects of language itself, and its relation to thought and world.

Before we try to review the position of the LRH and the issues involved, it seems wise to obtain more insight in the theoretical aspects of language. With that aim we will search the literature of the philosophy of language.

5. LANGUAGE AND PHILOSOPHY.

5.1. Introduction.

The main purpose of this chapter is to obtain a picture of the wider theoretical issues involving language, which we can use for guidance in assessing the position of the LRH and the methodological problems facing our study. It should be broad enough in order to prevent that important aspects of language remain out of sight. At the same time it should be geared to the special situation of our study.

With this objective in mind we turn to Blackburn, who starts his introduction to the philosophy of language as follows: "A philosophy of language attempts to achieve some understanding of a triangle of elements (see Figure 1):

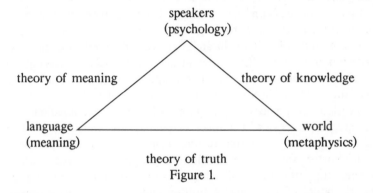

theory of truth
Figure 1.

The speaker uses the language. With it he can put himself into various relations with the world. He can describe it, or ask questions about it, issue commands to change it, put himself under obligations to act in it in various ways, offer metaphors, images, jokes, about what it is like. The task of the philosopher is to obtain some stable conception of this triangle of speaker, language, and world"[1]

Blackburn explains that "[a]t a given time, in a given philosophical tradition, one or another of the points of this triangle will appear prominent. That point will represent the primary source of understanding, so that the natural direction of enquiry is to use that knowledge to aim at conclusions about the other

---

1   Blackburn, 1984, p. 3.

elements."[1] He gives examples of how in the past "the individual, with his particular capacities for experience and reasoning," or "scientific naturalism, in which the results and (alleged) method of the natural scientist are regarded as the real philosophical data," have been dominant. "But ideologies change, and it has become natural to give the nature of language considerable autonomy, and even sovereignty over the other elements of the triangle. An individual's psychology becomes whatever is needed to enable him to understand the language which stands revealed, and the world becomes whatever is necessary to make true the true statements made with that language. This is the 'linguistic turn', for better or worse, of most of the important philosophy this century"[2]

It does not seem necessary for us to explore all these relations in detail. Our target is not an exhaustive theoretical treatise of language, but a limited theory which will assist us in our study. But since, beforehand, we do not know exactly what aspects of language will be important in our case, it seems wise to base ourselves initially on an approach to the area which pays adequate attention to all its aspects. During our considerations we can gradually leave out those points which look irrelevant and concentrate on the crucial items.

So we will start in paragraph 5.2. with a short outline of the most comprehensive theoretical approach to language which we have been able to find, viz., the four axioms of Bühler. In addition, we will briefly mention two further positions on one of the fundamental aspects, namely its having the character of a sign. At the end of that paragraph we will make an initial attempt to assess the situation in view of our investigation. On the basis of that assessment, we mention two points which require some further examination.

In the next paragraphs, we review a number of publications which cover these points: a more extensive survey on the relation language / world in paragraph 5.3. and a much shorter one on the relation language / man (receiver) in paragraph 5.4. The data gathered in this chapter and in the previous one lead us to devise a theory/model of language of limited and special scope, especially adapted to the needs of our own study. This is the topic of paragraph 5.5.

5.2. Language-theory.

5.2.1. The axioms of Bühler.

The theory of Bühler comprises four axioms, which we will consider subsequently. In axiom A, Bühler, following Plato, considers language to be an instrument for doing certain things, an organon. In order to get some idea of the role of language in this respect he gives a picture (see Figure 2) which

---

1   o.c. , p. 4.
2   o.c. , p. 4 - 6.

shows what entities and relations are involved.[1]

There are three 'entities' at the corners of the outer triangle: sender, receiver, and 'objects and atomic facts.' In the middle we find the entity Z which comprises a circle and a triangle. According to the explanation by Bühler:

"Der Kreis in der Mitte symbolisiert das konkrete Schallphänomen. Drei variable Momente an ihm sind berufen, es dreimal verschieden zum Rang eines Zeichens zu erheben. Die Seiten des eingezeichneten Dreiecks symbolisiren diese drei Momente. Das Dreieck umschließt in einer Hinsicht weniger als der Kreis (Prinzip der abstraktiven Relevanz). In anderer Richtung wieder greift es über den Kreis hinaus, um anzudeuten, daß das sinnlich Gegebene stets eine apperzeptive Ergänzung erfährt. Die Linienscharen symbolisieren die semantischen Funktionen des (komplexen) Sprachzeichens. Es ist Symbol kraft seiner Zuordnung zu Gegenständen uns Sachverhalten, Symptom (Anzeichen) kraft seiner Abhängigkeit vom Sender, dessen Innerlichkeit es ausdrückt, und Signal kraft seines Appells an den Hörer, dessen äußeres oder inneres Verhalten es steuert wie andere Verkehrszeichen."[2] As is apparent from one of his comments to this axiom, the author, by underlining the importance of the other functions tries to restrict the "Dominanz der Darstellungsfunktion der Sprache."[3]

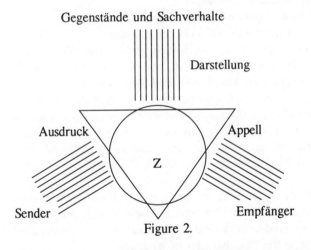

Figure 2.

The second axiom says: "Die sprachlichen Phänomene sind durch und durch zeichenhaft."[4] Under this heading Bühler discusses the way in which 'phonemes' are being joined together to form 'words,' and wonders whether to what extent the 'sign-character' of these entities is of similar nature. He also points to two

---

1   Bühler, 1982, p. 28.
2   o.c. , p. 28.
3   o.c. , p. 30ff.
4   o.c. , p. 33.

extreme attitudes towards signs, which both deny their sign-character. One, the "konsequente Stoffentgleisung," only takes into account the phenomenal, material side of the sign; the other one, the "'magische' Denken," only considers the 'other thing' of which the sign is a "Darstellung," and does not honour the 'distance' between the two.[1]

In his third axiom, Bühler distinguishes between four "Momente (Seiten), vier Fronten sozusagen, am Gesamtgegenstand der Sprachwissenschaft ...: Sprechhandlung und Sprachwerk; Sprechakt und Sprachgebilde."[2] He puts them together in the following scheme:

	I	II
	I	II
1.	H	W
2.	A	G

This table contains two types of distinctions. The first one considers language phenomena:

"I. Als subjektsbezogene Phänomene.

 II. Als subjektsentbundene und dafür intersubjektiv fixierte Phänomene.

.... Und was die andere Dichotomie angeht, so kann der Sprachforscher, was seine 'Sinne zu rühren' imstande ist, bestimmen:

1. Auf einer niederen Formalisierungsstufe als Handlungen und Werke.

2. Auf einer höheren Formalisierungsstufe als Akte und Gebilde."[3]

In the fourth axiom Bühler emphasizes:"[D]ie Sprachgebilde sind Wörter und Sätze. Nicht der eine oder der andere Terminus ist zum Range einer Kategorie zu erheben, sondern beide gehören zusammen und sind nur korrelativ zu definieren."[4] In a language the words are symbols which perform their syntactic function in the 'Symbolfeld' of the language. In this way language as a whole is able to achieve what other signalling systems cannot, namely: "mit einem beschränkten Schatz von Konventionen und dementsprechend von Sprachgebilden unbeschränkt Mannigfaltiges hinreichend differenziert und exakt zur Darstellung bringen."[5]

On the basis of the literature we studied we believe that these four axioms cover the essential functions of human language. In view of their importance for the subject area of our study, we would like to add two more detailed approaches which both relate to the sign-character of language.

5.2.2. Two additions.

The first one has been described by Apel, who bases himself on Peirce (see

---

1   see o.c. , p. 47.
2   o.c. , p. 48.
3   o.c. , p. 49.
4   o.c. , p. 70.
5   o.c. , p. 76.

Figure 3.): "Der Grundgedanke von Peirce, von dem ich ausgehe, ist die These, daß die Zeichen-Relation bzw. Zeichen-Funktion ('Semiosis') eine nicht weiter reduzierbare dreistellige Relation ist. Die prinzipielle Dreistelligkeit der Zeichen-Funktion liegt nach Peirce in dem Umstand, daß ein Zeichen (I) für einen Interpreten (II) etwas (III) bezeichnet (genauer: etwas in einer Hinsicht - als etwas-, die durch den sog. 'logischen Interpretanten' festgelegt ist, d.h. durch die Interpretationsregel, die das normativ richtige Zeichen-Verständnis und zugleich das daraus idealiter resultierende Verhalten des Zeichen-Interpreten unter allen nur denkbaren Bedingungen reguliert.)
Jedes der 3 Glieder der Zeichen-Funktion setzt demnach in seiner Funktion die beiden anderen schon voraus, und eine Nichtberücksichtigung dieser Voraussetzung hat nach Peirce unweigerlich eine 'abstractive' bzw. 'reductive fallacy' zur Folge. Da nun die menschliche Erkenntnis immer zeichenvermittelte, genauer: sprachvermittelte Erkenntnis ist, so läßt sich die semiotische Grundthese schon nach Peirce auch epistemologisch explizieren. Sie besagt dann:
1. Das Zeichen (I) kann in seiner Funktion nicht verstanden werden, ohne prinzipiell das zu bezeichnende Reale (III) und die Existenz des Zeichen-Interpreten (II) vorauszusetzen. (Bloß 'intentionale Objekte', Fiktionen oder dergl. können die Stelle III nicht ausfüllen),...
2. Das interpretierende Erkenntnis-Subjekt (II) kann nur gedacht werden unter der Voraussetzung realer Zeichen (I), die auch einen materiellen Aspekt haben, und der zu bezeichnenden Realität (III).
3. Das Reale selbst (III) kann von uns als das Reale nicht gedacht werden, ohne daß seine Interpretierbarkeit (II) vermittels Zeichen bzw. Sprache (I) vorausgesetzt wird. Ich nenne das im folgenden den transzendental-semiotischen Ansatz."[1]

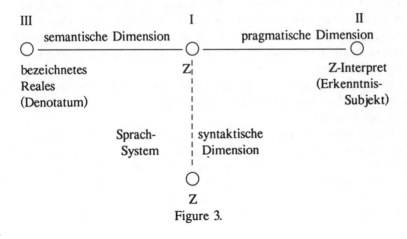

Figure 3.

1   Apel, 1974, p. 285 - 287.

On the basis of this approach, Apel demonstrates that various schools in the philosophy of language suffer from one or more reductive fallacies and thus fail to cover the phenomenon of language in all aspects of its use.

We will not follow him in his explorations, but mention two aspects of his approach which we believe to be important for our study. In the first place his emphasis on language as a system with a syntax which, at least for the individual signs, seems to add a fourth dimension to the three indicated by Bühler. Secondly, the approach of Apel regarding the semantic dimension of language and the reality of the "Denotatum" provides more specific ideas on an aspect of Bühler's work which is of interest to our study.

Our second addition to Bühler's axioms also relates to his distinction between the syntactic and the semantic dimension of the sign. It has a long history, but in present linguistic research usually the formulation by Frege is being used, who distinguished between sense and reference (Sinn und Bedeutung)[1] The sense of a sign has to do with the way in which it can be connected to other signs of that language, the reference is connected with its relation to the 'outside world.' The term reference figures heavily in recent literature on language, so it is necessary to consider it.

5.2.3. A preliminary impression.

Having completed our brief summary of the (expanded) axioms of Bühler, we will now make an initial attempt to consider them in some detail, in order to arrange them in such a way that we can use them for a further clarification of the theoretical and methodological problems which we meet in our study.

As a start we look at figure 2. It contains entities of three types:

a. Both sender and receiver belong to the category 'human'.

b. In his explanation of the picture, Bühler gives the central entity Z in particular an audible character, but from the rest of his book it seems clear that also linguistic signs of written character are included. So, we can call this entity Z 'text/language,' bearing in mind that the relation between language and text requires further explanation.

c. The third entity Gegenstände und Sachverhälte seems to refer to the whole 'extra-linguistic world.' In agreement with what we did in the previous chapter we will simply call it 'world.'

In figure 2, Bühler only considers the relations in which the central entity is involved. But when we take into account the three entities at the outer corners of the triangle, we see that more relations are possible. Sender and receiver have a relation with the world and with each other. In some cases this relation is a form of direct contact, in other cases it is of an indirect nature. It also requires further exploration and for the time being we shall call this relation simply 'contact.'

---

1   see Nuchelmans, 1978, p. 34 - 35.

On the basis of these considerations, we can modify the picture of Bühler's first axiom as indicated in figure 4.

Within the big triangle, three smaller ones can be distinguished. The two, which contain the top entity world, are very similar to the one used by Blackburn (see figure 1). The lower one is the well-known triangle frequently used to elucidate the communication process. So our preliminary considerations resulted in a figure (figure 4) presenting a scheme which seems to cover the whole area of language.

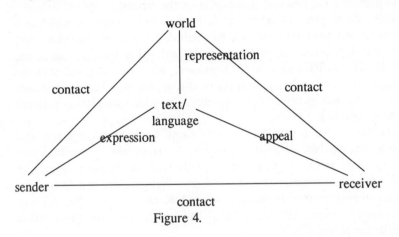

Figure 4.

Our first use of it will be in an attempt to obtain a rough picture of the mutual relationships between the main current approaches to language and linguistics. Chapter 4, in which we concentrated on one particular topic which figures in this area (linguistic relativity), indicated the complicated situation in these disciplines. A comprehensive survey of recent work on language and its philosophical aspects is beyond our capability and is not required for our investigation. In this connection we refer to recent textbooks.[1] In our exploration of the theoretical and methodological issues which impinge on our investigation, it will be helpful to have some idea where to locate the main lines of current linguistic involvement in figure 4.

The investigation of the structure of the central entity, text/language, receives a lot of attention. It is possible to distinguish between a text-oriented approach, which is mainly based in Europe (Jakobson, Coseriu, Van Dijk), and a language-oriented approach, which is concentrated in America (Chomsky, Fodor, Katz). Much of their study is mainly 'technical,' in the sense that it tries to find out how languages and texts are being structured. Our discussion of the work of Langacker (see above sub-section 4.3.4.) and Jackendoff (see above sub-section 4.4.4.), who both belong to the 'Chomsky-school,' shows however, that very

---

1   Lyons, 1981; Nuchelmans, 1978; Simon, 1981; Stegmüller, 1978, 1986.

often broader issues may be involved, in this case, the relation to the sender. The approach by some so-called super-structuralists of French origin (Foucault, Derrida), seems to extend the 'linguistic turn,' by letting text/language absorb all other elements of the triangle: "Il n'y a pas d'hors-texte."[1]

The use of language as a tool (see the third axiom of Bühler) receives much attention in a number of approaches, such as that of Austin (speech-acts) and Grice (intentions). Similar to the approaches discussed in chapter 4, they relate in particular to the expression-relation in figure 4, but in distinction to these, they tend to emphasize the role and possibilities of the sender.

They form one side of present-day interest in human communication, which also comprises a side that pays attention to the relation between text/language and the receiver (the appeal-relation in figure 4). In connection with the latter, the names of Gadamer and Ricoeur can be mentioned, who are concerned with the role of hermeneutics. A special application of this approach to literary criticism can be found in the 'reader-oriented hermeneutics,' to which we already referred (see above paragraph 3.5.).

As compared with the intensive involvement with text/language and communication, i.e. the bottom part of figure 4, the relation with world, seems to receive much less attention. This is only partly true. In the work of two of the most influential philosophers of this century, Wittgenstein and Quine, the world plays an important role. In addition, the whole discussion on the status of theories in natural science (Popper, Kuhn) has implications for the relation between text/language and world.

We hope that this short summary of recent philosophical approaches to language/text makes clear that figure 4 provides a suitable starting point for a further consideration of the methodological problems which we face in our investigation.

At first, it will be necessary, however, to obtain more insight into the nature of the relations between the various elements it contains. In chapter 4 we collected much information on the relation between text/language and sender, but those between text/language and world, and text/language and receiver have not yet been covered adequately. Hence the subsequent paragraphs will contain more detailed surveys of these relations.

5.3. Text/language and world.

5.3.1. Introduction.

In this paragraph, we will review a few general publications on language with the particular objective of getting more insight into recent ideas about the relation between text/language and world. Once again it should be emphasized that, in agreement with the view which we outlined in the previous paragraph,

---

1   Derrida, 1967, p. 227.

we do not wish to isolate this relation completely from the other aspects of text/language. So, if required, we will cover these as well.

It was necessary to make a choice from the available publications on this broader philosophical aspect of language. We will restrict ourselves to four publications from the last decade which approach the relation of text/language and world from different angles and, as a consequence, tend to emphasize different aspects of it. In section 5.3.2., we survey a publication by Grace, who places himself in the tradition of Herder and W.von Humboldt, a tradition which also had a heavy influence on Whorf (see above paragraph 4.2.). The next section discusses the philosophy of language of Devitt and Sterelny, who find their sources in a completely opposite direction, namely in realism and naturalism, and who also lean heavily on the nominalist approach of Quine. In the remaining two sections of this paragraph we present briefly the ideas of two British scholars, who, each in his own characteric way, carry forward certain ideas originated by Ludwig Wittgenstein. The linguist Harris considers the nature and limitations of linguistic rules, also as far as their use is concerned. The book of the philosopher Blackburn, to whom we already referred above (see paragraph 5.1.), covers all aspects of figure 1, but we will concentrate on his survey of the relation between language and world.

In our review of these publications in this paragraph, we will give initial comments only. Assessing them in detail and incorporating their ideas into the over-all picture, the shape of which we gave in our preliminary impression in section 5.2.3., will be the subject of paragraph 5.5.

5.3.2. The reality-construction view of language; Grace.

The starting-point of Grace is the difference between the mapping view of language, which he considers to be the one adhered to by most linguists, and the reality-construction view, which he considers to be more satisfactory. So in his book he attempts "to show that the mapping view in the long run conceals more than it reveals about the nature of language and the role of language and language differences in a wide range of human affairs. It will attempt to show how a generally more revealing view of language - what we are here calling the 'reality-construction' view - can be developed in a satisfactory way."[1]

In his introductory chapter, Grace discusses extensively the fundamental assumptions of both views. "The basic epistemological assumption of the mapping view might be stated as follows: there is a common world out there and our languages are analogous to maps of this world. Thus, this common world is represented or 'mapped' (with greater or less distortion) by all languages. ....

In the reality-construction view, the imperfectness of our access to knowledge of the real world assumes central importance. Emphasis is placed upon the fact that

---

1   Grace, 1987, p. 13.

we do not have direct access to the real world itself, but only to the data about it provided by our senses. And these senses provide very incomplete information. ....

Thus, in the reality-construction view, our sensory data are regarded as falling seriously short of constituting an adequate picture of the real world. They are considered to be very incomplete and unsystematic, are seen as not adding up to anything like a representative sample of what is out there. On the contrary, all we can do (according to this view) is invent explanations for the sensory data which are attempts to make sense of the whole of the sensory input. To put it differently, all we can do is to theorize about reality, or to put it more precisely still, to construct models of it. These models are our constructed realities, and they are reflected in the languages we speak.

Of course, these realities are not assumed to be fabricated out of the whole cloth. The real world imposes some constraints. The experiences of people in different cultures are not assumed to be totally random with respect to one another."[1]

Grace believes that there is one main assumption which contains in a nutshell the essence of the mapping view of language; that is the "intertranslatability postulate: anything can be said in any language."[2] According to him, this assuption leads to further ideas, such as considering each language as a universal encoder, and a strong insistence upon the independence of language from everything else. This emphasis on the autonomy of language on its turn leads to belittling the role of language in human life.

Grace defends a different set of assumptions which are the opposites of the ones of the mapping view and on their basis he develops an alternative view of language.

He first addresses the problem of the relation between linguistic expressions and reality. He rejects the ideas of the 'mapping view,' because "it conceives of linguistic expressions as if their relation to real-world situations were an immediate one. .... I believe, on the contrary, that we cannot understand the relation between a linguistic expression and a real-world situation to which it refers unless we recognize the mediating roles played by the speaker and by the context of the speech event."[3] His own views he summarizes as follows: "The linguistic construction of reality may be thought of as occurring on two levels. A language as a whole may be spoken of as reflecting a particular constructed reality. Such realities will be called Conceptual Worlds .... On a quite different level a single speech act, or rather the linguistic expression which serves as the vehicle of a speech act, also reflects a constructed reality. The constructed realities represented by sentence-level signs will be referred to as Conceptual

_____

1   o.c. , p. 6.
2   o.c. , p. 7.
3   o.c. , p. 26 - 27.

Events."[1] The relation between these two levels he describes as "the rather fixed constructed reality represented by a language as a whole and the ad hoc reality constructed as part of an individual speech act ...."[2]

According to Grace, the conceptual world as operated by a particular language, is not once and for all given. It is "constantly being modified in use." Its influence is also restricted: "Thus, although the conceptual world as it exists at any particular moment is a strong influence upon our preceptions and our thought, it nevertheless does not confine us in unyielding restraints.[3] In line with these ideas Grace develops the following view of the LRH: "It seems that actually much of the effect of language on thought and of thought on language is to be found in the way of talking rather than in the most rigid conventionalized parts of the language. It appears that the entering wedges of much linguistic change are to be found there."[4]

It is interesting to see in what way Grace uses the idea of 'conceptual world,' which seems to be related to similar ideas (world-view, projected world, etc.) , which we found with some authors whose work we discussed earlier. On one hand he connects it clearly with language; on the other hand he also acknowledges that it is based on "ways of talking about the subject matters" which the human mind "invents."[5] On one hand it seems to have a more or less fixed structure which influences thought, but on the other hand the human mind does not seem to be completely determined by it. Perhaps this unclarity is caused by the fact that he does not explain what is the precise relation between the conceptual events and the conceptual world. In this connection it should be noticed that he also considers the role of the culture of speakers on the characteristics of their linguistic behaviour.

5.3.3. A naturalistic approach; Devitt and Sterelny.

The authors explain that their approach to language is naturalistic in two respects. "First, a theory of linguistic phenomena has just the same status as a theory of any other phenomena: it is empirical and conjectural. We are confronted with a mysterious and complex world and have developed theories to explain and render tractable these complexities: theories in physics, biology, the social sciences and the like. The theory of language is just another such theory; another part of our total theory of nature. ... [It] must fit in with the rest of our beliefs about people and the world. This brings us to the second respect in which our approach is naturalistic: it is physicalistic.

We think that people are best seen as part of the natural world. They are not

---

1   o.c. , p. 31.
2   o.c. , p. 38.
3   o.c. , p. 113.
4   o.c. , p. 123 - 124.
5   o.c. , p. 112.

special except in detail and complexity. (a) They are part of the animate nature, part of the biological world. (b) The biological differs from the inanimate only in complexity: no vital essence distinguishes the living from the non-living. To be living is only to have a special, if complex, chemistry. .... Any linguistic facts there are must be, ultimately, physical. Semantic notions like meaning, truth and reference can be used only if they can be explained in non-linguistic terms; they are not 'primitive,' not theoretically fundamental."[1]

On the basis of these presuppositions, the authors develop a theory of meaning, which in the most general case which they consider - that of 'artefactual kind' terms - they call a "descriptive-causal theory" of meaning: "The descriptive element is taken over from the description theory. It is the description of physical characteristics ('graphite' for 'pencil,' 'back' for 'chair'). The causal element arises from groundings in samples. Whereas on the description theory, the reference-determining function is fixed by an associated description of the function, on the descriptive-causal theory it is fixed by the objects in the sample used to ground the term. The term refers to any object (with the physical characteristics) that has the same function as the objects in the sample.[2]

This approach assumes that man has a direct relation to the world and is able to establish a more or less fixed relation between world and language. The authors demonstrate similar ideas in the part of their book entitled "Language and Realism," from the beginning of which we give a few quotations: "It is hard to talk about language without talking about the world. .... A theory of language is bound to be influenced by a theory of the extra-linguistic world. Should a theory of that world be influenced by a theory of language? One would think not. Language, after all, is a local phenomenon, probably confined to humans. It is hard to see why our ideas of the stars, of biochemistry and geology, should be influenced by our ideas of language."[3] In the remainder of these chapters the authors give a defense of realism, which they describe as "a metaphysical doctrine with two dimensions. First it is a doctrine about what exists, and second it is a doctrine about the nature of the existence. Concerning the first, it holds that such physical entities as stones, trees and cats exist ('are real'). Concerning the second, these entities do not depend for their existence or nature on our minds, not on our awareness, perception or cognizance of them. Realists thus speak of these entities as being 'independent' of and 'external' to the mind."[4] On the basis of this realism, the authors attack relativism mainly on the ground that it starts with a theory of language: "The philosophy of language is exactly

---

1   Devitt and Sterelny, 1987, p. 7 - 8.
2   o.c. , p. 77.
3   o.c. , p. 187.
4   o.c. , p. 187.

the wrong place to start metaphysics."[1] In addition, they consider the argument that explanatory theories of the world have changed drastically in the course of time, as not damaging to their thoughts: "As theories have changed, have we abandoned our belief in the entities that we previously thought to exist? First, consider observables. Theoretical progress certainly results in the addition of new observables, terrestrial and celestial, to our catalogue. But there have been very few deletions. Cases like witches and Vulcan .... are relatively rare. There have been some mistakes, but there is nothing in our intellectual history to shake our confidence that we have steadily accumulated knowledge of the make up of the observable world. We have been wrong often enough about the nature of those entities, but it is their nature we have been wrong about. We have not been wrong about the fact of their existence. In brief, theory change is no threat to common-sense realism."[2]

The approach of these authors has many things in common with the mapping-view of language, which Grace attacks so heavily. It seems to favour the dominance of world over language. There exists a more or less fixed relation between 'worldly entities' and linguistic terms,' which is based on an initial linkage and an additional history. This makes their approach to all further problems concerning language clear and concise. But figurative, metaphoric, poetic, etc. use of language appears to remain out of sight.

5.3.4. Integrational linguistics; Harris.

A completely different approach is adopted by Harris, who in 1981 published a book in which he opposes a view of language which he calls the language myth and which he describes as follows: ".... the language myth assumes that a language is a finite set of rules generating an infinite set of pairs, of which one member is a sound-sequence or a sequence of written characters, and the other is its meaning; and that it is knowledge of such rules which unites individuals into linguistic communities able to exchange thoughts with one another in accordance with a prearranged plan determined by those rules. .... Such a model is said to be 'bi-planar'; that is to say, it envisages language as separable into the two planes of form and meaning, which are interconnected but distinct."[3]

Harris believes that this myth is "the product of two interconnected fallacies: the telementational fallacy and the determinacy fallacy. ....

According to the telementational fallacy, linguistic knowledge is essentially a matter of knowing which words stand for which ideas. For words, according to this view, are symbols devised by man for transferring thoughts from one mind to another. Speech is a form of telementation. This theory can be traced back .... to Aristotle, [who] .... says: 'Words are symbols or signs of affections or

---

1   o.c. , p. 209.
2   o.c. , p. 205.
3   Harris, 1981 , p. 11.

impressions of the soul', ... [which] themselves .... are the same for the whole of mankind ....

The determinacy fallacy, or 'fixed code' fallacy (as it might alternatively called) provides the explanation of how the telementational process works, and indeed of how telementation is possible. This fallacy too has Aristotelian roots. If we agree with Aristotle that all men are provided by Nature with the same ideas, then all it needs is for men to agree upon some fixed set of correlations between ideas and verbal symbols, in order to provide themselves with a viable system for exchanging thoughts. Languages are, precisely, systems of this kind. A language community is a group of individuals who have come to use the 'same words' to express the 'same ideas' supplied by Nature, and to combine those words in the same ways into sentences for purposes of connected discourse."[1]

After considering a number of aspects of language, Harris, in his final chapter, develops an alternative view of language, which he calls "integrational linguistics", and which in his opinion should proceed on the following general principles:

"First and foremost, an integrational linguistics must recognise that human beings inhabit a communicational space which is not neatly compartmentalised into language and non-language. The consequences of this 'non-compartmentalisation principle' are basic for the methodology of linguistic studies. It renounces in advance the possibility of setting up systems of forms and meanings which will 'account for' a central core of linguistic behaviour irrespective of the situation and communicational purposes involved. But it is important to note that this consequence does not automatically destroy the concept of a language community. What it does, rather, is to demand that the concept of a language community be reformulated in more realistic terms than those of the regimented sameness postulated by the language myth."[2]

These considerations lead Harris to emphasize the importance of the "individual linguistic act in its communicational setting. .... The basic principle which an integrational linguistics will be concerned to give adequate expression to is that language is continuously created by the interaction of individuals in specific communication situations. It is this interaction which confers relevance upon the participants' past experience with words; and not, as orthodox linguistics would have us believe, past experience (that is to say, mastery of 'the language') which determines the communicational possibilities of their present interaction.[3]

On its turn, the emphasis on the "individual linguistic act" leads him to recognize "certain indeterminacies which underlie all human communication. .... Insofar as what is meant is determinate, it can be only a provisional

---

1   o.c. , p. 9 - 10.
2   o.c. , p. 165.
3   o.c. , p. 166, 167.

determinacy, relativised to a particular interactional situation. One consequence of adopting this standpoint is that linguistic behaviour is thereby placed on a par with all other forms of voluntary human action, in which indeterminacy both of intention and interpretation is the rule."[1] Harris subsequently discusses several forms of indeterminacy, of which, within the framework of this section of our study, "referential indeterminacy" is the most relevant. He describes it as "failure to determine whether a given thing x and a given expression E are related in such a way that x counts as one of the things to which E may properly be applied or not," and sees it in a rather broad sense: "To avoid tying the notion of referential indeterminacy too narrowly to an approach to language which looks like some form of labelling theory, we may treat referential indeterminacy as one variety of indeterminacy of employment. For referential factors are not the only factors relevant to the appropriate use of linguistic expressions."[2] In line with his broad approach to the indeterminacy of language, Harris considers many aspects of it in human communication, at the end of which he concludes to "the fact that there is no way in which language can provide explicitly and specifically for all conceivable eventualities. What language can and must do, however, is provide mechanisms for participants to resolve possible communicational uncertainties."[3]

In the final part of his book, he discusses the relation between the fixed and the open sides of language. His conclusion will be clear from the following quotations: "To summarise, the enigma of rational speaker-hearers is that although they apparently require some fixed linguistic framework which would enable them to exercise their rationality, the moment we try seriously to identify and inspect that framework, it vanishes before our eyes. .... The search for some fixed point of linguistic reference outside that continuum of creative activity which itself is language encounters a typically Archimedean predicament. Such a search in the end is vain."[4]

Here we meet an approach to language which is almost directly opposite to that of Devitt and Sterelny discussed in the previous section. Its advantage is that it certainly tries to account for the creative and indeterminate aspects of language, and even makes these the cornerstone of its approach. But it uses a number of concepts which remain rather unclear. For example, what exactly is meant by 'communicational space'? Is it similar to the concept world, which is used generally? Another problem is the question of the 'fixed linguistic framework.' How far does it extend? Does it constitute a restriction to Harris's statement that language is 'continuously created'? If it 'vanishes before our eyes,' does that mean that it has limited influence only?

---

1   o.c. , p. 167.
2   o.c. , p. 169.
3   o.c. , p. 192.
4   o.c. , p. 203, 204.

Despite all these questions, it must be said that Harris's approach offers many stimulating ideas, in particular regarding those aspects of language which are more or less neglected by the 'standard theories.'

5.3.5. A projective account; Blackburn.

In paragraph 5.1. we already paid attention to the introduction to the "Groundings in the Philosophy of Language" by Blackburn.[1] We will now consider some elements of his approach to the relation of language and world.

He starts his discussion of this topic with a question: "How do we tell when we are discovering objects 'as they really stand in nature,' and when we are doing some other thing, such as projecting onto them our own subjective sentiments? .... This is the issue between realists and their opponents."[2] He investigates a number of anti-realist approaches, in particular by following "through a variety of attitudes to some particular area of commitments. This will give us a sense of the options locally. But by coming to appreciate local issues, arising, say, in the philosophy of value, or of mathematics, we can work our way into more general problems of realism and truth, and get a sense of why the global issues fall out as they do."[3] This choice involves a 'bottom-up procedure,' as Blackburn himself calls it, starting with considering a certain limited area (e.g. ethics), and afterwards expanding to broader fields.

After having investigated the approach which completely rejects the whole area, and the one that reduces it to others, he gives his own view in his discussion of the approach that regards "the commitments as expressive rather than descriptive. The commitments in question are contrasted with others - call them judgements, beliefs, assertions, or propositions - which have genuine truth-conditions."[4] He calls this approach an "expressive theory," which "must be sharply distinguished from more naive kinds of subjectivism. An expressive theory does not give a moral utterance a truth-condition which concerns the speaker. .... The point of expressive theories is to avoid the metaphysical and epistemological problems which realist theories of ethics .... are supposed to bring with them. Again it is important to remember the overall motivation. This is to explain the practice of moralizing, using causal language, and so on, in terms only of our exposure to a thinner reality - a world which contains only some lesser states of affairs, to which we respond and in which we have to conduct our lives."[5] In a further discussion of this attitude Blackburn calls its core activity 'projection': "Suppose that we say we project an attitude or habit or other commitment which is not descriptive onto the world, when we speak and

---

1   Blackburn, 1984.
2   o.c. , p. 145.
3   o.c. , p. 145 - 46.
4   o.c. , p. 167.
5   o.c. , p. 169.

think as though there were a property of things which our sayings describe, which we can reason about, know about, be wrong about, and so on. Projecting is what Hume referred to when he talks of 'gilding and staining all natural objects with the colours borrowed from internal sentiment,' or of the mind 'spreading itself on the world.'"[1] After having considered the view that this projection is a mistake, he wonders: "But perhaps there is no mistake. I call the enterprise of showing that there is none - that even on anti-realist grounds there is nothing improper, nothing 'diseased' in projected predicates - the enterprise of quasi-realism."[2]

In the subsequent chapter of his book, he develops this concept of quasi-realism in more detail. Figure 5 illustrates this "projective account of some commitments."[3]

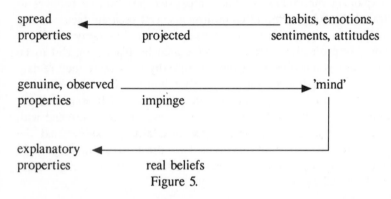

Figure 5.

In support for this approach, Blackburn mentions three motives: "The first of these is economy. The projective theory intends to ask no more from the world than what we know is there - the ordinary features of things on the basis of which we make decisions about them, like or dislike them, fear them and avoid them, desire them and seek them out. It asks no more than this: a natural world, and patterns of reaction to it. ....

The second argument for preferring projective theories is metaphysical. It concerns the relation between the values we find in the world, and the other properties of things of value. The argument arises from the common claim in philosophy that one kind of state supervenes upon another. The idea is that some properties, the A-properties, are consequential upon some other base properties, the underlying B-properties. This claim is supposed to mean that in some sense of necessary, it is necessary that if an A-truth changes, some B-truth

1   o.c. , p. 171.
2   o.c. , p. 171.
3   see o.c. , p. 181.

changes; or if two situations are identical in their B-properties they are identical in their A-properties. A-properties cannot (in this same sense) vary regardless of B-properties. .... This argument for a projective moral theory is in effect a development of the simple thought that moral properties must be given an intelligible connection to the natural ones upon which they somehow depend. It generates a metaphysical motive for projectivism.

The third and last motive I shall mention comes from the philosophy of action. Evaluative commitments are being contrasted with other, truth-conditional judgements or beliefs. This contrast means that to have a commitment of this sort is to hold an attitude, not a belief, and that in turn should have implications for the explanation of people's behaviour."[1] While discussing this motive Blackburn realizes that the precise relationship between moral commitment and action is difficult to establish. He acknowledges the influence of desires, choices, etc. Without exploring the details of this complicated problem, he believes to have demonstrated the role of 'moral commitments' as a separate factor in this process, and uses this as support for his 'projective account' of morality.

Many details of this projective account as advocated by Blackburn, had to be omitted from our discussion because of their complexity or because they remain unclear even in the exposition of the author. But it has a few characteristics which suggest that it might be very useful in our situation. It considers the element world not as a homogeneous entity, but as one with structure and with 'properties' of different kind, origin and effect. In addition it shows that the relation between world and man involves two directions ('impinge' and 'project'/'believe'). It looks promising to connect this approach with some other ideas which we described earlier.

5.4. Text/language and the receiver.

In this paragraph we will briefly address the third relation involving text/language in figure 4. As we mentioned already above (see section 5.2.3.), it receives much attention in the branch of science called hermeneutics. The results of the study in this field enjoy the interest of many scholars in the biblical sciences. So we limit ourselves in this respect to discussing a publication which was also mentioned in a book by Lundin et al. ,[2] which we already reviewed in paragraph 3.5. In their survey of new ideas on literary criticism, emphasizing in particular "reader-response hermeneutics," they quote Stanley Fish, who is, according to Thiselton, "the most radical exponent of reader-response

---

1   o.c. , p. 182, 183, 187, 188.
2   Lundin, Thiselton, Walhout, 1985.

hermeneutics."[1]

In 1980 Fish published a book on the authority of interpretive communities, which contained two essays with the same title "What is Stylistics and Why Are They Saying Such Terrible Things About It?", one originally published in 1973 and the second in 1980. In his 1973-paper he criticizes in particular the way by which 'stylisticians' move from description to interpretation. According to him a serious defect in their procedures is "the absence of any constraint on the way in which one moves from description to interpretation, with the result that any interpretation one puts forward is arbitrary. ...... (T)ypically, a stylistician will interpose a formidable apparatus between his descriptive and interpretive acts, thus obscuring the absence of any connection between them."[2] As a way out of these problems Fish suggests not to link the descriptive and interpretive acts but to make them one. This step entails quite some changes of attitude and outlook, as will be evident from the following quotations:

"It is hardly necessary to say that this kind of analysis is not without problems, and the problems are for the most part a direct consequence of its assumptions about what it means to be human. It can have no rules in the sense of discovery procedures, since the contextualizing ability that characterizes being human is not circumscribed by its previous performances, performances which, while they constitute the history of that ability, do not constitute its limits. Thus the value a formal feature may acquire in the context of a reader's concerns and expectations is local and temporary; and there is no guarantee that the value-formal feature correlation that obtains once will obtain again (although an awareness that it has obtained once is not without interest or usefulness). All you have when you begin is a sense of this finite but infinitely flexible ability and a personal knowledge of what it means to have it. You then attempt to project the course that ability would take in its intercourse with a specific text, using as the basis of your projection what you know, and at the same time adding to what you know by the very effort to make analytical use of it. There are other things that can help. Formal linguistic characterizations can help, if, as I have said, one views their content as potential cues for performing acts. Literary history can help, if one views its conventions in the same way; a description of a genre, for example, can and should be seen as a prediction of the shape of response. Other minds can help, because they know what you know, but with the same lack of distance between themselves and their knowledge which makes the effort so difficult. Analyses of perceptual strategy can help, because they acquaint us with the past performances of the ability we are trying to know. (Our trying is itself just such a performance.) Finally, however, you are left only with yourself and with the impossible enterprise of understanding understanding; impossible because it is endless, endless because to

---

1   Thiselton, 1985, p. 93.
2   Fish, 1980, p. 72 - 73.

have reached an end is to have performed an operation that once again extends it beyond your reach. In short, this way lacks the satisfaction of a closed system of demonstration and is unable ever to prove anything, although, paradoxically, this makes rigor and precision more, not less, necessary; but these very deficiencies are the reverse side of its greatest virtue (in both the modern and Renaissance sense): the recognition that meaning is human."[1]

In his 1980-essay the emphasis of the criticism of Fish has shifted to the nature of the formal patterns of the text: "Here my thesis is that formal patterns are themselves the products of interpretation and that therefore there is no such a thing as a formal pattern, at least in the sense necessary for the practice of stylistics: that is, no pattern that one can observe before interpretation is hazarded and which therefore can be used to prefer one interpretation to another. The conclusion, however, is not that there are no formal patterns but that there are always formal patterns; it is just that the formal patterns there always are will always be the product of a prior interpretive act, and therefore will be available for discerning only so long as that act is in force. Or, to end with an aphorism: there always is a formal pattern, but it isn't always the same one."[2]

In general we agree with the critical comments by Thiselton which we reported above (see paragraph 3.5.). More specifically, within the framework of our literature search on the wider implications of text/language, we notice that Fish puts all emphasis on the mind and situation of the receiver, on his 'creative abilities.' In this connection he seems to work parallel to Harris's approach of man as 'sender.' The main question remains how to link this creative activity to the 'given basis' of text/language.

5.5. Summary.

Before we start to summarize the results of the whole of the literature search as presented in this chapter and the previous one, it is wise to consider its limitations. It has been undertaken with a particular objective in mind, viz. obtaining more information regarding the position of the LRH in connection with the methodological issues of our study. In order to stay in line with this objective the search had to remain rather superficial, but at the same time had to cover many aspects and philosophical implications of language/text, and so it became a rather broad enterprise. In agreement with this approach it may be expected that its results will lead to a wide but rather superficial picture. But we believe that it is exactly such a picture that we need in order to obtain the desired clarity regarding the methodological problems of our study. We do not wish to give a complete and thorough philosophy of language.

In this paragraph and in chapter 6, we will make an intensive and extensive use

---

1   o.c., p. 95 - 96.
2   o.c., p. 267.

of the data which we collected in our search. In a number of cases we will mention the source to which we refer in particular. But in order to prevent the text becoming overloaded with quotations we will restrict ourselves to the main items. We hope that, in general, the reader will be able to recognize the sources we used, from their description in the survey-parts of chapter 4 and 5.

As a starting-point for our summary we choose figure 4 which we introduced in our provisional impression (section 5.2.3.), using the approach by Bühler, together with some additions. It provides an over-all view of all entities and relations involved in the role of text/language.

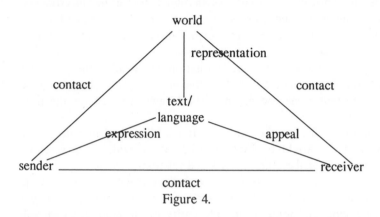

Figure 4.

As a first approximation of how things behave in this picture, we might consider all elements to be clearly defined: all entities are independent from one another, and their mutual relations are fixed according to certain rules. This view supposes that there is a world 'out there,' which man can perceive with his senses, in which he lives, and about which he can express himself using his language. In addition there are his fellow-men, together with whom he lives in this world, and with whom he can communicate about himself and the world, using that same language. The main advantage of this view is that everything seems clear and straightforward, and that any possible gaps in our knowledge of it could be filled provided the technical means were available. The approach as employed by Devitt and Sterelny comes close to this view (see section 5.3.3.).

But many other publications explain that things cannot be considered that simple. The literature of linguistics covered in our search[1] indicates that the entities man and text/language are not completely independent, but that they influence each other, which complicates their mutual relation. And although there is a lot of controversy about the type and direction of the influence, and some investigators even doubt whether it will ever be possible to establish the precise nature of the relation between man and text/language, it is evident that

---

1   see e.g.: Langacker, 1976; Talmy, 1983, Jackendoff, 1985.

the approach mentioned above does not provide an adequate explanation for all results of scientific investigation.

A similar situation appears to exist in the other areas of the triangle: the relation between man and world and also that between world and text/language are of a complex nature.

One of the ways out of such a complicated situation would be to put all emphasis on one of the entities involved, at the cost of the role of the others. We already mentioned Blackburn's illustrations of this attitude (see paragraph 5.1.). We admit that in order to obtain insight into a certain situation, it may be useful to reduce the entities and relations involved, to certain specific and well-defined phenomena. In fact this is one of the corner-stones of every scientific investigation. But such a reduction should fulfill at least two requirements:

a. It should be 'open' in view of the total situation surrounding the particular area of research; the factors not covered by the investigation should not be denied any existence, but rather be given a 'fixed value,' at least for the time being.

b. It should not be maintained to the extreme; after it has served its purpose the results obtained with it should be incorporated into a wider theory which honours the complete role of the other entities and relations as well.

From this point of view it will be clear that we believe that the 'linguistic turn' should not be carried through to the extreme, so that text/language would absorb all other elements and remain the only entity in the picture. So we will not follow those (super)structuralists who move into that direction (see above section 5.2.3.). This does not mean that we believe that investigation of the structure of text/language is not useful. On the contrary. One of the attractive features of Bühler's axioms is that they allow for and stimulate a wide variety of approaches to language, including the study of its structure (see his fourth axiom). But the results of these investigations should be incorporated into a picture of the role of language in the larger area of the triangle.

For the same reason we do not favour the attitude which puts all emphasis on material and natural aspects (the physicalist's approach), and reduces all elements (man, world and text/language and their relations) to material phenomena only. This seems to be a different type of reductionism, which does not remove the other elements of the triangle, but reduces the role they are able to play to a minimum by assigning a supreme role to one entity.

Some statements of proponents of the reader-oriented hermeneutics, and the literary critics quoted by them, appear to simplify the matter by attributing dominance to man and his judgment. Fish with "the recognition that meaning is human," provides a good example of this attitude (see paragraph 5.4.).

None of the emphasizing or reducing approaches to the triangle which we discussed so far seems to be able to account for all the diversity which its elements show. We will have to accept that language/text has intense and complicated relations with a number of aspects of human life, as we will have to accept that the three aspects involved in particular, text/language, world and man, are not of a simple, homogeneous and uniform nature. Our summary of chapter 4 already showed that the more recent literature on the LRH points to the complex nature of each entity.

At first sight, this idea seems to make things more complicated. Unfortunately, figure 4 is not suitable for including this diversity of the entities. But it seems possible to account for this feature by adding to its flat triangle, vertical directions perpendicular to the plane of the drawing. It would then become something like figure 6.

For sake of clarity we abbreviated the entities and left out the names of the relations.

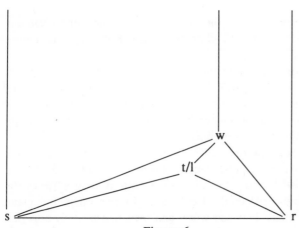

Figure 6.

In figure 6 it is possible to indicate a certain diversification of each entity alongside the vertical axis. It is not our objective to explore all of its possibilities in detail. But we will use it to illustrate some of the results of our literature search, and to demonstrate how they can be viewed together in elucidating the position of the LRH and the methodological issues involved in our study.

In the case of the world, we assume that the bottom of the axis represents the physical side of worldly objects, those properties which impinge upon human senses. Somewhat higher up we allocate the 'theoretical constructs,' those aspects of objects, or those supposed objects, which we use in our theories in order to explain certain phenomena. Higher still we place the ideas which we use in describing and explaining human behaviour, such as desires, honesty, love, selfishness, etc. And somewhere at the top we find concepts like faith, spirit, sacrifice, etc.

Similarly we operate alongside both axes originating from the two entities which are human. Somewhere at the bottom is the (highly unconscious) operation of the sense organs, a little higher up the workings of logic and reasoning, and more near the top activities which could be characterized as believing, creating, etc.

Regarding the axis based on the text/language entity, at its bottom it represents this entity in forms mainly involving the physical side of the world and human perceptive activity. Moving upward along the axis we meet it in a more abstract and theoretical shape. And at still higher levels it takes a more figurative and indeterminate character.

What we outlined above is only a brief and rudimentary description of this 'third dimension' to each of the entities. But we hope that it is sufficient to show a few things:

a. The 'movement' along each axis is in agreement with what we have found in our literature search.

b. It appears that the movements along the four axes show the same direction: from more or less confined patterns to phenomena which display and require more freedom and flexibility.

The next step is to look more closely at the shape of the relations in figure 6. On the basis of the more or less parallel movement along the vertical axes originating from the entities, we assume a gradual change in the nature of the relations within the 'basic triangle' when we move upward along the axes: from more or less fixed to more flexible and mobile.

This assumption also reflects a number of results from the literature search, for example, Blackburn's approach, as presented in figure 5 in section 5.3.5. The relation in the middle, called 'impinge' comes at the bottom area, whereas the other two, 'real beliefs' and 'projected,' are located higher up in the plane representing the relation 'contact' between world and man, and possibly also that between man and man, in figure 6.

The openness and flexiblity which we assume to exist in the higher areas of figure 6, refer to a more or less ideal situation. In practice, many things will to a certain extent be kept constant in order to make human life bearable:

- Particular beliefs will held to be true in order to provide for some feeling of security in a strange world.

- Linguistic rules are being followed in order to make a reasonable form of communication possible.

Nevertheless, these beliefs and rules are to a certain degree different from the fixed relations prevailing in the bottom area of figure 6.

- they show more diversification, from person to person, or from community to community.

- they are more easily subject to change or adaptation, depending on the situation.

Figure 6 thus incorporates a number of data from our literature search and presents a bird's eye view of the area of the methodological issues of our study. In a next step we will use it for a discussion of the three points mentioned at the end of paragraph 3.6., which formed the focal points for our literature search reported in the chapters 4 and 5 and which we already considered earlier in paragraph 4.5.

1. The position of the LRH.

In paragraph 4.5., we already noticed that the LRH on one hand seems to represent an idea considered to be true by many scholars, but on the other hand seems to fall short of solid confirmation by empirical investigation. Looking at figure 6, this situation could be accounted for by assuming that the LRH applies in particular to the relations between the various entities of the triangle at the higher levels of the vertical axes, whereas its testing usually is made at the lower levels, where the relations are different. But this view on the position of the LRH leads to the question how possible strong claims of the LRH in the upper regions of figure 6 can be reconciled with the fact that this is precisely the area where the creative and deliberate use of language by man seems to have its strongest possibilities.

So it seems better to admit that the results of our search make it impossible to maintain a general LRH which covers the whole of figure 6. Linguistic relativity, or better, the extent to which language and thought influence each other, seems to be determined by many factors which vary from case to case. So in every situation in which both entities are involved, it will be necessary to investigate what the conditions are and how they affect the relation between them.

The merit of the LRH and the discussion connected with it is that it points to phenomena which easily escape attention, both in daily life and in scientific study. In this way it forms an important contribution to our knowledge in the field of language and cognition. But it should not be given the status of a 'law,' which more or less automatically governs the relation between thought and language in every conceivable situation.

2. The concept of world-view.

In view of the complicated relations between the entities, and in order to prevent more confusion, it seems wise to restrict the use of the concept world-view to man only. In the end it is not his language, but he himself who views the world. That is not to say that his language does not play a role in his viewing the world. Perhaps, using ideas found with Grace and Harris, we could compare the role of language to that of projecting systems which cartographers use when they prepare maps of certain areas of the world.[1] Each projecting system has its own characteristic way of 'translating' the properties of the curved surface of the earth into the two-dimensional plane of the map. In the same way each language seems to have its own characteristic way of translating

---

1   see e.g. Wolters-Noordhoff, 1988, p. 8.

the "mysterious and complex world"[1] into the human mind. This does not mean that we agree completely with the 'mapping view' of language as described and rejected by Grace.[2] We believe that both views, which he contrasts, present useful approaches to the role of language: the mapping view with the more or less fixed form of the relations between the entities in the lower area of figure 6, and the reality construction view in which the mutual relations have a more flexible shape, in the areas higher up in the figure.

Owing to these diversified shapes of the mutual relations the role of language seems to vary as well. At the bottom area where stimuli from the world and their perception by human senses seem to be dominant, the role of language seems to be more straightforward and direct. Every language enables people who use it to refer to these 'more physical aspects' of the world. There may be differences between languages, but in essence each of them is bound by the 'impinge relation' as used by Blackburn. But for areas higher up in the figure, where human projecting and creative activities become more important, language seems to play a more complicated role. On one hand it has more influence since it provides its user with an available system to refer to that part of the world, a system which reflects previous use and is adapted to a certain way of coping with the world and viewing it. In fact this is the basic idea of the LRH.

But at the same time, it must be acknowledged that exactly in this area the human mind is most active in processing its perceptions and thoughts into a 'projected world,' and we must assume that it also includes language in this 'creative process.' This last point is the main topic of the final chapter of Harris's book.[3]

These considerations on the role of language underline its importance. But we hope to have made it clear that it is the human mind which uses language in its referring to the world. According to some philosophers this is the 'real world as it is given,' according to others it is the 'projected world' or 'conceptual world' as 'produced' by man. Again the situation may be different at different levels of figure 6. Perhaps the 'construed world' at the lowest level contains more features which can be related quite directly to features of the 'world out there' than at higher levels. But it would certainly be outside the scope of our investigation to become involved too heavily into the ontological and metaphysical problems which loom in this connection. Let it be sufficient at this point, to say that, whatever the status of the world out there and the character of the human world-view, language refers, either to one or to both of them.

If we compare language with the projecting system, we could compare the result of human use of language with a map. Using the terminology of Blackburn we

---

1   Devitt, Sterelny, 1987, p. 7.
2   Grace, 1987.
3   Harris, 1981, p. 150 - 204.

can say that every human utterance 'expresses' part of the world and enables those who receive that utterance to obtain some picture of that piece of the world. Thinking along this line, a text could be considered as a map of a certain part of the world made by somebody who perceives that world from a particular point of view and expresses himself using a more or less given projecting system. This idea leads us to make four remarks:

a. A map is not exactly congruent with the area it is supposed to represent. This is caused by the characteristic properties of the factors involved, viz. the area to be represented, the mapping system, and the plane of projection. Nevertheless the map gives some idea of the area. In the same way we assume that a text gives some idea of that part of the world to which it refers. In this sense a text constitutes a picture of part of the world, which can be observed, described, and evaluated. Like a map, the precise shape of that picture will also depend on the properties of the part of the world it refers to, the projecting system (=language) used and the plane of projection (=cultural environment) on which it is made.

b. In cartography a projecting system is adapted to the peculiar properties of the area of the world to which it is applied. The same holds true for languages: they also reflect the 'worlds' to which they refer. This is the phenomenon which is often illustrated by mentioning the fact that the language of Eskimos has many words for snow, etc. But the same phenomenon also can be illustrated for areas in the higher parts of figure 6, where the world reflects a greater influence of human thought. In this connection it should be borne in mind that the 'projecting system' of a language covers the whole of it, not only its lexicon, but also its syntax, idiom, etc.

c. If we see the mapping system of a language in such a broad sense, the properties of this concept seem to be comparable to the (linguistic) Weltansicht, as used by Gipper (see section 4.3.2.), Koch (see paragraph 3.5.), and others. In this respect we only agree partly with Gipper's ideas about its relation to the (scientific) Weltbild and the (ideological) Weltanschauung. It goes too far to say that the latter two are founded upon the former. Language, as a mapping system, will certainly play a role when man develops his Weltbild and Weltanschauung, and perhaps an even stronger one, when he expresses himself about them. But both these human activities involve creative processes which severely reduce the decisive role of language in this respect.

d. In reader-response hermeneutics, which we discussed earlier, it is common to say that a text calls into being a 'world' within the reader. This fits nicely with the view of a text as a map of part of the world. Maps may be observed for aesthetic reasons, and people may enjoy them without worrying about the whereabouts of the areas to which they refer. At the same time it should not be forgotten that they are maps, i.e., they express part of the world, be it the real world or the thought world or imaginary world of the originator of the text. It is perfectly acceptable when people enjoy a map for all kinds of reasons, but as soon as they wish to use it as a means of orientation in the world, they cannot do away with its origins and 'technical details.' In other words: they have to take

137

into account its referring character.

3. The structure of thought.

As a start, we look at the distinction made by Steinfatt: logic, cognitive structure and world-view, and perception, individual cognitions or areas of cognition. His placing of perception at the higher level seems to contradict our attitude which places it somewhere at the bottom of figure 6. This is probably due to the fact that Steinfatt uses the term perception for the relationship between man and world as a whole, something which we call 'contact' (see figure 4). In agreement with common practice in psychology it seems better to restrict perception to that part of the relationship between man and world which is dominated by the physical aspects of both, i.e. the human sense organs and the material/physical objects and aspects of the world. And the area of perception in this latter sense seems to be one of the processes which are fundamental to human cognition.[1]

The close connection of this area with the material side of man and world is the main reason which led us to assume that the relations between the entities in it are rather fixed and confined. They may be rather complicated, but as compared with the relations in areas higher up in figure 6, they are more readily accessible for empirical research, and usually can be described in a systematic way. This applies not only to the relation between man and world, but we suppose it to be true for the relation between language and world as well. The research by Rosch on colour terms can be mentioned in support of this idea.[2] And the publications of Talmy and Jackendoff (see sections 4.4.3. and 4.4.4.) on spatial terminology also seem to underline the rather straightforward connection between words and worldly features in this respect. Finally we quote Gipper, who writes that space "wesentlich leichter sprachlich objektiviert werden kann" (see section 4.3.2.).

If the relation between world and man and that between world and language are more or less fixed and confined, it is reasonable to suppose that the relation between man and language is fixed and confined as well. Again, this is not to say that it is simple and direct. We doubt whether Jackendoff is right when he more or less equates the two entities involved: "to study semantics of natural language is to study cognitive psychology" (see section 4.4.4.). But we agree that as a rule the relation between the two is not 'open' enough as to allow for a considerable determining influence of language on human thought in this area. This makes understandable the failure to 'prove' the LRH using data from it.

From the literature it is clear that the further structuring of thought and cognition in general, on the basis of the more fundamental phenomena of logic and perception, is a very complicated process, the details of which have only been partially the object of empirical investigation and scientific theoretical

---

1   see Anderson, 1980, p. 21 - 59, Vernon, 1977.
2   Rosch, 1980.

consideration.[1] Neuro-physiological research in this respect is still in its initial phase.

Regarding the perception of space, we already mentioned the investigation of the use of spatial terminology in the expression of thoughts in other areas.[2] We agree that this approach provides valuable insights into the way people think; in fact this is one of the motives for performing our study. But, as we already indicated above, we do not believe that investigations like this yield direct access to human thought patterns, as supposed by Jackendoff. For areas higher up in figure 6 the relation between language and man becomes more complicated, and on the basis of our present knowledge it seems impossible to draw definite and specific conclusions on the structure of human thought on the basis of linguistic research only.

At the end of this summary, we are in a position to locate our study of the perception of space in the Old Testament in figure 6. Its target area is in the bottom part of the figure and we may assume that the relations between the three entities involved are more or less fixed and confined. The problem is that the fact that we wish to study this phenomenon in the Old Testament poses a number of restrictions. These we will consider in detail in the next chapter.

---

1   see Anderson, 1980; Johnson-Laird, Wason, 1980.
2   see Jackendoff, 1985; Lakoff, Johnson, 1980.

6. AN INTERMEDIATE EVALUATION.

6.1. Introduction.

Having completed our explorations outside the field of Old Testament science, we now return to the target area of our study, the perception of space in the Old Testament. At the end of chapter 5 we placed the perception of space in general in the bottom area of figure 6. In the next paragraph of this chapter we consider the consequences of the fact that we want to study space perception in the Old Testament. In paragraph 6.3. we use the results of these considerations in an assessment of the relevant literature which we already reviewed in paragraph 3.2. Based on this assessment of the state of the art and on our methodological considerations, we devise an outline for a further investigation of the perception of space in the Old Testament in paragraph 6.4.

6.2. The study of the perception of space in the Old Testament in wider perspective.
6.2.1. A few general considerations.

Since the perception of space is located in the bottom area of figure 6, it seems reasonable to suppose that it more or less takes place in one horizontal plane of that figure. This means that in order to obtain a picture of it, we can use figure 4 which we have to accommodate to the conditions prevailing when investigating the Old Testament.

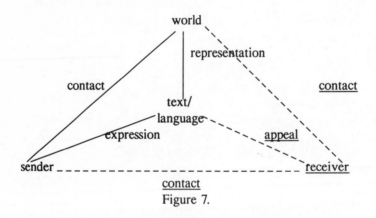

Figure 7.

Although we may consider ourselves as receivers of the texts of the Old Testament, we are this in a way which is different from that of the original receivers. This will affect all relations of this entity in figure 7. To emphasize the differences with figure 4 we have underlined the names of all elements

140

involved and indicated the relations by broken lines.

It is the big distance to the cultural environment from which the texts originated, and which is indicated in figure 7 by the upper-left triangle, which is the main cause of these differences. It is worth while to consider them in more detail for each of the relations involved.

a. The appeal-relation to the texts.

Owing to this distance, we cannot share with the senders their daily language which they spoke and in which they wrote their texts. Centuries of careful investigation of the Old Testament and thorough research into other ancient texts which have become known in the last two hundred years have given us an extensive knowledge of Old Testament Hebrew and cognate languages. But this knowledge remains theoretical and hypothetical. All our scholarly approaches will not be able to replace the intensive contact with the community actively engaged in using their language. And it is this 'field work' which is the basis of much modern research into foreign languages.

b. The contact-relation to man as sender.

The same distance causes important restrictions in our other contacts with the people who wrote the Old Testament as well. Interviews with consultants and tests with native-speakers, frequently used by experimental psychology in its study of the perception of space, are impossible. Even the study of pictorial and other material data is possible to a limited extent only, since the amount of these data, found in archaeological investigation of Israel, is relatively small. The main source which is available to us are written documents.

This does not mean that we have no idea at all about them. In a way similar to the one we mentioned under point a., the careful study of their texts, and of what remained of their environment and culture, enable us to construct a picture, a model of their 'way of life.' Our survey of recent developments in the field of language and cognition however shows, how difficult it is to obtain a sound picture of the thought-world and -structure of other people, even under ideal experimental conditions.

One of the methodological questions for our study is: how far can we get to obtain a well-founded picture of the perception of space of the people of the Old Testament, using these limited sources only? The best starting point seems to be an investigation of appropriate parts of their texts and language in order to find out how they expressed space and spatial relations. In this way we can discover what possibilities their language, Old Testament Hebrew, made available to them in this respect, and what use they made of these possibilities. This is about as far as we may expect to be able to get in this respect. We hope to detect some remarkable aspects in OTH and its use.

c. The contact relation to the world of the Old Testament.

It is again the 'cultural distance' which prevents us from having direct contact with this world. As referred to under b., investigation of its material remains can be of help in devising a picture of that aspect of the world of the Old Testament, and to which certain parts of its texts refer.

Seen in a wider sense, this is the main aim of much investigation of the Old Testament: to obtain knowledge of the world to which it refers, or rather, of Him to whom and to whose acts it refers. But if we formulate it in this way, it is clear that we address ourselves to the top areas of figure 6.

Although we hope it will be of some help in the study of the areas higher in the figure, the limited target area of our own study - the perception of space in the Old Testament - is located in the bottom areas of figure 6. This has the advantage that it mainly concerns physical objects and physical/material aspects in the world. Although we must assume that the precise shape and character of many objects in the world of the Old Testament are not the same as of their 'counterparts' in our world, and it is even probable that in that world objects were present that are completely unknown to us, there is bound to be some similarity between the two worlds. This similarity is based on the common physical characteristics which are shared by matter in the whole world. It seems wise to try to use that similarity in the study of the perception of space in the Old Testament.

6.2.2. A more specific application to our investigation.

In our opinion this can be done best by concentrating on Old Testament expressions in text/language, which specifically refer to a part of the world in which physical objects and aspects play an important role. Two approaches seem possible: investigation of a text in which spatial relations are expressed on a wide scale, or examination of that part of language which is used in this respect. But the latter approach can only be used properly if we already have some idea of what this part is like. In addition we run the risk that we will miss certain linguistic details which can only be discovered by carefully investigating the way in which objects and their spatial relations are being referred to in a text of reasonable size. So the best way seems to be examining a text which describes, or at least contains the description of, objects with obvious physical and spatial properties.

By choosing a text of this type we can use our own way of perceiving and expressing space as a kind of standard in assessing the characteristics of Old Testament Hebrew in this respect. Of course we are not able to observe the same objects directly, but as explained above, we may expect to have some idea of them.

Bearing in mind the complicated relationships between world, language, and thought, it does not seem justified, to devise a complete, 'psychologically motivated' model of space perception of Old Testament people, on that basis. We hope however, that the available evidence will enable us to discover a number of elements of this phenomenon. In addition, we intend to use that information for an initial exploration of the way in which the authors of the Old Testament use spatial terminology to express themselves about subject areas, which are higher up in figure 6.

6.3. Assessment of the relevant literature.

In paragraph 3.2. we reviewed four publications that investigate the experience of space in the Old Testament. In the final section of that paragraph we gave our initial reaction on their value as far as the investigation of the perception of space is concerned. In view of the methodological problems we had to postpone our final assessment, but now we have completed our explorations on this aspect, we come to give our ultimate evaluation. Below we will discuss the publications separately, and in the same order as in paragraph 3.2.

1. Boman.

His publication has already aroused a lot of critical reactions. In particular Barr attacked him on the way he used linguistic evidence (see above par. 3.3.). Our exploration of the wider relations between language, thought and world, enable us to see in more detail where he went wrong.

In the first place he did not use the linguistic evidence of the Old Testament properly. Barr already indicated that he investigated only part of the Hebrew language, and even that inadequately. But he also failed to examine that part of the linguistic evidence which is the most pertinent: texts which refer to parts of the world with characteristic spatial aspects. It is true that he mentions a few of them, but he does not provide a careful and detailed investigation of them.

In the second place it is clear that his conclusions go much too far. Statements such as: "[Die Israeliten] sehen die Gegenstände so, wie sie mit ihren Farben und Schatten sind, ... Konturen sehen sie aber nicht ..."[1] or "Wenn ein Israelit ein Gebäude sieht, beschäftigt sein Bewußtsein sofort mit dem Gedanken ...."[2] are impossible to defend on the basis of the given evidence. The present state of knowledge of the relation between language and thought does not allow us to draw conclusions of this nature.

It should be borne in mind that these considerations originate from our exploration of the wider methodological issues of the study of the perception of space in the Old Testament. They do not mean that Boman's publication has no value at all for this area. But his results (as summarized at the end of section 3.2.1.) cannot be used for constructing a picture of the perception of space in the Old Testament. They should rather be considered as working hypotheses which require confirmation by further investigation.

2. Childs.

In his publication Childs examines the role of mythical space in the Old Testament. He provides an analysis of this space, in which he refers to "the

---

1   Boman, 1977, p. 136.
2   o.c. , p. 61.

immediate contact of the individual with spatial reality" [1] but does not report in detail on what empirical data his further description is based. In addition he signals a number of points in which the Old Testament differs from this approach. But these differences appear to be located mainly in the broader field of the experience of space and the use of spatial concepts in the expression of religious thought.

So he provides no information which is directly relevant in connection with the objective of our study: to obtain a picture of the perception of space in the Old Testament.

3. Sawyer.

In his publication on spaciousness, Sawyer examines the occurrence of the words of a 'lexical group within a wider associative field' at various levels: denotation of physical dimensions, in a context of physical danger or distress, and in a context of psychological or spiritual distress. This approach is a nice example of the movement upwards in our figure: from the ground level of physical, matter-bound aspects, up to the area of psychological, mind-originating concepts.

Apparently he is interested more in these latter aspects, so his examination of the use of the words at physical level remains very limited and only covers a limited area of the perception of space, namely that related to 'wide, broad, enlarge.' As a consequence his contribution to our knowledge of the 'total' perception of space in the Old Testament is limited: Old Testament Hebrew has available a number of words for the aspect mentioned above. But how they relate to the words expressing other spatial dimensions has not been investigated. As outlined in paragraph 6.2., we believe that a broader investigation of all spatial dimensions within a particular text will yield more information regarding this point.

4. Stadelmann.

The main contribution of Stadelmann's exploration of the Hebrew conception of the world to our knowledge of the perception of space in the Old Testament is his description of the three systems of naming the directions of the horizon. But his discussion of how the origin and background of these names reflect the perception of these directions by the people involved seems of doubtful value. It is not the names or the words themselves, but their actual use, which possibly can tell us something in this respect. So, like Boman's, his conclusions can only be considered as hypotheses, which await further investigation.

But it is important to know that systems to describe the directions of the horizon were available in Old Testament Hebrew.

At the end of this final assessment of what is known about perception of space in the Old Testament, we must conclude that it is very little. Only a few publications have been found which contain relevant information, and on the basis of our methodological exploration, we have to consider this as hypothetical

---

1   Childs, 1962, p. 84.

only.

So in order to obtain more information on this area we will continue our study with an investigation, in which we will use the results of our exploration of the methodological issues. The general framework for this investigation will be outlined in the next paragraph.

6.4. The investigation of the perception of space in the Old Testament.

From our considerations in paragraph 6.2., it is clear that there is one question which will accompany us during whole our investigation: how far will an examination of text/language, being the main source of information available, assist us in formulating a well-founded picture of the perception of space by the people concerned? The best reply seems to be performing an analysis which is at the same time broad and thorough, in an attempt to obtain as much data as possible.

It will come as no surprise that our investigation will be directed towards a text and not towards a semantic field or a certain group of words. This text will have to refer to objects which have physical spatial aspects and will have to express these in particular.

Within the Old Testament there are a few texts of reasonable size which fulfill these requirements: Exodus 25 - 31, Exodus 35 - 40, 1 Kings 5 - 7, Ezechiel 40 - 43, 2 Chronicles 3 - 4. In our choice for Exodus 25 - 31 the following considerations played a role:

a. The number of textual problems within these chapters seems to be limited.

b. From a preliminary search of the literature on these chapters we concluded that most scholars who investigated their literary structure believe it to stem from one source, or from a few sources which are closely related to each other.

c. For this text, being part of the book of Exodus, a detailed computer-generated concordance is available.[1] We expect that this concordance will be of great help in our investigation of the text.

On the other hand, we also came across two problems relating to this text.

- Many scholars believe that it does not describe a physical reality, but an imaginary construction.

- Although the text-critical problems within Exodus 25 to 31 are limited, its relation to the 'parallel construction text' in the chapters 35 to 40 is complicated by a number of textual differences.

Both points make it the more necessary to carry out a more extensive literature search on the text. After having completed this, we will consider them in more detail (see below paragraph 7.4.).

For our choice of the method of analysis two publications reviewed in

---

1   Postma, Talstra, Vervenne, 1983, II.

paragraph 4.4. seem to be relevant: Talmy[1] and Jackendoff.[2] Comparison of the two reveals that Jackendoff pays more attention to the sentence structure as a whole, and his method of analysis seems deeper and more comprehensive than that of Talmy. On the other hand Talmy's approach seems to be more specifically directed to the more basic aspects of perception. Nevertheless, we decided to adopt the method used by Jackendoff, which we will modify to a certain extent, in order to make it applicable to a text of the Old Testament.

The initial objective of our analysis is to describe how the text structures space and spatial relations. In a further step we want to relate this structure to the structure of that part of the world to which the text refers. In this way, we hope to obtain insight into the possibilities of OTH for referring to space and spatial relations.

In this approach, we have to bear in mind that there is a chance that the structure for which we look is 'imposed upon the text' on the basis of our own background and general attitude towards language and text. We cannot avoid completely this possibility, which is inherent to this type of investigation. But we can take a few measures in order to diminish the chance of its taking place.

1. Following a 'bottom-up strategy.'

By starting at the level of the words in the text and from there moving carefully to levels which contain 'higher-order' constructs, we hope to prevent theoretically motivated concepts from invading the results from the outset of the investigation.

2. Considering other attempts to structure the text.

Apart from recent work in this respect, there exists a very old structuring of the Old Testament, namely, the one performed in the first centuries of our era by the Masoretes. We will incorporate their results in our investigation.

3. Simultaneous consideration of syntax and semantics.

With Talstra,[3] we believe that the investigation of the syntactic and semantic levels of a text cannot be separated completely. The frame of reference of the investigator will be an important factor both in the analysis of formal aspects and of meaning aspects of a text (see also point 1. above). So it seems best to adopt an open, self-critical attitude, which relates to all aspects of the text.

In this way, we also try to meet the points put forward by Barr, as we reviewed them above in section 3.3. It is true that by opting for the detailed investigation of a limited text of the Old Testament, we restrict our possible results to the people behind that text only, but it enables us to analyze the language of that text in a comprehensive way (point 2).

In addition, by using the analytical method of Jackendoff, we maintain a link with 'general linguistics' (point 3).

---

1   Talmy, 1983.
2   Jackendoff, 1985.
3   Talstra, 1982, p. 35 - 37.

Regarding the first point mentioned by Barr, our study as described in chapter 4 and 5, and our discussion of its result in paragraph 6.2., aim at complying with it as far as possible.

The considerations outlined in this paragraph so far led us to devise a method of analysis which consists of a number of steps, which are briefly described below:

1. To each word of the text is assigned the appropriate grammatical category.

2. The text is written out completely, while each word is replaced by its grammatical category, and it is divided according to the main Masoretic accents. This step results in a linear structuring of the text, which will be used in the next step.

3. The text is structured according to the method described by Jackendoff. The various types of phrases acquired in this step are discussed mainly in a formal and quantitative sense.

4. Based on the various parts of the world it refers to, the text is divided into smaller entities (fragments), each of which refers to a certain aspect of that world (e.g. ark, lampstand, etc.). This step is limited to those fragments which refer to aspects of the world which clearly have physical, spatial dimensions. A comparative analysis of these fragments is carried out, during which special emphasis is put on their internal structure.

5. Investigation of the words which are used in the text and of the referential functions which they and the phrases of which they are the 'head,' (can) have in the text.

6. On the basis of this analysis the possibilities of OTH to express space and spatial relations are formulated. In addition their use in the investigated text is discussed.

In chapter 8, in which we will report our investigation, each step will be described in more detail. Prior to this, we will survey the literature on Exodus 25 - 31. The results of this search are reviewed in chapter 7.

7. THE TABERNACLE TEXT OF EXODUS 25 TO 31.
A SURVEY OF THE LITERATURE.

7.1. Introduction.

The purpose of this review of the literature on this pericope is to obtain a general idea of recent research on these chapters in view of the investigation which we have in mind. Since it will be directed towards linguistic characteristics and structures, we are mainly interested in these aspects of the text. They cannot, however, be seen separate from its more general role, so we will pay attention to that as well.

According to common opinion, the chapters 25 to 31 belong to that part of the book of Exodus which is attributed to the Priestly material in the Pentateuch. Hence, we will pay attention to the literature on the Priestly source (P) in a somewhat wider scope and to the publications on Exodus 25 to 31 in particular.

In the next paragraph we will discuss the general aspects of the pericope, whereas in paragraph 7.3 we will review in particular the literature on its linguistic aspects. The final paragraph 7.4 contains a short summary of the results of the survey of the literature and considers a few points which are particularly relevant to our investigation.

7.2 Exodus 25 to 31 as part of the Priestly document.
7.2.1. Introduction.

In agreement with Utzschneider who recently published a study on the meaning of the 'Sinaitic sanctuary texts,'[1] we will discuss the general aspects of Exodus 25 to 31 including the role of P, in the following sections:

    7.2.2. Style-analysis.
    7.2.3. Literary-historical problems.
    7.2.4. The sources
    7.2.5. The theological concepts.
    7.2.6. Dating and meaning.

7.2.2. Style analysis.

In 1971 McEvenue published a monograph on "The Narrative Style of the Priestly Writer" in which he applied the methods of 'new criticism' to the

---

1   Utzschneider, 1988.

Priestly Document.[1] According to him, this new criticism "attempts to be scientific without ceasing to be a criticism of literature, i.e. without becoming a history of literature, or a philosophy of literature, or an ethical evaluation of literature, etc."[2] Its presuppositions and methods he found described in handbooks such as those by Wellek and Warren and by Kayser.[3]

While explaining his method, McEvenue emphasizes the importance of the object to be studied, i.e. the text itself:

"It is, of course, helpful to have seen various methods successfully used on other texts. But ultimately the researcher must simply stare at his text, or fumble with it, until acts of understanding begin to take place. After this he may discuss his method, in so far as this may be necessary to clarify or justify his conclusions. Beyond this the literary critic should not go, as he can only make a fool of himself (unless he is a philosopher as well).

In approaching the priestly document, the present author felt that the general categories applied to the priestly document up to now had failed to touch the essence of this writing. So he attempted to find a new entry by beginning with the minute rather than the general, beginning with grammar rather than literary form, beginning with stylistics rather than narrative structure, beginning with minor logic rather than Weltanschauung."[4]

He restricted his study to the narrative text of P, called Pg, for which he accepted the list given by Elliger[5] as hypothetical text. Subsequently he applied his method of analysis to three pericopes of Pg (Genesis 6 - 9; Numbers 13 - 14; Genesis 17) and arrived at the following conclusions:

"First of all, this is a written, not an oral creation. .... The most remarkable characteristic is its fidelity to the detail and to the order of materials, and at times to the vocabulary and syntax of its JE sources."[6]

"A second most remarkable characteristic of the priestly writer is his tendency to reduce all the story-telling qualities of his sources to an absolute minimum: action is replaced by idea, dialogue by discourse, suspense by symmetry, aspects of personal interiority and psychological interchange are simply eliminated, dramatic values give way to rhetorical ones. .... The secret of his presentation is principally to be found in simplicity of syntax, an extensive use of repetition and echo, a technique of writing in panels, a symmetry of organisation which adds dignity, and a variety in repetition which adds interest. Where he is narrating he tends to the motifs and dispassionate distance proper to fairy-tales. All of these qualities we have tried to understand in comparison with familiar children's literature, and in particular literature intended for children of

---

1   McEvenue, 1971.
2   o.c. , p. 10.
3   Kayser, 1969.
4   McEvenue, 1971, p. 11.
5   Elliger, 1952.
6   McEvenue, 1971, p. 179.

pre-school age."[1]

In line with this last point, McEvenue has explored extensively the idea of considering Pg as a catechetical work.

"A third important characteristic of the priestly style is the writer's unique manner of composing (i.e. organising, uniting, structuring) his work. .... If the priestly writer was not concerned to create a clear overall unity, he was most concerned to unite each unit within itself, and to link each unit with what precedes immediately and with what follows immediately. This he achieves by many techniques: by taw-aleph linking, by systems of stressed pronouns, by constant repetition of words or phrases within a unit, or by echo of words and phrases from unit to unit thus creating larger unities, by interweaving, by palistrophes either short or long, by parallel panels either short or long."[2]

Two of the technical terms used by McEvenue require some explanation:

- taw-aleph linking: "the last word of one unit is the first word of the next."[3]
- palistrophe: "the literary form which is called frequently 'concentric inclusion,' 'chiastic' or 'concentric' structure, or 'complex inclusion.'" According to McEvenue, its essential feature is 'return,' and this he wants to express by the term 'palistrophe' (= palin + strophe).[4]

Before drawing lines for future research, McEvenue summarizes his conclusions as follows:

"The priestly writer's deliberateness and careful ordering of materials, conjoined with his use of echo, palistrophe, and panel, result inevitably in a symmetrical structure of composition. However this is not the classical symmetry of balance and proportion. Rather the priestly writer seems to be at pains, not only to vary when he repeats, but also to confuse and interlock symmetries, and to disturb balance. The resulting effect is of order underlying chaos, of structure underlying disappearing and broken pattern.

We see the priestly writer, then, as a scribe in exile, writing a gospel of hope based entirely on written traditions, transforming these from story to restrained rhetoric, uniting his materials in tightly knit and interwoven unities, possibly for the catechesis of younger people. At this point, we can say no more about the 'Einheit und Individualität' of this writer."[5]

The words in German in the last line probably refer to Kayser who states that the concept of unity, which is contained in the concept of style, can only gain vital force in view of the individual object, be it work or personality or era.[6]

The book by McEvenue has been considered as an example of the recent progress "in refining descriptions of style and representation that may begin to

---

1   o.c. , p. 182.
2   o.c. , p. 183, 185.
3   o.c. , p. 40.
4   o.c. , p. 29.
5   o.c. , p. 185 - 86.
6   see Kayser, 1969, p. 280.

provide more controlled ways of testing source hypotheses."[1] Utzschneider takes a more critical stand, not so much as far as the work of McEvenue itself is concerned, but rather regarding the role stylistics can play in literary criticism. According to him, the fundamental problem is that stylistics does not lead to a literary-historic hypothesis. In fact it pre-supposes such a hypothesis, and can only be used to verify it. The main cause for this restricted role is that stylistics is in essence limited to the 'surface text' and cannot deal with the conceptional level of the deep structure.[2] Perhaps this criticism is understandable from the point of view and the objective of Utzschneider's investigation.

It cannot be denied, however, that stylistics can play an admittedly narrow but important role in literary criticism, as indicated e.g. by Deist.[3] He describes the use of statistical techniques in the analysis of the style of texts as a counterbalance against too strong an influence of subjective judgments in this matter. In this connection it should be seen as "ein nachträgliches, überprüfendes Verfahren."[4]

Relating to literary criticism in general we also point to the approach by Lundin and Thiselton[5] and the fundamental objections against the methods of the 'new criticism' by Fish,[6] which we discussed in paragraph 5.4.

In view of our interest in Exodus 25 to 31, it is worth while to note that McEvenue mentions these chapters repeatedly. In fact, he had in mind doing his research on this pericope "for the reason that it was a unit of sufficient length to permit recurrences of characteristic procedures, and a unit which P apparently considered important. However there was such a variety of styles within the unit, that one was led to suspect P had used sources here. How could one decide what was characteristic of P, and what was characteristic of his source?"[7] For these reasons he left this pericope out of his investigation. But in his conclusions, when discussing the ways of handing on a written source to a latter generation, he mentions it anew in a list of pericopes where the Priestly writer may have written over the source while interweaving new motifs throughout. In a note he adds: "For Ex 25 - 29 I can refer only to analyses as yet unpublished, in which the present author has discovered a unity of style in these chapters, which is thinly laid over a radical divergence of style from unit to unit."[8] A few years later he published his findings on Ex 25 - 31 in a separate article which we will discuss in paragraph 7.3.

Recently the Priestly style has been surveyed by Paran in a publication in

1   Gottwald, 1985, p. 158.
2   Utzschneider, 1988, p. 22.
3   Deist, 1977.
4   o.c. , p. 337.
5   Lundin, Thiselton, Walhout, 1985.
6   Fish, 1980.
7   McEvenue, 1971, p. 22.
8   o.c., p. 180.

Hebrew,[1] from the English abstract of which, we derive the following data. Basing his analysis on previous literature, he provides a number of points on the Priestly style and comments: "The points enumerated above, about which there is consensus, merit reexamination, both because their foundations were established more than a century ago, and because several of them are based even today more upon general consensus than upon the facts themselves."[2]

In order to answer the question: Is there a Priestly style? Paran examines "parallels between statutes found in P and those found in other Pentateuchal law codes."[3] His results "demonstrate the general principle that the priestly writer tends to expand, reduplicate and engage in various kinds of word play because of the joy of writing. The priestly writer enjoys playing with words as though they were building blocks which can be put together in a variety of patterns according to the whim of the writer."[4]

At the level of the sentence he notices that the "Priestly Code makes extensive use of a literary structure which we suggest calling 'the circular inclusio.' This is a syntactic-stylistic structure in which the predicate of the sentence is repeated even though the repetition is superfluous from the point of view of meaning or syntax. An example is Ex. 12:8 ...."[5] Paran admits that this phenomenon can also be found elsewhere, but in his opinion P uses it in a typical way, in which the predicate of the sentence is repeated along with a certain modification of the verb. Other features which are characteristic for P are "the alteration of qātal and yiqtôl forms of the verb in various ways, depending the necessities of incorporating the pattern in legalistic style and upon various things which the writer wishes to emphasize .... the use of pronouns .... a three member inclusio .... change of person within the inclusio ...."[6]

According to Paran, "It seems that by means of the repetition of less important words the essential words in the sentence are emphasized. By this means the writer is also able to emphasize two ideas in a single circular inclusio. The reason that he uses the same verbal root twice is connected with his mnemonic design."[7]

He subsequently discusses the occurrence of poetical elements in P, in particular "the reduplication of members in a rythmic manner."[8] He ascribes this pattern to several motivations, such as the desire for emphasis or to stress the grandeur of the matter, and rejects the idea that these poetic features can be "assigned to the remnants of early Epic Poetry ...."[9]

---

1   Paran, 1989.
2   o.c. , p. VI.
3   o.c. , p. VI.
4   o.c. , p. VII.
5   o.c. , p. VIII.
6   o.c. , p. VIII - IX.
7   o.c. , p. IX.
8   o.c. , p. X.

While discussing the structure of the pericopes, Paran mentions as the most important feature the 'closing deviation': "The priestly writers tend to construct the pericopes in an ordered manner based upon the principle of a single motif being altered intentionally at the end of a pericope. So, for example, many of the sacrifice laws are built up of short lines, each beginning with a verb. The actions are thus enumerated one after another without any digression. In the final sentence, however, the writer makes a sharp deviation by changing the order of the words. He places the verb in the middle of the sentence or at its end, thereby informing the reader that the matter with which he has been dealing is herewith concluded."[1] In addition, he notices that there are "enumerations of both seven and ten acts and even combinations of the two enumerations," which he considers as "aid to memorization ...."[2]

Regarding the words and terms, he believes that it is clear "that P tends to use most of his technical terms in a unique manner, distinct from that in which they are employed in the rest of the Bible. .... This points to a professional circle which does not employ the previously existing language as it is but which changes the language, adapting it to the needs of the circle.[3] On the basis of the examination of some thirty terms he concludes that "P's use of the terms has the same linguistic background as that of the early sources," which leads him to accept "M. Haran's claim that P was hidden and that it was made public only after the return ...."[4]

The work of McEvenue and Paran reminds us of the relation between style and structure. Style seems to be associated with the preference and specific objective of the author(s), whereas structure appears to be connected with the requirements of the language and of the way it is being used in the society concerned.[5] In any case, their publications deserve careful consideration because they describe a number of features of the text and theorize about their background.

7.2.3 The literary historical problems.

Before we discuss the publications on the literary sources of P in more detail, it seems wise to pay attention to a few general aspects of the present situation of the literary-historical investigation of the Old Testament. Quoting Zenger, Utzschneider uses expressions as tiefen Krise and Chaosvision to describe it.[6] As far as the Pentateuch is concerned, the Documentary Hypothesis, although having been under attack ever since its 'modern formulation' by Graf and

---

1   o.c. , p. XII - XIII.
2   o.c. , p. XIII.
3   o.c. , p. XIV.
4   o.c. , p. XIV.
5   compare the levels described by Bühler (see above section 5.2.1.).
6   Utzschneider, 1988, p. 22, 23.

Wellhausen,[1] used to provide a starting-point and a familiar frame of reference for many investigations. But the increasing emphasis on its hypothetical character has led to increasing uncertainty and even confusion. Utzschneider, admitting that this is the case, does not consider this to be a bad development, but on the contrary, sees it as a healthy consequence of a scientific attitude which has the permanent duty to examine critically its own pre-suppositions.

In the light of this confusion and bearing in mind that his investigation of Exodus 25 - 31 is both comprehensive and of a recent date, it is important to examine in what way Utzschneider proceeds methodologically with his own investigation. As "grundlegende Voraussetzung" he formulates: "Ausgangs- und Zielpunkt ist der 'sinaitische Heiligtumstexte' genannte Textkomplex Ex 25 - 31; 35 -40; Lev 8 f und seine Auslegung. .... Der hier verwendete Terminus 'sinaitische Heiligtumstexte' signaliert vor allem, daß wir die literarhistorische Kategorie und Vorstellung der 'Priesterschrift' nicht zur selbstverständlichen Voraussetzung unserer Auslegung machen wollen. .... Möglicherweise ist die 'Krise' der alten, den gesamten Penta-, bzw. Hexateuch übergreifenden Erklärungsmodelle, zu denen die 'Priesterschrift' gehört, tatsächlich so schwerwiegend, wie es den Anschein hat. Gerade dann aber darf im Getümmel um die Gültigkeit der alten und die Möglichkeit neuer Erklärungsmodelle das Eigengewicht der Texte nicht verloren gehen. Deshalb beschränken wir uns auf die Auslegung eines überschaubaren Textkomplexes."[2]

When outlining his concept of meaning (<u>Bedeutung</u>), Utzschneider, quoting Lyons, puts much emphasis on its communicative aspect. "Bedeutung ist eine Frage der Kontextualität."[3] The meaning of utterances is dependent, both on the intention of the sender and on the reception by the receiver, and not on the first factor alone, as is often assumed.

In this connection, it is interesting to see what role Utzschneider assigns to the text in its present form. He agrees that it is composed of very complex texts which usually have a long history of oral transmission, codification, editing, re-writing, etc., a history which is very difficult to describe exactly. However he does not agree with those scholars who, in view of all uncertainties (the crisis) in our reconstruction of the historical development, prefer to restrict exegesis to the present text only. He clearly sees a task for literary criticism in recognizing, through a process of analyses, simple (or at least more simple) texts in the present complex text, and subsequently placing these text-fragments in a relative chronological order, so that the historical situations from which they originated

---

1   See Houtman, 1980.
2   Utzschneider, 1988, p. 2.
3   o.c. , p. 18.

and in which they were joined together can be clarified (redaction history).[1] This literary-critical procedure should lead to a hypothetic model of the historical evolution of the text, which Utzschneider calls the 'text-hypothesis.'[2] It is this hypothesis which should answer the question: How is it possible to get from the complex texts which have been transfered to us in written form, to the historical texts, to the utterances? The historical situation of the utterances is decisive in determining their meaning.

For investigating the textuality (Texthaftigkeit) of the resulting historical texts, Utzschneider uses two criteria, namely cohesion and coherence. The first criterium refers to the way in which the components of the surface-text, i.e. sounds, words, clauses and sentences are mutually connected. It is mainly a formal criterium. Coherence, however, relates to the conceptual, deep-structural (tiefenstrukturelle) elements that connect words and sentences.[3] He makes it very clear that in his opinion cohesion alone is not sufficient as a criterium in text-analysis; it should always be used in combination with coherence. In this respect he takes a different attitude than Richter who gives priority to the formal aspects.[4]

It is from this point of view that he examines the present position of P. As we will discover in the next section, the cornerstone of many literary-critical investigations of P is formed by the so-called 'Grundschrift,' Pg. Until recently, it was generally assumed to have mainly a narrative character, but in the last decade, some scholars have attempted to describe its theological structure (see below sections 7.2.4. and 7.2.5.).

At the end of his methodological considerations, Utzschneider gives a summary of his objections against the 'Grundschrift-Hypothese':

"1. Entgegen ihrem Anspruch hat die Erzählungshypothese zunehmend Schwierigkeiten, die Grundschrift als Oberflächentext tatsächlich vorzuweisen.

2. Die 'Strukturhypothese' ist darüberhinaus bestimmt von einem u.E. fragwürdigen 'Gattungspostulat.'

3. Die Grundschrifthypothese insgesamt ist überwiegend an Texten der Genesis entwickelt und erprobt. Die Andersartigkeit der Texte der Sinaiperikope wird nicht hinreichend berücksichtigt.

4. Die Grundschrifthypothese geht von einem grundlegenden textlinguistischen Axiom aus: Kohärenz und Kohäsion gehen Inkohärenz und Inkohäsion voraus. Auf diesem Axiom beruht die Vorstellung, daß ein kohärent/kohäsiver Oberflächentext, eben Wellhausen's 'originaler Kern,' ergänzt, bearbeitet, ja 'zerschrieben' wird. Inkohärenz ist ein Ergebnis dieser 'sekundären' Vorgänge,

---

1   o.c. , p. 13.
2   o.c. , p. 15.
3   o.c. , p. 15 - 16.
4   o.c. , p. 17 - 18; Richter, 1971.

Kohärenz verdankt sich dem jeweiligen Original."[1]

In view of these objections, Utzschneider wants to consider a model, which explains coherence and lack of coherence within a text, by a process of complex and mutual interactions. This model is characterized in the literature by the keyword 'revision' (Bearbeitung). As an early example, he mentions the approach by Popper who as far back as 1862 pointed to the unique and characteristic way of presentation exhibited in the secondary processing of the tabernacle texts of Exodus 25 to 31 in the chapters 35 to 40 of the same book. According to Wellhausen this meaningless pericope would not have been missed if it had not been present, whereas Popper points to the more perfect and more correct form in which the original content is being explained and developed in the new version of the text. Utzschneider comments: "Ergänzung und Bearbeitung trägt nicht nur Inkohäsion und Inkohärenz in den Text ein, sondern schafft u.U. auch einen höheren Grad von Kohäsion und Kohärenz. Wohlgemerkt: Popper ignoriert keineswegs die literarhistorischen Komplexität der Texte, wie manchen Neueren. Vielmehr stellt er jenes Axiom der Literarkritik in Frage, das Kohärenz an Originalität bindet."[2]

It is clear that the 'revision-model' appeals to Utzschneider, and it is this model which he is going to use in his own exegesis of the Sinaitic sanctuary texts. Similar ideas have been suggested by Houtman,[3] Blum[4] and by Whybray, who writes: "The Pentateuch, then, it may be suggested, is an outstanding but characteristic example of the work of an ancient historian: a history of the origins of the people of Israel, prefaced by an account of the origins of the world. .... He had at his disposal a mass of material, most of which may have been of quite recent origin and had not necessarily formed part of any ancient Israelite tradition. Following the canons of the historiography of his time, he radically reworked this material, probably with substantial additions of his own invention, making no attempt to produce a smooth narrative free from inconsistencies, contradictions and unevennesses. Judged by the standards of ancient historiography, his work stands out as a literary masterpiece."[5]

7.2.4. The sources.

Having considered the underlying problems of the literary-critical approach of P, we proceed by briefly summarizing the main publications in this area. As a starting point, we choose the investigation of Von Rad published in 1934 and entitled "Die Priesterschrift im Hexateuch." In his preface, the author notices that since Wellhausen, P has received little attention from Old Testament

---

1   o.c. , p. 30.
2   o.c. , p. 31.
3   Houtman, 1980, p. 243 - 258.
4   Blum, 1990, see in particular p. 224.
5   Whybray, 1987, p. 242.

scholars. He wonders: "Vielleicht war die große Einstimmigkeit in der Ausscheidung ihrer Bestandteile daran Schuld, daß die Debatte, jahrzehntelang ruhte."[1]

Von Rad continues to explain, however, that the few detailed investigations which had appeared since then had indicated that the literary problems of P are more complicated than had been assumed. In his opinion even the work of Wellhausen himself contains signals of this situation. The purpose of his investigation is to overcome this backlog, at least partially. He apologizes that, in view of the lack of earlier work, he has to resort to "eine sehr unmodern scheinende Arbeitsweise."[2]

In the exposition of his results, Von Rad follows the chronological order in which he carried out his investigation and, hence, starts with a consideration of Gen. 9: 9 - 17. Careful examination of the doublets which occur in this pericope led him to conclude that material differences are involved: "Es gibt eine sachliche Differenz, die tatsächlich in den formalen Duplizität der Aussagen bis in die Einzelheiten hinein sichtbar wird. Die eine Bundesansage (V.11) wendet sich einfach an den Menschen und hat zum Inhalt, daß 'alles Fleisch' hinfort nicht mehr von der Flut vertilgt werden soll. In der anderen dagegen ist einerseits (V.9) in persönlicher Anrede Noah und seine Nachkommenschaft angeredet, andererseits (V.10) aber auch, deutlich davon abgesetzt, die gesamte Tierwelt in den Bund mit einbezogen. Und dieser Unterschied - hie Bundesschluß mit 'allem Fleisch,' dort Bundesschluß einerseits mit Noah, andererseits mit der Tierwelt - läßt sich in der Tat im ganzen Abschnitt aufzeigen."[3]

As a result of this analysis, Von Rad assumes that the pericope can be divided into two parts:
- A: v. 11a, 13, 16 , 17;
- B: v. 9, 10, 11b, 12, 14, 15.

"So liegen hier also zwei vollständige Versionen über das Wesen des Noahbundes vor, eine Textverlust ist nirgends sichtbar."[4] For several reasons, he assumes A to be the older version of the two and he describes the religious differences between them. The next part of his publication consists of an investigation of the whole of P in order to find out whether the two versions are present elsewhere as well.

Prior to this investigation, he asks himself two questions: "Sind etwa festgestellte Unebenheiten literarisch faßbar? Es gibt eine Art von Unebenheiten, die durchaus vorliterarisch bedingt ist. Viele alttestamentliche Überlieferungsstoffe haben sich vor ihrer literarischen Fixierung Wandlungen unterzogen - man

---

1   Von Rad, 1934, p. III.
2   o.c. , p. III.
3   o.c. , p. 1.
4   o.c. , p. 2.

157

denke an ursprünglich nichtisraelitisches Gedankengut -, von denen jetzt noch allerlei Risse oder Nähte Zeugnis ablegen. Solche sachliche Holprigkeiten literarisch erklären zu wollen, ist vielleicht eine große Versuchung, aber doch ein Fehlgriff. Da, wo wir oben den Spaten eingesetzt haben, glaubten wir allerdings, daß diese Spannung sehr wohl auf dem Weg einer literarischen Analyse gelöst werden kann. Ist diese Frage, die jeweils bei jedem Abschnitt neu zu stellen ist, zu bejahen, so folgt daraus die zweite: handelt es sich bei solcher literarischer Verflechtung um Zusätze von Ergänzern oder um Parallelrezensionen, die, wenn auch inhaltlich verschieden, tatsächlich doch im Grundzug der Erzählung einander parallel laufen?"[1]

At the end of his investigation, Von Rad concludes that indeed both sources occur throughout the whole of P: "Denn, mag auch manches an den Analysen verbesserungsbedürftig sein, sowohl die Tatsache der Zweigleisigkeit der priesterschriftlichen Überlieferung wie auch ihr erzählerischer Zusammenhang scheint uns gesichert."[2] He thus clearly defends the narrative character of both sources.

In his survey of the history of the traditions of the Pentateuch, Noth accepts that P in its main outline is an "Erzählungswerk," but he considers as unsuccessful Von Rad's attempt to show the existence of two parallel narrative layers of P.[3] He rather assumes a few literary sources which have been included by P into an original narrative document, to which later editors added more material. So he distinguishes between:
- a narrative 'Grundschrift' (Pg),
- later additions (Ps).[4]

The isolation of the original core of P, the Pg, is one of the topics which attracts much attention in recent research. Utzschneider remarks, that the underlying hypotheses which support this work, are that Pg is the coherence-shaping factor, which holds together all the divergent material of P, and that it is possible to reconstruct its <u>Wortlaut</u> more or less exactly.[5] In a brief survey, he shows that a process of reducing the original core of Pg has started, to which Elliger,[6] Noth himself[7] and Fritz[8] have contributed in particular. Utzschneider points to a dilemma that faces all those involved in searching for the original core-text of Pg: in order to arrive at a text, the coherence of which is higher than that of the Masoretic Text, they have to delete much material which shows no immediate cohesion at the level of the surface-text. The result

1   o.c. , p. 4.
2   o.c. , p. 161.
3   Noth, 1948, p. 9.
4   Noth, 1948.
5   Utzschneider, 1988, p. 24.
6   Elliger, 1952.
7   Noth, 1959.
8   Fritz, 1977.

of this process is a text of Pg, which on one hand is highly coherent, but at the same time is of very limited size, and in fact consists of a number of completely separated single elements only.

Whereas the authors quoted so far put much emphasis on the narrative character of Pg, more recently a few attempts have been made which put more emphasis on its (theological) structure.[1] In this approach the heuristic principle for retrieving the original text of Pg is formed by the important theological statements. This process also leads to a considerable reduction of the text, so that what remains in the end for Pg is only a kind of theological structural framework, "ein theologischer Traktat," as Utzschneider calls it.[2] According to him, this approach involves a "Gattungspostulat" which is inappropriate to the text.

Regarding the mutual dependence of the various sources, it is generally thought that the 'execution-texts' (Ex 35:1 - 39:30) are literally dependent on the 'instruction-texts' (Ex 25:10 - 28:43; 30:1 - 31:17). Regarding Ex 29 there is a difference of opinion: whereas many scholars (Noth, Rendtorff, Koch) assume that Lev 8 is dependent on Ex 29, there are others (Elliger, Walkenhorst) who try to defend the reverse. The latter see in the author of Ex 29 a 'copyist' who adopted the original text of Lev 8 to his own situation by changing words, explaining inprecise terms, etc. Utzschneider, who prefers to call the author of Ex 29 an 'exegete,' believes that "diese Auslegungsarbeit keineswegs als Einbahnstraße vom Original zum sekundären Gut darstellt, sondern einen höchst komplexen, lebendigen Prozess."[3] Unfortunately he does not give more details of this process which apparently plays a key-role in his revision-model.

Another problem concerns the genres of the sources. Koch's publication of 1959 has opened this field of investigation, at least as far as Ex 25 - 31 is concerned. In Ex 25 to Lev 16 he distinguishes two styles: the first one is characterized by longer sentence structures in which the imperfect is used by far the most. Koch calls it 'gefügter Stil,' in distinction to the 'formularhafter Rede,' which is characterized by simplicity and uniformity of sentence-construction and by the predominant use of we-perfectum. As a rule sentences are short in this style, and they do not contain any words which are superfluous. Since in the present text both styles are mixed together, a separation into pericopes which demonstrate one style only cannot be made readily. Only by a process of separating clauses of similar style, and combining these together into a re-constructed text, Koch is able to arrive at a genre of text very similar to the one described earlier by Rendtorff on the basis of an investigation of Lev 1 to 3, which he calls 'ritual' and of which he gives the following details: "Jedes Ritual besteht aus einer Anzahl von drei- bis viergliedrigen Kurzsätzen, die alle mit einem Verb im w-pf

---

1   Lohfink, 1979; Weimar, 1984.
2   Utzschneider, 1988, p. 28.
3   Utzschneider, 1988, p. 37.

beginnen und zu einer Reihe von drei, fünf, zehn, ja einmal sogar dreißig Gliedern zusammengestellt sind. .... Der festgeprägte, eintönige Sprachgebrauch läßt vermuten, daß die Rituale mündlich überliefert wurden und so noch P überkommen sind, sonst wären diese Reihen nicht mehr in solchen Umfang aus dem jetzigen Zusammenhang herauszuschälen. .... Mit der Aufnahme in den P-Zusammenhang werden die alten, für die mündliche Überlieferung gebildeten Reihen notwendig aufgelöst, sie werden zerschrieben. Die priesterliche Sinaigesetzgebung ist eine bezeichnendes Beispiel für den Wandel der Gattungen beim Übergang von der mündlichen zur schriftlichen Überlieferung ...."[1]

Utzschneider considers three critical remarks regarding the results of Koch.[2]

a. The rituals as recognised in Lev 1 - 3 concern cultic handlings which are performed at regular intervals, whereas the construction of a sanctuary, such as the tabernacle, refers to a unique event. Koch, who himself already mentions this difficulty, wonders whether the rituals in this case could not form a kind of cult-etiology.[3] But Utzschneider thinks that assuming such a new genre for explaining the Sinaitic sanctuary texts carries too far.[4]b. Whereas the rituals relating to the cult use verbs in 3 m. form, those for the instruction of building the sanctuary have been written in 2 m. According to Koch originally all rituals had been in 3 m. form, so apparently the partial transfer to 2 m. must have occurred at the re-writing by P. Utzschneider, however, wonders whether it is really probable that P consistently made this change for Ex 25 to 31, whereas he failed to do so for Lev 1 to 4.

c. Fritz[5] has criticized the separation of style used by Koch, because the verbal forms we-perfect and imperfect have close affinity to each other. He rather sees a <u>Stilbruch</u> in the occurrence in the text of both instructions for the construction of the sanctuary and clauses that only describe it. On the basis of this criterium, he considers much material in Ex 25 to 27 as secondary additions (all 'descriptive texts') and arrives at an original source document of limited size (an instruction for the construction of the sanctuary) which he characterises as Priestly, and considers to be Pg.[6] Utzschneider joins Fritz in his criticism on the stylistic criteria used by Koch, but at the same time raises serious objections against the alternative criterium chosen by him.

On the whole Utzschneider's judgment of Koch's publication is negative. "Im ganzen scheint uns K.Kochs Versuch, auf gattungskritischem Wege überlieferungsgeschichtliche Vorstufen der sinaitischen Heiligtumstexte herauszuarbeiten, im Ergebnis nicht geglückt."[7] He signals the fact that Görg,

---

1   Koch, 1959, p. 96, 97, 99.
2   see Utzschneider, 1988, p. 39 - 42.
3   Koch, 1959, p. 99.
4   see also Blum, 1990, p. 301, n.52.
5   Fritz, 1977.
6   o.c. , p. 117 ff.
7   Utzschneider, 1988, p. 41.

160

who had accepted Koch's results in an early publication, later abandoned that position. And concluding this paragraph of his survey of the literature he comments on Weimar's attempt to reconstruct the source-documents for Pg on the basis of an analysis of Ex 1:1 - 6:7.[1] He considers the resulting texts of this analysis to be rather "Systemtexte" than "reale 'kommunikative Ereignisse.'"[2] It is to be expected that the source document which Weimar recently constructed on the basis of an investigation of Ex 25 to 31[3] will receive a similar judgment of Utzschneider.

7.2.5. The theological concepts.

So far in this paragraph we mainly paid attention to the literary aspects of P. We now address the (theological) contents of this source.

As in the previous section, we start by quoting Von Rad. He refers to the fact that in his writings, P mentions many details which might lead us to try to explain each of them. But he asks for restraint in this matter: "Für uns wird die strenge Regel gelten müssen, nur die von P selbst gedeuteten Elemente zur Erklärung heranzuziehen; denn bei der Unzahl der allgemein genannten Einzelteile haben wir keine Sicherheit, die Grundgedanken des spezifisch-israelitischen Kultus und seiner Symbolsprache fassen zu können."[4] He describes the "einzigartigen Funktion dieser kultischen Anlage: Hier an diesem Ort vollzieht sich der Wechselverkehr zwischen dem heiligen Gott und dem Volk Israel. Das ist der theologische Scopus des Stifthüttengesetzes. Nicht den Einzelelementen gilt das letzte religiöse Interesse, sondern dieser Funktion der Stifshütte zwischen Gott und Volk ...."[5] In agreement with an earlier publication of 1931, in which he had distinguished between two conceptions of the presence of God: a lasting, cultic presence and a more occasional appearance of Yahweh, respectively of the כבוד,[6] he writes: "Die Lade .... ist überall im A.T. die Bürgschaft für Jahwes Gegenwart. Anders das Zelt; es ist nicht Wohnort Jahwes, sondern der dritte Ort, da Jahwe dem Volke 'sich stellt'; er erscheint in der Wolke von oben her, um für die Dauer eines Gespräches gegenwärtig zu sein. So ergibt sich, daß zwischen der Lade-Thronvorstellung und der Zelt-Moedvorstellung reinlich zu scheiden ist. Bei P sehen wir nun Zelt und Lade kombiniert. Ob das die Tat von P selbst war, entzieht sich unserer Kenntnis ...."[7] According to Von Rad, the ark and its theology seem to have been dominant in the literary sources before P, and even though they have been incorporated into the idea of the 'Moed,' their influence has not been cut off.[8]

---

1   Weimar, 1973.
2   Utzschneider, 1988, p. 43.
3   Weimar, 1988.
4   Von Rad, 1934, p. 181.
5   o.c. , p. 182.
6   see Von Rad, 1931, p. 110 - 111.
7   Von Rad, 1934 , p. 182.

Cross paid attention to the combination of the terms אהל מועד and משכן,
and concluded from his research on the root שכן: "Yahweh does not 'dwell' on
earth. Rather he 'tabernacles' or settles impermanently as in the days of the
portable, ever-conditional Tent."[1] Regarding the theological significance, he
remarks that the Priestly writers with their tabernacle account "strove after a
solution to the problems of covenant theology; the means through which the
breached covenant might be repaired, and the conditions under which a holy
and universal God might 'tabernacle' in the midst of Israel."[2] In a later
publication, Cross underlined how in the time of Solomon the conception of the
tent, to which David still had confined himself, was replaced by the conception
of the temple. According to him, this new concept is best viewed "as an
innovation conceived by Solomon alongside his other reversals of Davidic policy
and practice."[3]
The authors quoted so far assumed that the conception of the permanent
presence of God, which they connect with circles from Jerusalem, has been
critically revised by the incorporation of the 'appearance concept' by Priestly
writers. But others believe that the latter simply used the tradition of the Tent
for their own ideas, which were based on the Temple-concept. For example,
Haran comments: "After all, they were only writers, recorders of tradition which
provided a framework for their Utopia; they were not critically-minded
historians."[4] Janowski even argued that the Priestly writers did not answer the
problem of the presence of God in Israel by means of the concepts of Tent or
Temple, but on the basis of their idea about the Glory of Yahweh.[5] In his
conclusion he combines the various theological elements in the following
statements: "Als innerster Kern des 'Begegnungszeltes' (אהל מועד) ist die
כפרת der Ort der Präsenz Gottes in Israel: der Ort, an dem der transzendente
Gott als der im Sühnegeschehen begegnende Gott nahe ist, kondeszendiert.
Modus der Gegenwart Gottes ist das auf eine 'Begegnung' (יעד nif. , אהל
מועד 'Begegnungszelt') mit Mose bzw. Israel zielende 'Verweilen' (שכן) seines
כבוד 'inmitten der Israeliten' ebenso wie sein Mose, dem Repräsentanten Israels
geltendes 'Begegnen' (יעד nif.) auf der כפרת."[6]
At the beginning of his discussion of the traditional concepts, Utzschneider
defines them as "konzeptionelle Größen eines 'Weltwissens,' sie bestehen in
ihren Grundelementen über längere Zeiträume unverändert (diachron stabil)."[7]
This final point explains why the diachronic perspective is predominant in this

---

8   see o.c. , p. 184.
1   Cross, 1947, p. 68.
2   o.c. , p. 68.
3   Cross, 1981, p. 176-177.
4   Haran, 1978, p. 203.
5   Janowski, 1982, p. 302.
6   o.c. , p. 361.
7   Utzschneider, 1988, p. 44.

respect. But, in the opinion of Utzschneider, the synchronic approach has its own right as well: "Für Sender und Empfänger als den Beteiligten eines Kommunikationsvorganges steht ja in ihrer Gegenwart ein ganzes Set von traditionalen Konzepten bereit. So ist es ganz sicher bedeutungsvoll, auf welches oder welche der synchron vorhandenen traditionalen Konzepte ein Sender zur Formulierung seiner Aussage zurückgreift und auf welche nicht."[1]

In a comment on the differences of opinion on the precise shape of the 'presence theology' of P, Utzschneider remarks that in his opinion clarification in this matter could be obtained when additional conceptual and situational aspects from the contextual atmosphere will be considered in the research. However, according to him, in a diachronically oriented approach such aspects can hardly be distinguished.

In this respect, he discusses in detail the expression כבוד יהוה. Regarding the conceptual contents of this combination of words, he refers to Rendtorff and Westermann, who saw it related to the idea of theophany and Kingdom of God. Both the universal presence of the כבוד יהוה and its spatial limitation have been indicated, the latter in particular by Priestly writers. They seem to use this concept to legitimize and characterize the Sinaitic sanctuary. When they refer to the theophany in which the כבוד יהוה is involved, they notice that there is a movement 'from above down to the mountain,' and a 'movement from below up to the mountain.' This event provides the 'focal point' for the sanctuary, which is instrumental in maintaining the possibility for this two-way-movement throughout history. In this way the idea of "Begegnung" becomes important in the theological thinking of P. In this connection, Utzschneider also quotes Janowski, whom we mentioned above. He is concerned, however, about the 'high level of abstraction' of the results of research and also in this case he expects useful progress from a synchronic approach.

As an example of an attempt into this direction, he quotes Mettinger, who on the basis of his investigation of the name-theology of the deuteronomic-deuteronomistic literature, believes that in the exilic/post-exilic time at least three concepts of sanctuary-theology were available: the established cult-theology 'with its assurance of God's presence in the temple and protection of its city,' the name-theology and the kabod-theology. According to Utzschneider, this hypothesis raises a lot of interesting questions, such as: To what extent did the concepts and their adherents compete among each other? Did the choice for one type of theology entail certain options for the solution of social and political problems?

In a separate 'excurs' to this section of his review, he discusses the relation between the Sinaitic sanctuary texts and the primordial history as described in Genesis. Word-associations between the beginning chapters of Genesis and the final chapters of Exodus suggest that P sees some correspondence between the

---

1   o.c. , p. 44.

completion of the creation and the completion of the sanctuary. Analogies in chronological and other numerical schemes can be used in supporting this idea. It has also been suggested that the tabnit which plays a role in the sanctuary texts has some relation to the 'image-of-God-statements' in Genesis. In a recent study Weimar has pointed to the analogy of the Priestly sanctuary in Exodus and the ark in the flood-narrative.[1] In this matter as well, Utzschneider suggests that further investigation of the situative context will bring to light the validity of these ideas and their consequences for our understanding of the meaning of the texts concerned.

Hence, he examines himself the role of the Sinaitic sanctuary texts in the larger complex of the Sinaitic narrative of Exodus to Numbers. Under the heading of the dramatis personae and their functional roles, he subsequently investigates the roles of human groups, such as the people, human individuals, divine persons, and the functional relations of the ark, the building and the dwelling. On the basis of this investigation he distinguishes between the ark-dwelling concept, which has connections with a prophetic approach, and the ohel-moed concept. The relation between the two he describes as follows: "Diese, die 'Lade-Wohnungs-Konzeption' scheint uns überwölbt von einer zweiten, der 'Ohel-Moed-Konzeption' ...., in der die priesterlichen Handlungsanteile geradezu überwältigend in der Vordergrund treten. Überspitzt gesagt: Erst mit der Einbringung dieser Konzeption werden die sinaitischen Heiligtumstexte 'priesterschriftlich.'[2]

In the next step of his study, he investigates the 'macrostructure' and the conceptual fundamental lines of the Sinaitic sanctuary texts. He arrives at this macrostructure by re-narrating the surface-text in the form of 'elementary propositions,' and by summarizing these elements into a structured whole of macro-propositions.[3] These macro-propositions, in their turn, are summarized according to the functional role aspects formulated earlier, and the results of this coordinating step are examined together with comparable aspects in 'control-texts' outside the Sinaitic sanctuary texts. These examinations should make it clear whether, and to what degree of probability, the handling roles, expressed in the macro-propositions, can be coordinated into coherent concepts, or whether, and why, this is not possible.

After examining the functional role of prophet, king, people, and priest, Utzschneider concludes that in addition to the two concepts mentioned above, a third concept can be distinguished in the Sinaitic sanctuary texts: the people-sanctuary concept. This "Volk-Heiligtum-Konzeption" implies hat not only prophet and priest, but "auch das Volk, bzw. die Handelnden aus seiner Mitte Elemente, königlicher Handlungsrollen wahrnehmen und zwar als Stifter und als

---

1   Weimar, 1988, p. 384.
2   Utzschneider, 1988, p. 133.
3   o.c. , p. 135.

'weise' Hersteller des Heiligtums."[1] According to Utzschneider, this concept provides for a 'community-model' (Gemeinde-Modell).

In a detailed investigation of the surface-text of Ex 25 - 31, which we will discuss in paragraph 7.3., Utzschneider confirms the occurrence of these three concepts.

Blum, in a recent review on the "priesterliche Komposition," considers the possibilities of a spiritualizing explanation of these chapters: "Nimmt man die priesterliche Tradition beim Wort, dann geht es ihr gerade um konkrete Gottesgegenwart, die aber ohne ebenso konkrete, 'dingliche' Räume, Institutionen, Regelungen usw. weder für den heiligen Gott noch für das Volk, das dessen Gegenwart ausgesetzt ist, tragbar wäre! Eine Tradition, die sich dergestalt selbst aufhöbe, ist wohl eine moderne Projektion.

Überhaupt dürfte es schwer fallen, den (kommunikativen) Sinn dieser detaillierten Architektonik in einer generalisierenden Deutung zu bestimmen. Wahrscheinlich greifen verschiedene Weisen und Ebenen des 'Wirklichkeitsbezugs' ineinander."[2] He also refers to the correspondence of "Tempelbau und Schöpfung."[3]

A detailed account of earlier research on the theological implications of the concepts of Tent and Ark has been given by Schmitt.[4]

7.2.6. Dating and meaning.

The dating of P has been a matter of much debate between scholars, from the time Wellhausen formulated this literary source for the Pentateuch up to now. In his introductory chapter, Utzschneider provides an extensive survey of this debate, which is understandable from his methodological point of view (see above section 7.2.3.). The dating of the original text is one of the important factors in determining the historical situation, which at its turn is decisive in conceiving the meaning of the text. "In der Rekonstruktion des situativen Kontextes und der daraus erhobenen Bedeutung des Textes laufen alle Fäden der Auslegung eines Textes zusammen."[5] In this section we will follow the main line of Utzschneider's survey.

Regarding the dating of P, Utzschneider sees as the remaining contribution of Wellhausen, the setting of the key-dates for this source of the Pentateuch: its terminus a quo at the time of the exile, and its terminus ad quem at the time of Ezra. These dates have received general acceptance all over the years, and also Utzschneider is prepared to make them the starting-point of his investigation.

The ideas of Kaufmann, who dates P before D, have been rejected by many

---

1   o.c. , p. 183.
2   Blum, 1990, p. 304 - 05.
3   o.c. , p. 306.
4   Schmitt, 1972.
5   Utzschneider, 1988, p. 55.

scholars, mainly because they lack literary-historic 'depth of sharpness' (Tiefenschärfe), but Utzschneider thinks they should be critically examined from the purely historical side as well. Kaufmann's main reason for an early dating of P is that it does not appear to be aware of the struggle for centralization of the cult, which, according to him, had started with Hezekiah's reform. So it is this time which forms for Kaufmann its terminus ad quem. But Utzschneider believes that attempts to centralize the cult, and opposition to these, had already started much earlier; even David's transporting the ark to Jerusalem could be considered as an act of centralization of the cult. He wonders whether a document which is silent regarding this conflict could originate in that period.[1]

Haran explains P's silence at this point by assuming that it describes a kind of Utopia and only aims at a soft reform. He connects P with the reform of Hezekiah. In a later publication, he assumes that P, after its creation, had remained the exclusive possession of the Priestly semi-esoteric circle, until Ezra published it as part of the canonized Torah. An extended period of dating is also assumed by Friedman, who divides P into a pre-exilic and a post-exilic part. He believes that the (pre-exilic) Sinaitic sanctuary texts refer to a real tabernacle, which formed a part of the first temple in Jerusalem. He dates these texts in the time of Josiah.[2]

Utzschneider objects to this idea, because it does not explain the fact that these texts in fact describe a complete sanctuary, and not just a part of it. He acknowledges the affinity between the descriptions of the construction of tabernacle and temple, but maintains that these 'buildings' cannot be integrated simply. So he remains doubtful regarding this way of dating P, in the same way as he remains doubtful concerning all hypotheses which accept the centralization of the cult - which is not mentioned or referred to in the texts - as meaning-constituting context for the Sinaitic sanctuary texts. He believes that it is better to choose as a starting-point topics about which the texts are not silent, and he illustrates his position as follows:

"Die Texte beschreiben in aller Deutlichkeit die Gründung und den Bau eines Heiligtums. Eben dies aber war das Problem nach der Zerstörung des jerusalemer Tempels in der Zeit seines Wiederaufbaus und in der Zeit der Reorganisation seines Kultes. Die so umrissene Zeit deckt sich mehr oder minder mit der 'Zwischenzeit', die von den besprochenen Autoren zwischen Entstehung und 'Veröffentlichung' der sinaitischen Heiligtumstexte angesetzt wird. In dieser Zeit werden wir den bedeutungskonstitutiven Kontext für die sinaitischen Heiligtumstexte (nicht für die priesterschriftlichen Materialien

---

1   o.c. , p. 60, p. 61.
2   Friedman, 1980.

insgesamt) suchen."[1]

In this connection it is remarkable that Utzschneider only 'anhangsweise' points to recent attempts to establish a pre-exilic dating of P by 'style-historic means.'[2] As his main reason he states: "Das stilistische, sprachgeschichtliche Argument allein reicht zur Datierung nicht aus."[3] Though this statement may be true, we wonder whether it is justified to disregard the results of these investigations completely.

Regarding the meaning which has been attributed to the Sinaitic sanctuary texts by Old Testament science, Utzschneider distinguishes three basic designs:

a. The etiology-thesis, which sees the main objective of the Sinaitic sanctuary texts in the explanation of the cultic institutions, especially of the temple in Jerusalem. But this thesis tends to see the tabernacle, the Solomonic temple, Zion, the Josianic temple and the post-exilic sanctuary in one line.[4] Utzschneider does not deny the relation between the Sinaitic sanctuary and the Jerusalem sanctuary, but he thinks it to be questionable to call this relation an etiology.[5]

b. The thesis of the paradigmatic sanctuary. With regard to the writings of P as a whole, Lohfink has used the concept of transparency: "Zwar wird in Vergangenheitsform erzählt. Aber das, was erzählt wird, entspricht Situationen, Möglichkeiten, Erfahrungen und Problemen der angezielten Leserschaft. .... Jedes Ereignis ist transparent erzählt. Was einmal war, kann also wiederkehren. Die Strukturkongruenz erhellt die Gegenwart des Lesers, ja vielleicht jede mögliche Gegenwart. .... Dies ist ein Verständnis von Geschichte, für das es gewissermaßen einen Vorrat paradigmatischer Weltkonstellationen gibt, die alle schon da waren und die wiederkommen können."[6]

Utzschneider comments that in line with this view the Sinaitic Sanctuary texts contain a concept of sanctuary that not only claims to be paradigmatic for Israel, but for every possible sanctuary.[7] In agreement with his methodological attitude, Utzschneider recognizes in this approach an important aspect of the Sinaitic sanctuary texts: "Die Texte geben keine unmittelbar auf außertextuelle Größen beziehbaren Signale. Dies heißt aber nicht, ... daß die Texte aus ihrem situativen, geschichtlichen Kontext herausgenommen werden dürfen, oder daß ihnen eine solche Esoterik gar als Programm unterstellt werden dürfte."[8]

c. The thesis of the critical utopy, which sees the critical attitude towards the cult theology of Jerusalem as the most important aspect of the meaning of the Sinaitic sanctuary texts. Utzschneider quotes Fretheim who, after having

---

1   Utzschneider, 1988, p. 63.
2   Hurvitz, 1982; Zevit, 1982; see also Hurvitz, 1988.
3   Utzschneider, 1988, p. 64.
4   see o.c. , p. 65.
5   o.c. , p. 66.
6   Lohfink, 1978, p. 211, 213.
7   Utzschneider, 1988, p. 67.
8   o.c. , p. 68.

considered a number of scholarly ideas on the background of P's conception of the tabernacle, wrote in 1968: "The immediate impression these ideas give is that the Priestly writers did not expect their tabernacle to serve as a model for a more permanent temple. In fact, we suggest that they were opposed to the rebuilding of a temple after the return from the exile. Instead, they were calling for a return to the theocratic age, prior to kingship and temple, in their own day, with a people centered around a movable sanctuary."[1] Utzschneider believes that those scholars who see the Sinaitic sanctuary texts as referring to an utopian project very often suppose implicitly (or sometimes explicitly) a critical attitude of P towards the traditional cult. According to him, this thesis provides ideas which should be explored in more detail in the reconstruction of the situational context, and through that of the meaning-horizon of the Sinaitic sanctuary texts.

It is this reconstruction which Utzschneider describes in detail in his book and we conclude this section with a brief summary of his results.

At first he tries to describe the historical texts which correspond with the traditional concepts, which he had formulated earlier (see above, section 7.2.5.). Although, in none of the cases, he is able to provide a detailed and complete description of the historical text, he believes to have found in the present surface-text enough signals which enable him to conclude that for each concept there existed a historical text.

In the second place, he tries to find a connection between these historical texts and utterances or concepts which "[1] mit hoher Wahrscheinlichkeit einem synchronen Äußerungskontext angehören .... und die [2] den sinaitischen Heiligtumstexten und ihren Einzeltexten konzeptionell nicht oder nur zum Teil entsprechen."[2] In the framework of this comparison, he subsequently investigates: the 'law-less temple' (der gesetzlose Tempel), which he sees based on a number of texts from Jeremiah, the Solomonic temple, which he connects with parts from 1 Kings, and the second temple as put forward in Ezra and Haggai/Zechariah. In each case, he describes how the texts which he had found in connection with the traditional concepts given above contain features showing opposition against the alternative concepts.

In a concluding paragraph, he summarizes his ideas on the dating and meaning of the Sinaitic sanctuary texts. "In dem Jahrhundert nach dem Verlust der Eigenstaatlichkeit und des geistig-geistlichen Mittelpunktes, des ersten Tempels von Jerusalem .... votieren die sinaitischen Heiligtumstexte für das Heiligtum des Gottes Israels. Sie tun dies grundsätzlich und zeitbezogen zugleich. Sie votieren für das Heiligtum zunächst gegenüber einer Bestrebung, die nach der Zerstörung des ersten Tempels jedes Vertrauen in eine sichtbare Repräsentanz der Gegenwart Gottes verloren hat und an deren Stelle allein die fromme,

---

1   Fretheim, 1968, p. 315 - 16.
2   o.c. , p. 259.

gesetzestreue Gemeinschaft setzen will."[1]

7.3. Language and text of Exodus 25 to 31.

7.3.1. Introduction.
In this paragraph we bring together those publications which deal in particular with the linguistic aspects of Exodus 25 to 31 and give a bird's eye view of their scope.

We were unable to find publications which deal with the specific textual problems of these chapters. Gooding has investigated the text of the Septuagint, but concentrates on the 'second account' of the tabernacle in chapter 35 to 41, where the differences between the Masoretic Text and the Greek translation are largest. They relate to the order in which the subject matter is presented in the text and to deletions of complete passages of the MT by the Septuagint. In some cases, the Greek text is "drastically abbreviated or paraphrased."[2]

Gooding also points to differences in the Greek of the first (chapter 25 to 31) and second account. A number of Hebrew technical terms for objects described in the tabernacle text have been translated into different Greek words in the two accounts. He discusses all these differences in view of the problem of reconstructing the Hebrew text on which the translation into Greek was based, and of answering the question whether the translations of the first and second account were made by the same translator or by different ones. Regarding the latter problem, Gooding concludes that both accounts stem from the same translator, whereas he assumes that the order of the Greek text of the second account reflects the order and scope of its original Hebrew text.

The rest of this paragraph contains our review of a number of topics relating to Exodus 25 to 31. In the next section, we will review Utzschneider's work on this pericope. In addition, we will give a survey of the literary-critical and genre-critical analyses (section 7.3.3.) and those publications which describe the reconstruction of the tabernacle and the other objects (section 7.3.4.). Finally, publications which deal with general linguistic aspects relating to Ex 25 - 31 will be reviewed (section 7.3.5.).

7.3.2. The cohesion of Exodus 25 to 31.
In chapter 5 of his book, Utzschneider investigates the surface-text of the Sinaitic sanctuary texts.[3] He examines the syntax of the text, its structuring devices, and its context. In view of our interest most emphasis will be put on the first aspect mentioned.

In addition to the concept of cohesion, which we mentioned above (section

---

1   o.c. , p. 296 - 297.
2   Gooding, 1959, p. 3.
3   Utzschneider, 1988, p. 185 - 235.

7.2.3.), a central role in his investigation is played by the 'phoric,' which he defines as follows: "Unter 'Phorik' verstehen wir den Inbegriff aller jener Verweissysteme, durch die Textteile - vorwiegend im mikrotextuellen Bereich (von Satz zu Satz) - miteinander verknüpft werden."[1] With regard to the Sinaitic sanctuary texts he distinguishes between two systems: one based mainly on the way in which verbal forms constitute the connection between clauses (phoric of formations), and the second based on nominal elements of the texts, in fact, the way in which nominal and pronominal forms provide for a continuing account of the 'actors' (phoric of actors).

As far as the phoric of formations in Exodus 25 to 31 is concerned, Utzschneider distinguishes between a normal syntax, and a modified or a deviating syntax. The structure of the normal syntax "wird durch eine Reihe von weqatal-x-Formationen gebildet, die durch Nominalsätze einerseits und durch x-yiqtol-Formationen andererseits unterbrochen wird. Auffällig ist, daß die Nominalsätze asyndetisch im Zusammenhang der weqatal-Formationen stehen, untereinander aber meist verbunden sind .... Dagegen bleiben die x-yiqtol-Formationen, wenn sie (selten genug) nebeneinander zustehen kommen, auch untereinander meist unverbunden. Funktional sind die Nominalsätze wie die x-yiqtol-Formationen als asyndetische Umstandssätze anzusprechen."[2]

Using Ex 25:11-22 as an example Utzschneider explains that the phoric of formations and the order of contents are closely related. "Mit weqatal-Formationen werden jeweils neue Arbeitsvorgänge bei der Herstellung der Lade eingeführt. Demzufolge werden auch neue Einzelteile des Inventars oder der Ausstattung mit solchen Formationen eingeführt. Die besonderen Umstände dieser Arbeitsvorgänge oder weitere Qualifikationen der Einzelteile sind hingegen mit x-yiqtol-Formationen ausgedrückt. Die Nominalsätze sind nahezu ausschließlich für Maßangaben reserviert."[3]

This type of syntax Utzschneider recognizes in Ex 25:11 - 27:8; 28:6 - 39; 30:1 - 10, 17 - 21, 22 - 32, 34 - 37. It provides for a high degree of cohesion, especially for the pericope 25:11 - 27:8, but also for those parts of Ex 28:6 - Ex 30, which have been written in this style.

At the end of the section on the normal syntax, Utzschneider discusses three problems with regard to Ex 25 - 31.

- Most commentaries and monographs consider it to be written in the jussive, which is obvious for reasons of conceptual structure. However, it should be noticed that in those cases where it is possible to have a short form for the yiqtol-formation, with only one exception (Ex 25:15: יסרו), the long form has actually been used. Hence, Utzschneider concludes: "Von der morphologischen Seite her ist das iussivische Verständnis und die entsprechende Wiedergabe so

---

1   o.c. , p. 185.
2   o.c. , p. 192.
3   o.c. , p. 192.

sicher nicht."[1]

- Two times an imperative has been used (25:19 and 28:42), but a particular function for these forms cannot be recognized.

- "Die ca. 10 belege für die Formation we-x-yiqtol .... sind insofern signifikant, als ihr numerisches Verhältnis zu den x-yiqtol-Belegen .... ein Unterscheidungskriterium zu den Textteilem mit dem modifizierter Normalsyntax darstellt."[2]

This latter type of syntax, which is characterized by the more frequent occurrence of we-x-yiqtol forms as compared to x-yiqtol forms, Utzschneider finds in Ex 28:40ff; 29 and 30:11 - 16. Moreover Ex 29 is characterized by the fact that weqatal-formations dominate, but without the interruption by situation-sentences which is usual in the normal syntax. Nominal sentences appear in most cases as structuring sentences. Utzschneider remarks that this modified form of the normal syntax, especially in Ex 29, seems to be connected with the genre-characteristic syntax of the 'rituals,' as described by Rendtorff.[3]

In addition to these two main forms of syntax, he distinguishes another two deviating forms:

- In Ex 31:1 - 6 both wayyiqtol and x-qatal-formations occur together. This seems to be related to Yahweh's message to Moses, that it is He who has called both artisans.

- In two pericopes list-like compositions do occur (Ex 27:9 - 18; 31:7 - 11). Both are introduced by a verbal sentence which is followed by a number of clauses, to which the experienced reader could add the verbal forms (in the first pericope) or which he could consider as direct objects to the beginning sentence (in the second pericope).[4]

Under the heading of the second aspect of phoric - the phoric of the actors - Utzschneider discusses several problems. The first one relates to the you/they incohesion in Ex 25 to 36. He describes this problem as follows:

"In Ex 25:1 ff beauftragt Jahwe den Mose, bei den Freiwilligen ('sie', 'ihr') eine Abgabe zu erheben, damit 'sie' ein Heiligtum für ihn (Jahwe) herstellen; mit der Herstellung der Lade sollen 'sie' beginnen (V.8 - 10).

Dann aber richtet Jahwe ab Ex 25:11 bis 27:8a die Herstellungsanweisungen für die Lade, den Tisch, den Leuchter, die Wohnung und den Altar an ein 'Du', mit dem, nach der ab 24:15ff vorgestellten Szenen auf dem Berg nur Mose gemeint sein kann."[5]

This problem has become manifest in particular in the form וְעָשׂוּ in Ex 25:10. Already the Septuagint changed this form into 2 m.s. futurem, and most exegetes followed this line. Koch did not alter the text, but assigned the 3 m.p.

---

1   o.c. , p. 193.
2   o.c. , p. 193.
3   o.c. , p. 193 - 194.
4   o.c. , p. 194.
5   o.c. , p. 197.

to the source-document, which according to him, had used this form everywhere. Before him, Von Rad had also tried to solve the problem by assuming different sources - a 'Moses-tradition' and a 'you-source' - but it is not completely clear how his solution operates in all details. It is this idea of the two sources which Utzschneider uses to solve the problem. He points to the fact that after Ex 25:10 the next 3 m.p. form occurs in Ex 27:8. This sentence is very cohesive with the conclusion of 25:8.

According to him, in Ex 28:1-5f the you/they-incohesion is very clear again. The verses 3 to 6 show a continuous 'they-series,' whereas only from v.9 onwards the 'you-forms' return again. The 'they' in this pericope apparently are the 'artisans' (Kunstfertigen). This connects the 'they-section' of 28:3 with the corresponding section in 35:10, 36:1ff, in the same way as the 'volunteers' of 25:2 are connected phorically with 35:5, 20ff, and the order to offer for the sanctuary and to construct it, directed in 25:2, 8 to all Israelites, finds its fulfilment in 39:32. On the basis of these connections Utzschneider concludes: "In den durch die 'Sie'-Phorik verbundenen Stellen scheinen sich die Oberflächenorte der .... Volk-Heiligtums-Konzeption herauszuschälen."[1]

Utzschneider tries to find the connection between the 'they-phoric' and the 'you-phoric' in Ex 25:8f, where all possible pronominal morphemes (I, yu, they, their) actually occur. Moses alone receives the 'model' (tabnit) of the sanctuary, so it is understandable that Yahweh speaks to Moses, but it is not clear why the latter receives detailed instructions for building it, whereas originally the people as a whole had received the order for constructing it. Utzschneider considers this to be in the first place a problem of coherence, which he tries to solve by investigating cotexts, in which Moses received instructions for constructing things as well: Ex 34:1 and Deut 10:1. There, he is asked only to construct the tablets and the ark, not a complete sanctuary. Hence, Utzschneider concludes that the 'you-phoric' is related to the ark-dwelling-concept and that the you/they-incohesion of the surface-text is an outward sign of the coming together of the people-sanctuary concept with the ark-dwelling concept.

Another problem concerning the phoric in Ex 25 - 31 is the 'you/he-incohesion,' which occurs in 25:37; 27:20f; 30:6f, 17f. According to Utzschneider, all these cases refer to 'ceremonial instructions,' which occur in Ex 25 - 31 in increasing number besides the construction-instructions. He assumes that they relate to the ohel-moed concept, for which he mentions three reasons:

a. The term אהל מועד appears for the first time in the Sinaitic sanctuary texts at a 'he-place': Ex 27:21.

b. In all cases either Aaron himself or Aaron and his sons, are subject of the handling processes, hence all refer to 'priests-on-duty.'

c. "Von den aufgeführten Stellen sind zwei Zitate aus Texten und Textbereichen,

---

1   o.c. , p. 199.

die zweifelsfrei der Ohel-Moed-Konzeption zuzurechnen sind."[1]

The last aspect of the phoric of the Sinaitic Sanctuary texts which Utzschneider investigates is the way in which Yahweh speaks of Himself in the I-form, the first person. Although this does not involve a proper case of incohesion, Utzschneider discusses it under this heading, since it is remarkable that in a text which is dominated by the appellative (you ......), now and then the message (I .....) occurs as well. It may be expected that the longer text-elements in which this happens possess an important function in the totality of the text. Indeed they do, according to Utzschneider. Ex 25:16b, 21b, 22 refer to the (prophetic) ark-dwelling concept. In Ex 29:42 - 46 it is attempted to increase the constitutive elements of this concept with those of the ohel-moed concept.[2] Finally, Ex 25:2, 8f belongs to one of the text-ordering pericopes, and it is characterized by the fact that the people are the only 'factor' involved, both as 'actors': they should provide an offering and construct the sanctuary, and as 'recipients' of Yahweh's activity: He will live among them. Hence this pericope belongs to the people-sanctuary concept.

In his summary, Utzschneider concludes that the three pericopes written in the I-form, which to a certain extent seem to be independent from each other, can be clearly related to the three main concepts of the Sinaitic sanctuary texts. After he has listed his conclusions from the other forms of incohesion, he summarizes: "Es mehren sich also die Hinweise darauf, daß den drei Hauptkonzeptionen jeweils Teile des Oberflächentextes der sinaitischen Heiligtumstexte entsprechen."[3]

Under the heading text-arranging-signals (Textgliederungssignale), Utzschneider discusses refrain-like signals which occur repeatedly, such as the reference to the תבנית, and 'formulae' such as עולם (ות)חק or הוא-x. A second type of these signals which he investigates are the opening and concluding parts, such as Ex 25:1 - 10a, 28: 1 - 6, and other formulae such as כאשר צוה יהוה. He explains the function of these text-fragments as ordering-devices for the overall structure of the Sinaitic sanctuary texts.

The final aspect of the surface-text to which Utzschneider pays attention is the order in which the objects to be constructed and the rituals to be performed are being introduced. There is a remarkable difference between Ex 25 - 31, Ex 35 - 39, and the Septuagint-version of the latter. He summarizes the explanations for this phenomenon given in the literature, among which the one suggested by Von Rad, that Ex 35 - 39 is secondary, because it provides the 'better order,' has been widely accepted. Utzschneider expresses his doubts regarding this idea, because he is of the opinion that the Sinaitic sanctuary texts do not refer to one

---

1   o.c. , p. 205.
2   o.c. , p. 207.
3   o.c. , p. 210.

sanctuary only.[1] On the basis of an investigation of the order in Ex 26:30 - 37 and the general framework of Ex 25:1 - 27:8, he concludes that the former refers to the sanctuary of the ark-dwelling concept and the latter to the sanctuary of the people-sanctuary concept.[2]

7.3.3. Literary-critical analyses of Exodus 25 to 31.

At first, we give a list of some publications which provide a more or less detailed analysis of parts of the pericope Ex 25 - 31, often within the framework of an investigation of wider scope.

1. Ex 25 - 27	Fritz.[3]
2. Ex 25:17 - 22	Janowski.[4]
3. Ex 26	Görg.[5]
4. Ex 29:42 - 46	Görg.[6]
	Janowski.[7]
	Struppe.[8]
	Blum.[9]
5. Ex 30: 11 - 16	Janowski.[10]

As will be clear from sections 7.2.3. and 7.2.4., a number of scholars analyzed these chapters in order to isolate a text for the original source document, the 'Grundschrift,' Pg. The following list provides the result of some of them:

a. Von Rad: 25:2a, 8; 28:3 -5; 29:43, 45; 31:13 ab, 14a.

Additional comment from the author: "Natürlich ist es möglich, ja wahrscheinlich, daß noch mehr dieser ältesten P-Schicht zugehört hat."[11]

b. Elliger: 25:1 - 27:19; 28:1 - 41; 29:1 - 37, 42b - 46; 31:18.[12]

c. Lohfink: 25:1 - 2, 8, 9; 26:1 - 30; 29:43 - 46; 31:18.[13]

d. Weimar: (25:8, 9) 26:1ab, 2a, 6*, 7, 8a, 11ab, 15a, 16, 18*, 22 - 23*, (30; 29:45 - 46).[14]

Other publications do not restrict themselves to the Pg alone, but attempt to

---

1   o.c. , p. 226.
2   o.c. , p. 234, p. 235.
3   Fritz, 1977, p. 114 - 166.
4   Janowski, 1982, p. 339 - 346.
5   Görg, 1967, p. 8 - 34.
6   o.c. , p. 59 - 61.
7   Janowski, 1982 , p. 317 - 320.
8   Struppe, 1984, p. 31 - 62.
9   Blum, 1990, p. 297 - 301.
10   Janowski, 1982 , p. 161 -162.
11   Von Rad, 1934, p. 64.
12   Elliger, 1952, p. 175.
13   Lohfink, 1977, p. 198.
14   Weimar, 1988, p. 345 - 46.

describe more source documents. In this respect, Von Rad,[1] Koch[2] and also Utzschneider[3] can be mentioned.

7.3.4. The reconstruction of the tabernacle.

In a recent publication, Weimar writes: "Da die nur schwer miteinander harmonisierbaren Konstruktionsprinzipien des priesterschriftlichen Heiligtums primär von der dahinter stehenden theologischen Aussageabsicht gesteuert sind, wäre es verfehlt, diese auf die Möglichkeiten ihrer Realisierung hin zu befragen ...."[4]

On the other hand, it appears from the literature that many scholars have attempted to clarify details of the technical language used in Ex 25 - 31, or even tried to design a model of the sanctuary as a whole. A preliminary comparison of the pictures with which they illustrate their models leads to the conclusion that many details are uncertain, or, at least, can be interpreted in different ways. Without claiming completeness, we survey a number of publications on this subject.

In his commentary on Exodus, Galling distinguished between two sources which each have their own model: Pa with a proper tent, and Pb with a temple-like structure. The present text yields a picture of the construction of the tent, which is technically hardly feasible.[5]

Cross sees the Priestly tabernacle as it appears from descriptions in Exodus 26 and 36 as a 'portable temple.' His model has a rectangular shape, and like Galling, he recognizes two motives: "One derives from the desert and suggests its tent-shrine origins," and the other ".... points to the influence of Syro-Phoenician temple structure."[6]

Haran is of the opinion that despite a "unique combination of long-winded description on the one hand and total omission of various particulars on the other .... the general character of the structure is quite clear." His model is rectangular as well, and he pays much attention to possible alternative arrangements of the pillars.[7]

Modern mathematical construction theory was used by Pelzl to calculate the strength of the various parts of the wooden structure. He concludes that its construction is a feasible possibility.[8]

Friedman suggests an overlapping arrangement of the frames of the wooden structure, by which it is possible to arrive at a model of the tabernacle of such a

---

1   Von Rad, 1934.
2   Koch, 1959.
3   Utzschneider, 1988.
4   Weimar, 1988, p. 347, n. 33.
5   Galling, 1939, p. 135.
6   Cross, 1947, p. 55, p. 61.
7   Haran, 1978, p. 149 - 174.
8   Pelzl, 1975, p. 386.

size that it fits into the Holy of Holies in the first temple, beneath the wings of the cherubim.[1]

A survey of the older literature and of all problems relating to the tabernacle is provided by Henton Davies.[2] In addition to these publications which relate to the tabernacle as a whole, a number of others have been found which describe details or single objects of Ex 25 - 31.

7.3.5. General linguistic aspects of Exodus 25 to 31.

At first, we survey a few publications which investigate the language of P in broader perspective. In 1976 Polzin published an investigation of the historical typology of Late Biblical Hebrew (LBH). He did not base himself on the general idea of the documentary hypothesis, but only assumed that "if those scattered portions of the Tetrateuch called P actually represent a relatively late unified 'source' within it, this corpus should contain enough linguistic characteristics to indicate such a relative age. ..... That the typological nature of P's language established in this study on linguistic grounds alone happens to agree with its relative dating by source critics has no essential connection with nor assumes any corroboration of the documentary hypothesis as such. The isolation of those sections called P is one thing; the interpretation of that unity, once isolated, and its integration into a genetic theory of interpretation is quite another."[3] He further assumed that "the books of Chronicles provide us with the best example of what LBH looked like" and that "grammar and syntax provide a more objective and reliable basis for chronological analysis than do lexicographic features of a language."[4]

By means of an investigation of the language of Chronicles he determined a number of significant linguistic features of LBH. After that he studied the language of P and gave as his preliminary conclusion: "What is clear to me is that, whatever may be the suppositions leading to the isolation of that entity called P, such a unity makes sense linguistically and provides us with a definite stage in the historical development of BH prose."[5] As the text of P, he considered those parts of the Pentateuch which a number of scholars assigned to it, and restricted his investigation to the narrative parts, which he divided into Pg and Ps, for which he again used the "generally recognized corpus."[6]

On the basis of his comparison, he concluded the following historical order:

    JE   Court History   Dtr   Pg   Ps   Chronicles,
however, without specifying a period of origin for Pg and Ps.[7]

---

1   Friedman, 1980, p. 241.
2   Henton Davies, 1962.
3   Polzin, 1976, p. 1.
4   o.c. , p. 2.
5   o.c. , p. 86.
6   o.c. , p. 88 - 90, p. 101 - 102.
7   o.c. , p. 112.

Using a linguistic study of P and Ezekiel, an attempt to date P was made by Hurvitz, who, after having found "substantial differences in their linguistic profiles," describes how the following pattern emerged:

"(1) The texts belonging to P make intensive use of only early linguistic elements - and never of those identifiable as late.

(2) The texts belonging to Ez. use both early linguistic elements as well as those identifiable as late.

In our opinion, this situation allows for only one explanation: the presence in Ez. of late linguistic elements betrays the late background of this Book, while the absence of such late elements from P reflects the early background of the Priestly Source."[1]

After having considered a number of alternative solutions and questions still open to further investigation, Hurvitz maintains as his final conclusion: "Whatever the absolute dating of P and Ezekiel, then, it can definitely be stated that P comes first in a relative chronological order."[2]

The monographs by Hurvitz and Polzin contain a lot of information on details of the language of P, which seem to be useful for our investigation. The same applies to a number of books on grammatical aspects of OTH. For example, Andersen, in his study of the sentence,[3] and Niccacci, in his investigation of the syntax of the verb,[4] discuss in detail parts of Exodus 25 to 31.

Of course, the commentaries on the book of Exodus also form a valuable source of information. In particular, the extensive list of words occurring in Exodus given by Houtman in the first volume of his commentary on Exodus may be of help.[5]

A number of authors have compared the text of Ex 25 - 31 (or part of it) with other biblical or extra-biblical texts. Postma et al.[6] provided computer-generated verse-by-verse comparisons of the pericopes of Ex 25 - 31 with their counterparts in Ex 35 - 40.

Kearny[7] and Weimar[8] compared the tabernacle texts of Exodus with the creation- and the creation/flood-narratives of Genesis respectively.

Hurowitz[9] analysed the structure of the tabernacle-text and compared it with other accounts of building temples, as found in the Bible and Mesopotamian and Ugaritic sources. The tabernacle account in its canonical form is shown to be identical in pattern to these other accounts. It must be said that this identity

---

1   Hurvitz, 1982, p. 150.
2   o.c. , p. 155.
3   Andersen, 1974, p. 71ff.
4   Niccacci, 1990, p. 80ff.
5   Houtman, 1986, p. 24 - 82.
6   Postma, Talstra, Vervenne, 1983, I, p. 84 - 96.
7   Kearny, 1977.
8   Weimar, 1988.
9   Hurowitz, 1985.

does not cover, however, the detailed aspects of the technical building language. A similar comparison, but based on Ex 35 - 40 only, had been made earlier by Levine.[1]

In a separate publication, McEvenue reported the results of his study of the style of Ex 25 - 31. He made a comparison of two sub-pericopes: Ex 25: 31 - 36, 40 on the lampstand, and Ex 26: 1 - 11 on the dwelling. The stylistic techniques in either piece corresponded exactly to what he had found in the rest of Pg,[2] and he concludes: "The differences between these two pieces are sufficiently explained by the hypothesis that the lamp was somehow present, whereas the mishkan was not."[3]

7.4. Summary.

From our review of recent literature, it appears that both the Priestly document in general and the chapters Exodus 25 - 31 continue to be investigated quite intensively. Despite the 'crisis' of the Documentary Hypothesis, most scholars still operate within the framework of the more or less established formulation of P and related source criticism, and try to refine its possibilities. As examples, we mention the work of McEvenue and Paran on the style of P and all publications which try to isolate the Priestly 'Grundschrift' and its 'theological objective.'

In addition to these, we also found a few publications which clearly aim at alternative approaches. The one most relevant to us is Utzschneider's study of the Sinaitic sanctuary texts. Independent from the idea of the Priestly Codex, he uses a kind of revision hypothesis in order to arrive at the original sources of these texts and their accompanying theological concepts. In his approach, he puts heavy emphasis on the historical communication events, which he tries to reconstruct by a careful analysis of the existing text using the concepts of cohesion and coherence as 'yardsticks.' A thorough examination of his method falls beyond the scope of our study. The aspect of his publication which is most relevant to us are the extensive observations, which he makes on the text of Exodus 25 to 31. The same applies to the other publications discussed in this chapter.

In paragraph 6.4. , we gave a few considerations which played a role in our choice of Exodus 25 - 31 as the target text for our investigation. The results of our literature search enable us to make additional comments on two of these points.

ad. a. We did not find publications on particular textual problems of Exodus 25 - 31, so we assume that our original idea is right. The Septuagint text of the account of the construction of the tabernacle in Exodus 35 - 40 presents a

---

1   Levine, 1965.
2   see McEvenue, 1971.
3   McEvenue, 1974, p. 7.

number of problems which have been considered repeatedly in the literature. It is possible that the translator used a Hebrew original which is different from the Masoretic Text of most of these chapters. This means that, in case we wish to include these chapters in our investigation, we will have to pay attention to this point.

ad b. Despite the fact that recent scholarship shows a wide variety of approaches, our original assessment seems to be true. In general, literary-critical studies of Exodus 25 - 31 do not assume more than three independent sources and all of these are thought to stem from closely related circles.

Our literature search revealed another problem, however. It appears that many scholars consider the tabernacle, as referred to in Exodus 25 to 31 and 35 to 40, as a 'theological construction' only and, in their exegesis, tend to emphasize its theological and religious meaning.[1] On the other hand, other exegetes, while appreciating the theological objective of the author, assume that he (also) referred to a 'real tabernacle.' We believe that the available evidence does not permit one to decide which of these two positions is true. But we assume that, even if the author referred to something which existed in his mind only, he would have used his language in the same way, as if he had been referring to an existing tabernacle. Hence, we do not think this point to be strong enough to force us to abandon Exodus 25 - 31 as the target text of our investigation. But it may influence our result, so we will have to consider it again at the end of our study.

---

1   see Childs, 1974, p. 537.

8. THE TABERNACLE TEXT OF EXODUS 25 TO 31.
AN INVESTIGATION OF ITS STRUCTURE AND ITS WORLD.

8.1. Introduction.

In this chapter we report our investigation of Exodus 25 to 31 as outlined in paragraph 6.4. Each of the subsequent paragraphs covers one step of the analysis of the text and consists of a number of sections which discuss its various aspects. In each case the final section contains initial remarks regarding the step involved.

In agreement with the scheme of this analysis, the next paragraph describes the assignment of grammatical categories to the words of the text. Paragraph 8.3. surveys how the text is divided into units according to the Masoretic accents. The structuring of the text according to the X-bar theory is the subject of paragraph 8.4. A number of general aspects of the resulting phrase structure is investigated in paragraph 8.5., whereas the subsequent paragraph examines the relation between referential functions, phrases and words. The final paragraph (8.7.) summarizes the results of the application of all steps of the analysis in view of its objective.[1]

As explained in chapter 6, our goal is not the complete exegesis of the text, but to find out how it structures space and spatial relations. As a consequence, paragraphs 8.5. and 8.6. do not cover the text completely, but concentrate on those parts which are most relevant for achieving this objective.

8.2. Grammatical categories.

8.2.1. The text and the words.

The investigation has been carried out on the Masoretic Text of Exodus 25 - 31, as given in the BHS. The corrections of Ex 27:7 and 30:24, as proposed by Postma et al.[2] have been accepted.

Each string of consonants separated by a blank or maqqef, has been considered to be a word. This means that a word may comprise a number of grammatical categories, e.g., a verb and a suffix which refers to a noun, or a prefixed preposition and a noun.

A complete list of all categories which have been used is given in table 8;1. This list has been developed in the course of the analysis and reflects a number of decisions which have been taken mainly for practical reasons. As a result, some

---

1   In this chapter, we will quite often present the Hebrew wording of the Masoretic text. As a rule, only the consonants will be given.
2   Postma, Talstra, Vervenne, 1983 II, p. VII, n.2.

Table 8;1. List of codes and categories.

Verbs
V1 Perfect
V2 WePerfect
V3 Imperfect
V4 WaImperfect
V5 Imperative
V6 Participle
V7 Infinitive
V8 WeImperfect

Suffixes
S1 First pers. sing.
S2 Second pers. sing.
S3 Third pers. sing.
S4 First pers. plur.
S5 Second pers. plur.
S6 Third pers. plur.
S7 ה-locativus

Nouns
N0 Noun (general)
N4 measure length s.
N5   „   dual.
N6   „   plur.
N7 measure, contents or
    weight

Adverbs
A0 General
A1 לא
A2 זה
A3 שם
A4 בן
A5 סביב
A6 תמיד
A7 לבד
A8 אם

Prepositions
P0 General
P1 אל
P2 ב
P3 ל
P4 על
P5 מן
P6 כ
P7 לפני
P8 תחת
P9 את

Conjunctions
C0 General
C1 אשר
C2 כי
C3 ו, ו
C4 את
C5 או
C6 Conjunctive acc.
C7 Maqqef

Pronouns
R0 General
R1 Personal
R2 Demonstrative

Quantifiers
Q0 General
Q1 Unspecified
Q2 Numeral
Q3 חצי
Q9 Article

Dimensions
D0 General
D1 ארך
D2 רחב
D3 קומה

Solid Materials
M0 General
M1 זהב
M2 כסף
M3 נחשת
M5 עץ עצי
M6 אבן
M9 שטים

Soft Materials
O0 General
O1 תכלת
O2 ארגמן
O3 תולעת
O4 שני
O5 שש
O8 עור
O9 עזים

Fluids
L0 General
L1 שמן
L2 דם
L3 מים

words have been grouped under headings which do not exactly correspond to
their grammatical category as reported in the main stream of the literature. All

these cases relate to individual words, which, in the rest of the analysis, have been treated according to their proper grammatical category.

The following categories have been distinguished: verbs, nouns, pronouns and particles. These will be discussed separately in the subsequent sections of this paragraph.

8.2.2. Verbs.

The following verbal forms have been assigned a separate category:

V1 Perfect (Suffix-conjugation).
V2 WePerfect.
V3 Imperfect (Prefix-conjugation).
V4 WaImperfect (Imperfectum consecutivum).
V5 Imperative.
V6 Participle.
V7 Infinitive.
V8 WeImperfect.

As a rule, it is not difficult to choose the proper category for verbal forms. The distinction between waw-copulativum and waw-consecutivum (or waw-relative[1]) is not always easy to make. Therefore, in the case of the Perfect all forms with prefixed waw have been assigned to V2 (WePerfect), whereas in the case of the ו+Imperfect a distinction has been made between WaImperfect (V4) and WeImperfect (V8).[2] As a result of this decision, five forms of the finite verb have been distinguished, which is in agreement with recent practice.[3]

The imperative has been assigned a separate category, despite the problems with its formal distinction from other verbal forms.[4]

Sometimes it is not clear whether a word should be considered as a noun or as a participle, e.g. מִשְׁקְדִים in 25:33, 34. In cases like this, purely formal categories are not sufficient for taking a proper decision and it is necessary to consider syntactic and semantic factors as well.[5] In this step of our analysis, all words for which we met with this problem have been assigned the category V6 (participle).

8.2.3. Nouns.

Since in OTH there is no formal distinction between substantives and adjectives,[6] all nouns have been given the same category. In view of the use of the data in the further analysis of the text, some groups of nouns have been given separate entries, such as: measures of length, (construction) materials, dimensions.

---

1 WO'C, p. 519.
2 see Johnson, 1979, p. 19 - 20; WO'C, p. 521.
3 see Niccacci, 1990, p. 12; WO'C, p. 456.
4 see Schneider, 1985, p. 200; WO'C, p. 567 - 68.
5 see Hardmeier, Talstra, 1989, p. 421 - 22.
6 see GKC, p. 221; WO'C, p. 65 - 66.

A few individual nouns each received their own entry in the section of adverbs, but have been treated as nouns in the remainder of the analysis.

Names have been treated as simple nouns, whereas suffixes that refer to nouns have been given separate categories according to (grammatical) person and singular/plural. The ה-locativus also got a separate entry in the section on suffixes.

8.2.4. Pronouns.

Personal and demonstrative pronouns have been assigned separate categories. The same applies to the demonstrative pronoun זה. It has been arranged under the heading adverbs, however, because in the earlier parts of the text it functions as a demonstrative adverb.[1]

The 'relative pronoun' אשר has been included under the heading of the conjunctions. The article, which is considered to be a pronoun in many grammars, has been given a separate category as well.

8.2.5. Particles.

These have been divided into adverbs, prepositions and conjunctions. Most of the words which belong to this category, receive a separate entry, while general groups are available for the others.

In OTH, it is not always clear whether a word is a preposition or not. "All words which by usage serve as prepositions, were originally substantives."[2] In our analysis only words 'generally considered' to be prepositions, have been classified as such. Prepositions in prefix-form sometimes combine with an other preposition or with a noun to form a word which can be considered as a complex preposition. Some of these received a separate entry, like לבד: A7, and לפני: P7. But most of these combinations have been coded as complex words, e.g. מלמעלה has been represented as P5P3P0. Of course, it is a matter of choice whether to code מעלה as a preposition, as a noun or as an adverb. In addition, the word is complex due to the presence of the final ה, which has been considered as a ה-locativus.[3]

Jackendoff considers words like 'here' and 'there' as intransitive prepositions.[4] Following the practice of Hebrew grammars, we will include them under the heading adverbs.[5] A few nouns have been included under this heading as well (see 8.2.3).

The heading C (conjunction) also includes a few other items:

a. The 'nota accusativi', את, which "is one of the most difficult grammatical

---

1   see Joüon, 1947, 443; WO'C, p. 307.
2   GKC, p.297; see also WO'C, p. 188.
3   Hoftijzer, 1981, p. 152 - 53.
4   Jackendoff, 1985, p. 161
5   see WO'C, p. 657.

morphemes in Biblical Hebrew."[1] The main reason for placing it here is its role in the text as indicator of a connection between a verbal form and a substantive. b. The most important conjunctive accents of the Masoretes (number 19 - 21 in the list of BHS) and the maqqef. These data have been included in view of the further analysis of the text.

8.2.6. General remarks.
Apart from those mentioned in the sections above, this first step does not present any difficulties.

8.3. Dividing the text into units according to the Masoretic accents.

8.3.1. Introduction.
The importance of the Masoretic accents for the investigation of the text of the OT has been emphasized time and again. Schweizer writes: "Die Frage für uns heute ist: können wir beanspruchen, ein Sprachgefühl für Hebräisch zu entwickeln, das so sicher ist, daß es derartige Hilfen der Masoreten außer acht lassen kann?"[2] And he continues by quoting Sawyer, who had written a few years earlier: "A further criticism of existing grammars is that, although the Hebrew text is divided into phrases and clauses by a system of stress marks, most grammars ignore these entirely and a valuable aid to sentence analysis is wasted." In this connection, it is worth while to note, that in a recent introduction to the syntax of OTH, the authors comment: "The complex accentual systems added to the text by the Masoretes represent an important understanding of the text, one that complements the study of Hebrew grammar but one that needs to be taken up independently."[3]
In order to make the fullest possible use of the Masoretic accents it is necessary to know more about their background and function. In his introduction to the Tiberian Masorah, Yeivin writes: "Altogether the accents perform three functions. Their primary function, as already noted, is to represent the musical motifs to which the Biblical text was chanted in the public reading. This chant enhanced the beauty and solemnity of the reading, but because the purpose of the reading was to present the text clearly and intelligibly to the hearers, the chant is dependent on the text, and emphasizes the logical relationships of the words. Consequently the second function of the accents is to indicate the interrelationship of the words in the text. The accents are thus a good guide to the syntax of the text; but, since the reader was naturally presenting meaning, not structure, and accentuation marks semantic units, which are not always

---

1   WO'C, p. 177.
2   Schweizer, 1981, p. 38, n. 42.
3   WO'C, p. 633; see also p. 29.

identical with syntactic units."[1] According to Yeivin, the third function of the accents is to mark the position of the word stress.

It should be borne in mind that apparently the length of the verse has influence on the way the Masoretes placed the accents. Although scholars differ in opinion on the exact formulation of the principles which governed them in this respect,[2] the statement with which Yeivin ends the section on this topic should be underlined: "The longer the verse and the more complex the phrase, the more difficult it is to analyze this feature."[3]

In a discussion of the possibility of using the Masoretic accents for determining the limits of sentences in OTH, Andersen concludes: "The systems [of accentuation] are unfortunately of little value, for they are geared to written texts, they reflect liturgical artificiality and the units of 'verses' and subverses bear only partial correspondence to sentences as grammatical units."[4]

Despite these negative comments, we undertook the analysis of Ex 25 - 31 on the basis of the Masoretic accents to see what kind of structure it would yield. Only the main distinctive accents (nrs 1 - 7 in the list of BHS) have been used to divide the text into small entities, which we will call 'units'. In this way, it is possible to distinguish them from the text-entities which we hope to obtain in our next step and which we will call 'phrases.' Within each verse, the units have been numbered consecutively and arranged accordingly, e.g. : 26:201; 26:202, etc. The next page gives a sample of the result of this analysis.[5]The result of this step presents the structuring of the text according to the formal criterium of the Masoretic accents. It displays a number of features which can be considered remarkable from the point of view of modern, Western ideas on the structuring of texts. Sometimes units are 'too long'; they contain words which we would assign to a different unit. In other cases we feel they are 'too short'; we would not consider them as a separate unit, but incorporate them into a larger one. We will discuss these features in a number of sections, each of which corresponds to one of the most important grammatical categories, which we mentioned in the preceding paragraph. Hence, this paragraph contains sections on verb units (VU), noun units (NU), prepositional units (PU), and adverbial units (AU). The final section (8.3.6.) considers the result of this step of the analysis in general and assesses its value.

8.3.2. Verb units (VU).

All units which contain at least one verb form have been considered to be a VU. It is possible that a unit contains more than one verb form. This does not

---

1   Yeivin, 1980, p. 158.
2   o.c. , p. 171 - 176.
3   o.c. , p. 175 - 176.
4   Andersen, 1974, p. 21.
5   The complete result is available from the author at request.

Analysis of Exodus 25 - 31 according to the Masoretic accents.
(Example)

26;202	Q2	N0		
26;211	C3 Q2 C6	N0 S6	M2	
26;212	Q2 C6	N0		
26;213	P8 C6	Q9 N0 C6	Q9 Q2	
26;214	C3 Q2 C6	N0		
26;215	P8	Q9 N0 C6	Q9 Q2	
26;221	C3 P3 N0 C6	Q9 N0	N0 S7	
26;222	V3	Q2 C6	N0	
26;231	C3 Q2 C6	N0	V3	
26;232	P3 N0	Q9 N0		
26;233	P2 Q9 N0 S6			
26;241	V8	N0	P5 P3 P0	
26;242	C3 N0 S3			
26;243	V3	N0	P4 C7	N0 S3
26;244	P1 C7	Q9 N0	Q9 Q2	
26;245	A4 C6	V3	P3 Q2 S6	
26;246	P3 Q2 C6	Q9 N0	V3	
26;251	V2	Q2 C6	N0	
26;252	C3 N0 S6 C6	M2		
26;253	Q2 C6	Q2	N0	
26;254	Q2 C6	N0		
26;255	P8 C6	Q9 N0 C6	Q9 Q2	
26;256	C3 Q2 C6	N0		
26;257	P8	Q9 N0 C6	Q9 Q2	
26;261	V2	N0	M5 C6	M9
26;262	Q2			
26;263	P3 N0 C6	N0 C7	Q9 N0	Q9 Q2
26;271	C3 Q2 C6	N0		
26;272	P3 N0 C6	N0 C7	Q9 N0	Q9 Q2
26;273	C3 Q2 C6	N0		
26;274	P3 N0	N0 C6	Q9 N0	
26;275	P3 N0	N0S7		
26;281	C3 Q9 N0 C6	Q9 N0	P2 P0 C6	Q9 N0
26;282	V6			
26;283	P5 C7	Q9 N0	P1 C7	Q9 N0
26;291	C3 C4 C7	Q9 N0	V3	M1
26;292	C3 C4 C7	N0 S6	V3	M1
26;293	N0	P3 Q9 N0		
26;294	V2	C4 C7	Q9 N0	M1
26;301	V2	C4 C7	Q9 N0	

present a problem when only one of these is a finite form. All forms coded as V can be considered to be finite verbs, apart from V6 (participles) and V7 (infinitives).

Indeed, by far most VUs contain one finite form only, but 14 cases have been found with two or more. From a modern, Western view on the structure of language, it is surprising to include more than one finite verb form in one unit, but apparently it did not bother the Masoretes too much. The following verses contain a unit which shows this phenomenon:

25:40; 26:11; 28:07, 32, 35, 41, 43; 29:20, 27, 33; 30:20, 34; 31:11, 14.

It might be due to the fact that the verses concerned are of greater length than average, and, indeed, the average verse length of the chapters 28 and 29, which contain most of these cases, is somewhat higher than that of the other parts of the text. But the differences are relatively small and closer examination of the individual cases reveals that this factor can only account for a few cases (e.g. 29:20). We must therefore assume that other aspects play a role, such as the wish to indicate the close connection between the words concerned, or to put emphasis on another word or word-group. This latter point could be the case in 25:40 where בְּתַבְנִיתָם is singled out, and in 31:17, where וּבַיּוֹם הַשְּׁבִיעִי becomes a separate unit.

The grammars of OTH consider participles as occupying "... a middle place between the noun and the verb. In form they are simple nouns and most nearly related to the adjective."[1] It has already been pointed out that it is sometimes difficult to establish whether a word is a participle or a noun(see 8.2.2). Participles can form a unit on their own, such as מְשֻׁלָּבֹת in Ex 26:17, or govern a unit, such as סֹכְכִים בְּכַנְפֵיהֶם עַל־הַכַּפֹּרֶת in 25:20. But they occur also in units which are clearly dominated by a finite verb form.

The infinitives also have a position between verb and noun. In Ex 25 - 31 most infinitives occur preceded by a prepositional prefix. Only in three cases the infinitive absolute occurs, twice together with a finite form of the same verb, i.e. in the expression מוֹת יוּמָת in 31:14, 15. The infinitive stands on its own completely only once, i.e. in 30:36 וְשָׁחַקְתָּ מִמֶּנָּה הָדֵק.

8.3.3. Noun units (NU).

As expected the number of nouns in the text is very high, but most of them are constituents of other units. One noun or a series of nouns can form a separate type of unit which we call 'noun unit.' Occasionally a preposition may be incorporated in such a unit, as the following examples illustrate:

26:262 חֲמִשָּׁה;
26:211 וְאַרְבָּעִים אֲדָנֵיהֶם כֶּסֶף;
29:133 וְאֵת הַיֹּתֶרֶת עַל־הַכָּבֵד.

From a Western point of view it is quite surprising to notice that pieces of text

---

1   GKC, p. 355 - 356; see also WO'C, p. 612.

like these have been selected to form separate elements in the ordering of the whole text. It may be that they concern cases of 'casus pendens,'[1] in which certain parts of the text receive extra emphasis.

In addition there are units which are similar to the so-called 'nominal sentences,' e.g.25:102 אמתים וחצי ארכו.

8.3.4. Prepositional units (PU).

Although OTH contains a number of prepositions which can stand on their own, like למעלה, no units have been found which consist of one preposition only. But units which are clearly 'headed' by a preposition occur very frequently, e.g. Ex 25:124: על צלעו האחת. And in VUs, prepositions can play an important role, e.g. 25:161: ונתת אל־הארן.

8.3.5. Adverbial units (AU).

It is understandable that adverbs occur together with verbal forms in VUs. But a few cases have been found in which they occur apart and form a separate unit, which can be called an adverbial unit. In Ex 25:334 we find the following example: כן לששת הקנים.

8.3.6. General remarks.

Having completed this step, we would like to make the following remarks:

a. The Masoretic accents have their place in the linear sequence of the text: they separate words or put them together. It is not possible to arrive at a multi-layered structure, such as the 'trees' of modern linguistic analysis. An attempt to differentiate between units based on similar accents, brought to light that the 'value' of the accents is not absolute, but indeed seems to be dependent upon the textual environment.

b. Using only part of the distinctive accents has something arbitrary about it. Using all of them, however, would have led to a fragmentation of the text into very small word-groups, which could hardly be used in describing a structure of the text. So we decided to take a 'middle-route,' which would lead to reasonable results.

c. The linear structure which we obtained in this step, however, displays so many awkward phenomena that it is impossible to use it as the basis of an analysis of the text which also tries to remain within the sphere of the main modern views on language. So it is not suitable as the basic structure for our investigation.

d. At the same time it provides a lot of data about the ideas of the Masoretes regarding the problem of which words in the text should be grouped together and which should be kept separate. These data will be used in the next step, when we will analyze the text with a modern Western method.

---

1   see Gross, 1987; WO'C, p. 76 - 77.

8.4. Structuring the text according to the X-bar theory.

8.4.1. Introduction.
In this step of our investigation of Exodus 25 to 31, we analyze the text using a modern approach to the structure of language. In the next section we survey a few details of this approach and discuss some problems which we meet when applying it to OTH. The analysis results in a phrase structure of the text and the subsequent sections discuss the various types of phrases and their roles in the whole of it. Hence the separate sections bear the titles:

8.4.3. Verbal phrases (VP).

8.4.4. Noun Phrases (NP).

8.4.5. Prepositional Phrases (PP).

8.4.6. Adverbial Phrases (AP).

The so-called nominal sentences in OTH are considered in a separate section 8.4.7., whereas the final section discusses the general implications of this step of the analysis.

8.4.2. The X-bar theory and Old Testament Hebrew.
In section 4.4.4. , we already reviewed in some detail the work of Jackendoff on the structuring of space and spatial relations by language. We now concentrate on the more general aspects of the method he employs. The general outlines of this X-bar theory have been described by Jackendoff as follows:

"A primary distinction is customarily made between the lexical categories (or parts of speech) - e.g., Noun (N), Verb (V), Adjective (A), and Preposition (P) - and the phrasal categories - e,g., Noun Phrase (NP), Verb Phrase (VP), Adjective Phrase (AP), Prepositional Phrase (PP), and Sentence (S). Each phrasal category contains a head - a member of one of the lexical categories - plus a variety of possible modifiers, which are typically other phrasal categories. Corresponding to each lexical category there is a major phrasal category which maximizes the possible modifiers of the lexical category. The major phrasal category corresponding to N is NP; that corresponding to V is S."[1]

A major phrasal category may dominate a constituent belonging to a double-primed phrasal category (or X"); this in turn may dominate a constituent belonging to a single-primed phrasal category (X'), which itself may dominate the corresponding lexical category. The following scheme provides an illustration for the general case:

---

1   Jackendoff, 1985, p. 63 - 64.

Major phrasal category

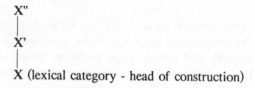

X''
|
X'
|
X (lexical category - head of construction)

Part of an example given by Jackendoff may further illustrate this approach:

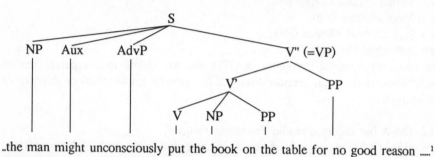

..the man might unconsciously put the book on the table for no good reason .....[1]
An introductory description of the application of the X-Bar theory to the Dutch language has been given by Scholten et al.[2] Leech discusses the historical and theoretical background of the transformational grammars to which it belongs.[3]
An advantage of its application by Jackendoff is that he starts from the surface-text and develops the phrase structure on that basis. This is in agreement with our wish to use a bottom-up strategy (see paragraph 6.4.). It also involves a method which covers language in its broadest sense, because it takes into account the various types of words within a particular language and the different phrases based upon them. At this point we meet a restriction, however: our knowledge of the details of properties and coordination of phrases in OTH is still limited, and this makes it impossible to use all aspects of the theory in their fullest detail.
In this connection, it should be kept in mind that the objective of our analysis is not the complete description of the structure of the text. As explained in chapter 6, we need a method of analysis which is broad enough to cover the whole of language (and of world), but our main aim is to investigate the text only in relation to a limited part of the world: space and spatial relations. In fact, the main reason for choosing the X-Bar theory for our analysis has been its use by Jackendoff for a similar purpose. We intend to discuss our results with its application to Exodus 25 to 31 in the light of other approaches to the structure

1   see o.c., p. 64 - 65.
2   Scholten, Evers, 1981, p. 76 - 98.
3   Leech, 1981, p. 342 - 348.

of texts in OTH.

Before we start the detailed description of this analysis, it is necessary to consider a few general points.

From the description of the theory given above, it is clear that one of its main phrasal categories is the sentence. It is not easy to give a proper definition of what a sentence is in OTH. Some grammars do not mention this problem at all and just start using the concept 'sentence' without any introduction.[1] Others simply declare that they do not wish to give a definition or think it to be superfluous.[2] In our opinion it is appropriate to give at least some indication of what is intended with the term sentence. As such we will use the definition given by Waltke and O'Connor: "We define a sentence as a linguistic unit not as large as a discourse but larger than those grammatical elements that cannot exist independently, but are syntactically dependent on one another within this larger linguistic unit; namely, the clause, the phrase, the word, the morpheme."[3] Of course, this definition does not specify exactly what a sentence is, but it gives some indication of its level and role within the analysis which we intend to perform: the sentence brings together a number of phrases into a structural entity, or singles out one phrase into that role.

At the same time, this definition calls for another problem: How do we determine the boundaries of a sentence? Schneider writes: "Zu einem Satz gehören alle Wörter, die sich in der Umgebung eines finiten Verbs diesem Verb zuordnen lassen."[4] Along the same lines, he states for nominal sentences, which he defines as sentences which contain ".... mindestens zwei Nomina oder Nominalgruppen .... , die so aufeinander bezogen sind daß eine Aussage vom Typ: 'A ist B' entsteht": "Zu einem solchen Satz gehören alle Wörter, die sich einem der beiden Glieder der Aussage zuordnen lassen."[5] It is clear that in this approach the judgment of the investigator will sometimes be necessary. It is possible to use the wellknown sentence opening forms of OTH, such as verbal forms starting with ו, and a number of particles, such as כִּי, אֲשֶׁר, etc. Very often we can consider as a separate sentence each opening form together with all phrases which follow it, up to the next opening form in the text. But there are cases in which this procedure fails, because no proper opening form is present in the boundary-area between two sentences. In that case a decision on how to assign phrases to different sentences has to be made by taking into account either the relative importance of the Masoretic accents or factors from context or contents.

The nominal sentences which we defined above occur quite frequently in OTH.

---

1   Lettinga, 1976; Sawyer, 1976.
2   Brockelmann, 1956; Schweizer, 1981.
3   WO'C, p. 79.
4   Schneider, 1985, p. 159 - 60.
5   o.c. , p. 160.

This means that, whereas it is true that the major phrasal category corresponding to V is the sentence S, in OTH not all sentences contain a V as their main lexical category.

Some scholars consider all sentences which do not have a verb form in their first position as nominal sentences. Schneider distinguishes between simple nominal sentences (which have no verb form at all) and "Zusammengesetzte Nominalsätze," which have a verb form in one of the later positions of the sentence.[1] In line with Jackendoff's method of analysis, we will include our discussion of these 'complex nominal sentences' under the heading of the appropriate verbal phrases in section 8.4.3.

Since we decided earlier not to distinguish between substantives and adjectives, in the present step we will have one phrasal category covering both, which will be called Noun Phrase (NP). The other phrasal categories in our analysis are Verb Phrase (VP), Prepositional Phrase (PP), and Adverbial Phrase (AP).[2] In addition to these phrases the following particles have been included into the structure of the text: אֲשֶׁר = C1; כִּי = C2; ו or וֹ = C3; אֵ = C5.

Using the approach which we described above, the whole text of Exodus 25 - 31 has been divided into phrases and all phrases have been grouped into sentences. Within each verse, the sentences have been distinguished by assigning them a code consisting of the notation of the verse and a letter, e.g. 26:20A; 26:20B, etc.

Sometimes sentences are clearly connected with a NP which, either directly or through another phrase, is part of another sentence. These 'embedded sentences' have not been included into the main structure of the text.

Noun Phrases which occur at the same level and play a similar role in a sentence, and stand beside each other or are joined together by the conjunctive וֹ (C3), have been coded as one phrase NPL. Noun Phrases within series like this to which an embedded sentence has been attached have been coded separately, in order to be able to show clearly, at what point of the main sentence, the embedded sentence is attached.

In the printout of the analysis, every verbal form has been indicated as a separate verb phrase, whereas the type of the verb has been specified in agreement with table 8;1. Every group of phrases belonging together and containing one verbal phrase has been considered as a sentence. In the printout, all phrases belonging to one sentence have been written on one line; this applies to the nominal sentences as well. In case the sentence is too long, it is continued on the next line, which carries the same code. Sentences within the main structure of the text start at the beginning of the line; embedded sentences start below the phrase to which they are attached and have the same code as the main sentence with an additional number.

---

1   Schneider, 1985, p. 161; see also Niccacci, 1990, p. 23.
2   This abbreviation is used in a way which is different from Jackendoff's.

A sample page of the result is given on the next page.[1]

8.4.3. Verb Phrases (VP).
8.4.3.1. Introduction.
Since most sentences within the text are headed by a VP, we include in this section of the paragraph a discussion of the sentence structure of the text in general. Table 8;2 collects some data in this respect. The first column gives the type of the sentence, whereas the subsequent columns list the total number of sentences of that type, the number of those occurring in the main structure of the text and of those that are embedded sentences. The table also specifies data for the nominal sentences and for the total number of all sentences together, according to our analysis of Exodus 25 - 31.

In our discussion of its sentence structure, we will pay attention to Niccacci's presentation of the syntax of the verb. Following Weinrich, he distinguishes between "two sets of tenses with separate functions. Group I 'discourse' or 'comment'; Group II functioning as 'narrative.' The first or second person is used chiefly in Group I, the third person in group II."[2] In addition, he considers two other aspects of the text: emphasis, which he differentiates into foreground and background, and linguistic perspective, where he has three categories: "retrieved information (flashback, 'antecedent' to the ensuing account), degree zero (the level of the story itself), anticipated information ('disclosure,' reveals the end of the story)."[3] Although he describes these latter two aspects for narratives only, in the course of his book it appears that he uses them in a similar way for discourses.

Table 8;2.

Type of phrase	Total	Main structure	Embedded sentences
V1P	15	5	10
V2P	220	220	
V3P	143	125	18
V4P	9	9	
V5P	11	11	
V6P	37	11	26
V7P	64		64
V8P	5	5	
Total verbal sentences	504	386	118
Nominal sentences	172	154	18
Total number of sentences	676	540	136

---

1   The complete result is available from the author at request.
2   Niccacci, 1990, p. 19.
3   o.c. , p. 20.

Analysis of Exodus 25 - 31 according to the X-bar theory.
(Example)

26;19A	C3	NP	V3P	PP		
26;19B	NP	PP	PP			
26;19C	C3	NP	PP	PP		
26;20A	C3	PP	PP	NP		
26;21A	C3	NP	NP			
26;21B	NP	PP				
26;21C	C3	NP	PP			
26;22A	C3	PP	V3P	NP		
26;23A	C3	NP	V3P	PP	PP	
26;24A	V8P	NP	PP			
26;24B	C3	NP	V3P	NP	PP	PP
26;24C	AP	V3P	PP			
26;24D	PP	V3P				
26;25A	V2P	NPL	NP			
26;25B	NP	PP				
26;25C	C3	NP	PP			
26;26A	V2P	NP	NP	NP	PP	
26;27A	C3	NP	PP			
26;27B	C3	NP	PP			
26;28A	C3	NP	PP	V6P	PP	PP
26;29A	C3	NP	V3P	NP		
26;29B	C3	NP	V3P	NP		
26;29C	NP	PP				
26;29D	V2P	NP	NP			
26;30A	V2P	NP	AP			
26;30A1			C1	V1P	PP	
26;31A	V2P	NP	NPL			
26;31B	NP	V3P	NP	NP		
26;32A	V2P	NP	PP			
26;32A1			V6P	NP		
26;32B	NP	PP				
26;33A	V2P	NP	PP			
26;33B	V2P	AP	PP	PP	NP	
26;33C	V2P	NP	PP	PP	C3	PP
26;34A	V2P	NP	PP	PP		
26;35A	V2P	NP	PP	PP		
26;35B	C3	NP	PP	PP		
26;35C	C3	NP	V3P	PP		

A preliminary look at Exodus 25 - 31 makes clear that it belongs to the discourse-type of text. It starts with a narrative introduction: וַיְדַבֵּר יְהוָה אֶל־מֹשֶׁה לֵּאמֹר, which is followed by an imperative: דַּבֵּר. The remainder of the text can be considered as the consequence of this imperative.

In the following parts of this section, we will briefly examine the various types of sentences as distinguished by their verb phrase.

8.4.3.2. Verb phrases with Perfect (V1P).
These occur 15 times, 10 of which are relative clauses starting with אֲשֶׁר and forming embedded sentences. In all of them, the VP immediately follows אֲשֶׁר and in six cases it is clear that they refer to past information.

All five sentences which belong to the main structure of the text occur in chapter 31. Three are in 1 c.s. conjugation and two in 3 m.s., whereas all of them refer to יְהוָה as the acting subject.

8.4.3.3. Verb phrases with We-Perfect (V2P).
With 220 occurrences this type of verb phrase is the most frequent one used in the text. This is in agreement with Niccacci's presentation of this verb form as one of the 'continuation forms' of the discourse. It looks as if these sentences fulfill more than one role in the text. Those who are in the 2 m.s. conjugation can be seen as continuations of the imperative style of the discourse. But those for which the conjugation depends on the subject seem to play another role. This applies to all forms of this type of the verb הָיָה. In paragraph 8.6., where we hope to examine the structure of a number of parts of the text in more detail, we will come back on this point.

Because of its nature, this verb form is always the opening word of the sentence. Two cases have been found where it forms the whole VP, and thus the whole sentence:

Ex 28:07 וְחֻבָּר, and Ex 28:43 וָמֵתוּ.

In both cases, the Masoretes included the words into larger units, which contained more than one finite verb form (see section 8.4.3.1.). In the rest of the phrases the V2P is followed by a number of NPs and PPs, which in 80 percent does not exceed two. Hence most of the verbal phrases with We-Perfectum belong to one of the following types:

V2P	NP	
V2P	PP	
V2P	NP	NP
V2P	NP	PP
V2P	PP	NP
V2P	PP	PP

Because of these conditions V2Ps exhibit a somewhat uniform character, and do not have the possibility of variation which other types of VP can demonstrate. At the same time it must be said that longer V2Ps occur, e.g.

וְעָשִׂיתָ עַל־הֲרֹשֶׁת אַרְבַּע טַבְּעֹת נְחֹשֶׁת עַל אַרְבַּע קְצוֹתָיו (Ex 27:04), the phrase structure of which reads: V2P PP NP PP.

8.4.3.4. Verb Phrases with Imperfect (V3P).
In total 143 phrases headed by a V3 have been found in the text, 18 of which occur in embedded sentences, which means that only 125 belong to the main structure of the text.
All 18 embedded sentences start with the relative pronoun אֲשֶׁר and in all of them the verb phrase immediately follows the pronoun. In many cases it is clear from the context that they refer to the future.
None of the V3P-sentences in the main structure of the text start with the verb phrase. This means that all of them belong to the class of the complex noun clauses, as distinguished by Niccacci. As in the previous sub-section, this is in agreement with his approach of discourse-texts.[1]
Usually sentences of this type contain a number of NPs, PPs and APs, which in 75 percent of the cases does not exceed 2. Some exceptionally long ones occur as well. Because it is possible to start with a NP or PP they show more variation in the order of the sentence than the sentences with V2Ps. In paragraph 8.6., we will consider the possibility that these various forms of this sentence fulfil different roles in the text.

8.4.3.5. Verb Phrases with Wa-Imperfect (V4P).
This verb form, which is typical for the narrative form of text, occurs 9 times. Seven of these relate to the speaking of the Lord: וַיְדַבֵּר יהוה אֶל מֹשֶׁה לֵאמֹר (25:01; 30:11, 17, 22; 31:01) or וַיֹּאמֶר יהוה אֶל מֹשֶׁה (Ex 30:34; 31:12). They have been used to arrange the text in seven units, which, however, are of very unequal size.
The other two cases occur in the last verses of the text. The form וַיִּנָּפַשׁ (31:17) is unique, since in the result of our analysis, it forms a sentence on its own. But the Masoretes saw no problem in leaving it within the same unit as the preceding perfect verb form. The form וַיִּתֵּן is the first word of verse 31:18, which seems to be a concluding remark of the whole text in narrative form.

8.4.3.6. Verb phrases with We-Imperfect (V8P).
This form only occurs five times, three of which are the direct continuation of a sentence which contains an instruction: 25:02; 27:20 and 28:28. In 31:02, it has the l.c.s. conjugation and seems to refer to a future action following an initial announcement.
Regarding the fifth case (26:24), other textual witnesses suggest that it should be considered as a WePerfect.

---

1   o.c. , p. 170.

8.4.3.7. Verb phrases with Imperative (V5P).

A number of sentences with an imperative occur after reports of the speaking of the Lord (in the narrative form): 25:02; 30:23, 34; 31:02, 13. In 29:01, it also forms the beginning of an instruction from the Lord.

Ex 25:40 contains two imperatives, the first one of the verb רָאָה, the second one of עָשָׂה. The first one seems to act as a kind of introductory formula (see also 31:02), whereas the emphasis is on the second one. In 28:01 the phrase וְאַתָּה seems to fulfil this role.

In 25:19 other textual witnesses read an Imperfect, which, if true, would be the only sentence in the text starting with this form (see above 8.4.3.4.).

It is remarkable that in most cases the imperative phrase does not form the first word of the sentence.

8.4.3.8. Verb phrases with the Participle (V6P).

As already mentioned, participles are thought to have a position half-way between verbs and nouns (see above section 8.3.2.). In order not to lose any forms with verbal function, we decided to consider a participle as forming a NP only in those cases where it was clearly attached to a noun in an adjectival function. Examples of these are מָאְדָּמִים in Ex 25:05 and מָשְׁזָר in 26:01. In all other cases the participle has been counted as a verbal form, and hence as the head of a V6P.

Three of these sentences, however, were found to contain a V3P as well. The latter was considered to be the head of the phrase (and thus of the sentence), with the V6P seen as one of the constituents.

In 26 cases, it is possible to explain in a reasonable way that a V6P is attached to a NP belonging to a sentence of the main structure of the text. All these sentences have been considered as embedded sentences.

As a result, only 11 cases remain in which a V6P-sentence belongs to the main structure of the text; e.g.: מִן־הַקָּצֶה וְהַבְּרִיחַ הַתִּיכֹן בְּתוֹךְ הַקְּרָשִׁים מַבְרִחַ אֶל־הַקָּצֶה (Ex 26:28).

8.4.3.9. Verb phrases with an Infinitive (V7P).

All three cases of Infinitive Absolute have been considered as constituents of the phrases to which they belong, and which are headed by other (finite) verbal forms.

The other 64 V7-forms all occur as constituents of a PP in sentences in the main structure of the text or in embedded sentences. All of these have been considered to act as head of an (additional) embedded sentence. The result is that all infinitive constructs occur outside the main structure of the text. Sometimes these embedded sentences only consist of the verbal form, e.g. לֵאמֹר in Ex 25:01, sometimes they contain a few additional phrases,e.g. לָשֵׂאת אֶת־הָאָרֹן בָּהֶם in 25:14.

This type of phrase shows an uneven distribution over the text: only 7 of them occur in Ex 25 - 27, whereas the chapters 28 - 31 contain 57.

197

8.4.4. Noun Phrases (NP).

The Noun Phrases within the text show a considerable diversity.

The most simple are those consisting of one noun, pronoun or suffix only. In case one noun is modified by the nota accusativi or the article it is also not difficult to determine the extent of the NP. The same applies to a suffix with nota accusativi.

Problems arise, however, when it is possible to consider a number of nouns, each of which forms a simple NP, as forming together a NP of higher level. As far as English is concerned, this point has been discussed by Jackendoff,[1] whereas for OTH useful data are available in the grammars under headings such as 'modification of nouns' or 'genitive.'[2]

We will illustrate this problem for this step of our analysis by discussing a few examples from Ex 25 to 31:

a. The first phrase of Ex 25:10 reads: וְעָשׂוּ אֲרוֹן עֲצֵי שִׁטִּים; in the (simplified) code of the previous step this reads: V2 Na Nb Nc . The words Nb and Nc are connected in two ways:
- by the grammatical concept of status constructus;
- by a conjunctive Masoretic accent.

So it seems justified to consider them together as one NP (or N' in the terminology of Jackendoff).

The following point to look at is: do this N' and Na together form another 'NP of higher order'? Between Na and the first word of N', we find a tifha, one of the distinctive accents and a clear grammatical signal is lacking. From the absence of the article with Na, it might be concluded that N' is intended to give Na a definite status, which means that both belong together, and should be translated as "the sittim-wooden ark." Nevertheless, it seems justified to keep them separate, which leads to the following phrase-structure for this sentence: V2P NP NP.

b. Ex 25:13 demonstrates another problem. Its first words are: וְעָשִׂיתָ בַדֵּי עֲצֵי שִׁטִּים. Here there is a clear case of status constructus between Na and the first word of N'. But again, we find a distinctive Masoretic accent (tifha). In this case, where we are confronted with conflicting formal signals, it was decided to give priority to the Masoretic accents, which led to separated phrases, and the same phrase-structure as in the previous case: V2P NP NP.

c. Sometimes many nouns of the same or similar scope follow each other in the text, such as in Ex 28:06: וְעָשׂוּ אֶת־הָאֵפֹד זָהָב תְּכֵלֶת וְאַרְגָּמָן תּוֹלַעַת שָׁנִי וְשֵׁשׁ מָשְׁזָר מַעֲשֵׂה חֹשֵׁב. The atnah is between הָאֵפֹד and זָהָב, so in line with the preceeding example we will consider אֶת־הָאֵפֹד as one NP, which is clearly separate from the rest of the verse. On formal grounds we can

---

1   Jackendoff, 1985, p. 66.
2   GKC, p. 410 - 429; WO'C, p. 73 - 74, 136 - 160, 226 - 234.

also see together as separate NPs שֵׁשׁ מָשְׁזָר and מַעֲשֵׂה חֹשֵׁב, since in each case both nouns are connected by a conjunctive accent. In addition we recognize in the series of words from תְּכֵלֶת to מָשְׁזָר a combination of materials which occurs in the text a number of times.[1] So it seems justified to consider these nouns together, as one lengthy Noun Phrase, a NPL. The other 'materials', זָהָב and מַעֲשֵׂה חֹשֵׁב, have been maintained as separate NPs. So the structure for 28:06 reads: V2P NP NP NPL NP.

d. There are also cases in which the object to be constructed and the construction-material to be used are connected together; for example in 25:11, the end of which reads: וְעָשִׂיתָ עָלָיו זֵר זָהָב סָבִיב. Here the only words which are connected by a conjunctive accent are זֵר and זָהָב, so that the phrase structure becomes: V2P PP NP NP. It should be noticed that the word סָבִיב, which has been coded as an adverb, is considered as a noun in this step of the analysis.

From these examples, it will be clear that the demarcation of the NPs within the text, is not always a simple matter. Quite often, the available 'formal criteria' alone are not sufficient for obtaining a proper decision. Even the incorporation of the meaning of the nouns concerned does not solve all the problems involved. In sentences with verb phrases, it is necessary to consider also the features of the verb concerned. In this respect, the maximum number of 'objects,' which the verb can 'coordinate,' is important.

As expected, NPs show a wide variety and have a wide occurrence in the text. They may be constituents of Prepositional and Adverbial Phrases. They also fulfil many referential functions as will become apparent in the paragraphs to follow.

8.4.5. Prepositional Phrases (PP).

The structure of PPs is very simple. They always consist of a preposition followed by a NP or a verbal infinitive. The last group of PPs has already been considered in sub-section 8.4.3.9. Regarding the first group, occasionally the problem of determining the end of the phrase is similar to that of determining the end of NPs, as discussed in 8.4.4.

Sometimes prepositions occur together in what seem to be, 'fixed combinations,' e.g. מִחוּץ לַפָּרֹכֶת (Ex 26:35) and בֵּינִי וּבֵין בְּנֵי יִשְׂרָאֵל (Ex 31:17). These have been considered as separate PPs, so that the phrase structure of these text-fragments becomes: PP PP, and PP C3 PP, respectively.

Most PPs are included in sentences with VPs or in nominal sentences. Only rarely they stand on their own and then often in an embedded sentence with אֲשֶׁר, as in the second part of 25:26, the phrases structure of which reads:

V2P NP PP   וְנָתַתָּ אֶת־הַטַּבָּעֹת עַל אַרְבַּע הַפֵּאֹת

Cl PP   אֲשֶׁר לְאַרְבַּע רַגְלָיו

---

1   see Ex. 26:31, 36; 27:16; 28:08, 15.

8.4.6. Adverbial Phrases (AP).

An AP may consist of an adverb alone, e.g. לֹא, שָׁם, כֵּן, or of an adverb (possibly in prefixed form) with a NP to which an embedded sentence (with אֲשֶׁר) may be attached. The words כַּאֲשֶׁר and כְּכֹל אֲשֶׁר have been considered as an AP in the sentence of the main structure, with an embedded sentence attached to them.

It should be borne in mind that NPs and PPs also may have an adverbial function. But in this step of the analysis, we only discuss the phrases as based on the grammatical category of their major constituent.

8.4.7. Nominal Sentences (NS).

These are sentences which do not have a Verb Phrase as their heading category. They consist of one or more NPs, PPs or APs.

Also in this case we meet the problem of determining the boundaries of each NS. In this respect we will adopt a 'generous attitude,' which means that we will accept as many separate NSs as is reasonably possible. Two examples may illustrate the application of this attitude:

a. In the final part of Ex 25:10, we recognize the following three NSs:

NP NP	אמתים וחצי ארכו
C3 NP NP	ואמה וחצי רחבו
C3 NP NP	ואה וחצי קמתו

which have the phrase structure indicated at the left.

b. Ex 26:02 contains 4 separate NSs:

NP NP PP	ארך היריעה האחת שמנה ועשרים באמה
C3 NP NP PP	ורחב ארבע באמה
NP	היריעה האחת
NP NP	מדה אחת לכל־היריעת

the phrase structure of which is again given at the left of each sentence.

Both examples also show a number of types of NSs, which indeed occur in a wide variety of structure. Perhaps the most noteworthy is the occurrence of an NS, consisting of one NP only. Of course, it is possible to assign it to one of the neighbouring sentences. But it is clearly demarcated by Masoretic accents and seems to fulfill a double role: summarizing the previous sentence and introducing the following one. For these reasons, it was decided to consider it as a separate NS.

From table 8;2, it is clear that NSs represent a substantial proportion of the sentences in the result of our analysis of the text. According to Niccacci, who calls them simple noun clauses (SNC), they can mark both the foreground of the communication and its background in discourse type of texts.[1] The word order in nominal sentences has been discussed recently by Waltke and O'Connor.[2]

8.4.8. General remarks.

a. Although the X-bar theory has been developed for Western languages, it has proved possible to use it for the analysis of a text in OTH. This analysis resulted in a structure using phrases as the basic components and coordinating these phrases stepwise into higher order constructs.

b. In our analysis, we distinguished between a limited number of types of phrases only. As with Jackendoff's investigation, it may be that a further refinement will be required, in view of the relation between the various roles within the whole of the text, and the types of phrases used to fulfill these roles.

c. In this paragraph, we compared the result only briefly with the ideas as outlined by Niccacci.[3] There seems to exist general agreement as far as the relation between the distribution of types of sentences and the nature of the text is concerned.

8.5. The structure of the text: a survey in some detail.

8.5.1. Introduction.

In the previous paragraph we applied the X-Bar theory to the text and gave an initial description of the resulting phrase structure. In this paragraph we continue our investigation by studying in more detail a number of aspects of this structure.

The text has been divided into a number of fragments, each of which describes the instructions regarding a certain object. Since the aim of our investigation is the study of space and spatial relations, we limit our detailed examination of the text to those fragments covering topics which are thought to be relevant in this respect. These fragments have been grouped under three headings which will be reviewed in sections 8.5.3., 8.5.4. and 8.5.5. of this paragraph. The inventory at the top of page 202 shows what individual fragments of the text can be found in the separate sections.

In our selection of these fragments, we left out those parts of the text which are of introductory character or describe procedures and materials for the cult. It was not always possible, however, completely to separate relevant and irrelevant parts of the text in a reasonable way, so it has been accepted that some of the fragments contain a number of less relevant sentences.

---

1   Niccacci, 1990, p. 171.
2   WO'C, p.130 - 135; see also Andersen, 1970.
3   Niccacci, 1990.

8.5.3. Objects for the cult.

a.	The ark	Ex 25:10 - 16
b.	The mercy seat	17 - 22
c.	The table	23 - 30
d.	The lampstand	31 - 40
e.	The altar of burnt offering	27:01 - 08
f.	The altar of incense	30:01 - 10
g.	The laver of bronze	17 - 18

8.5.4. The tabernacle and court.

a.	The curtains of linen	Ex 26:01 - 06
b.	The curtains of goats' hair	07 - 14
c.	The frames	15 - 25
d.	The bars	26 - 30
e.	The veil	31 - 37
f.	The court	27:09 - 19

8.5.5. The garments.

a.	The priests and their garments	Ex 28:01 - 05
b.	The ephod	06 - 14
c.	The breastpiece	15 - 21
d.	The chains, etc.	22 - 30
e.	The robe	31 - 35
f.	The golden plate	36 - 38
g.	The coat	39 - 43

All fragments contain more or less elaborate instructions for making the object concerned and most of them end with a statement saying what to do with the object or how to use it. Usually this is of small size and has been included in the fragment as explained above. As a result, the division into fragments generally follows the division of the text in the BHS. Only in the case of the altar of incense and of the laver (8.5.3.f. and g.), the final verses, which describe its use, are much larger in number as compared to those giving the orders for its construction. So in these two cases, we decided to limit the fragment to the 'construction verses' only.

It appears that there are some aspects regarding the types of sentence used in the text which are common to all fragments. These will be discussed in the next section, 8.5.2., prior to the sections which contain the more detailed review of the fragments of each heading according to the list given above. Following this survey is a section (8.5.6.) in which we pay attention to the relation between the type of sentence and the role(s) it can play in the text. The final section (8.5.7.) contains the general remarks concerning this step of the analysis.

202

8.5.2. General features of the fragments.

The majority of the fragments use a limited number of phrase-types as will be apparent from table 8;3 (see next page). The first column of this table specifies the object concerned, whereas the total number of phrases in the main structure of the fragment is given in the second one. The following three columns contain the number of the most frequent phrase types, whereas column 6 specifies in each case the less frequent types of phrases in the main structure of the text. The next column gives the total number of embedded sentences which is followed by two columns giving the number of V7P-phrases and that of Nominal Sentences, whereas again the final column specifies the other types of phrases.

From a comparison of table 8;2 (see above sub-section 8.4.3.1.) and table 8;3, it appears that the distribution of sentence-types in those fragments selected for our detailed analysis is very similar to that of the whole text. It is true, however, that the fragments collected under heading 2 differ from those in the other two headings by having a much higher proportion of Nominal Sentences. In addition, within each heading there are one or two fragments which show a pattern which deviates considerably from that of the other fragments in it.

The sentence-types occurring most frequently in the main structure, are:
- WePerfect sentences (V2Ps);
- Nominal sentences (NSs);
- Imperfect sentences (V3Ps).

As already noticed above (see section 8.4.8.), this is in general agreement with the presentation of the syntax of the Hebrew verb as outlined by Niccacci.[1] It should be remembered that Koch used the various types of sentences to distinguish between two main styles in the text, which led him to assume the existence of different genres and sources.[2] His approach has been criticized heavily, however (see above section 7.2.4.), in particular by Utzschneider, who himself recognizes a number of syntax-types in the text.[3] According to him the WePerfect-forms are used to introduce new activities in the construction of the ark and the other objects. In his concluding remarks of his analysis of Exodus 25 - 27, Niccacci seems to agree with this: "A chain of coordinated weQATALs expressing a series of orders/instructions is attested. The chain can be interrupted by a simple noun clause to describe a detail within the discourse or it can be interrupted by a compound noun clause of the (WAW-)x-YIQTOL type to emphasize a detail of this kind. The chain of narrative WAYYIQTOLs corresponds to the weQATAL chain, the (WAW-)x-QATAL construction corresponds to (WAW-)x-YIQTOL, while the simple noun clause remains

1   Niccacci, 1990.
2   Koch, 1959.
3   Utzschneider, 1988, p. 190 - 194.

unchanged."[1] This final comment relates to a comparison of the structure of the 'instruction-text' of Ex 25 - 31 with the 'execution-text' of Ex 35 - 40.

Table 8;3.

1. The objects of the cult.

verb	a	b	c	d	e	f	g	total
Main structure.								
V2P	9	6	12	4	12	7	3	53
V3P	3	4	2	4	5	4		22
V4P							1	1
V5P		1		2				3
V6P				4				4
NS	5	3	3	9	5	7	1	33
tot.	17	14	17	23	22	18	5	116

Embedded Sentences.								
V1P					1			1
V3P	1	2	1			1		5
V6P		2		3				5
V7P	1		1		2	1	2	7
NS	-	2	1	-	-	2	-	5
tot.	2	6	3	3	3	4	2	23

2. The tabernacle and the court.

verb	a	b	c	d	e	f	total
Main structure.							
V2P	4	9	3	3	11	1	31
V3P	6	3	7	2	2		20
V6P	2		1	1		1	5
V8P			1				1
NS	4	10	10	3	3	23	53
tot.	16	22	22	9	16	25	110

Embedded sentences.							
V1P				1			1
V6P		3			1		4
V7P		1					1
NS	1	1		-	-		2
tot.	1	5		1	1		8

---

1   Niccacci, 1990, p. 85 - 86.

3. The garments.

verb	a	b	c	d	e	f	g	total
Main structure.								
V2P	3	8	2	13	5	7	10	48
V3P	2	5	6	2	4	1	5	25
V5P	1						1	2
V8P				1				1
NS	2	3	8	—	4	1	2	20
tot.	8	16	16	16	13	9	18	96

Embedded sentences.								
V1P	1							1
V3P	1					1		2
V6P		2						2
V7P	4			3	3		4	14
NS	—	1		1	—	—	—	2
tot.	6	3		4	3	1	4	21

The following scheme gives the totals of all types of sentences for both the main structure and the embedded sentences of all fragments together:

	V1P	V2P	V3P	V4P	V5P	V6P	V7P	V8P	NS	Tot
main struct.	-	132	67	1	5	9	-	2	106	322
embedd. sent.	3	-	7	-	-	11	22	-	9	52

But Andersen has already indicated that some of the WePerfect forms "predict standing results, and do not prescribe specific acts."[1] In addition, Talstra has pointed to the fact that in a number of cases the verbal forms in Ex 25 - 31 are the same as in Ex 35 - 40.[2] These are indications that the assignment of a particular role in the text to a certain sentence-type is a complicated process which requires careful consideration of all factors which may be of influence.

From the quotation of Niccacci given above, it appears that he assumes three roles and three sentence-types which can nicely be coordinated, according to a one-to-one distribution:
- order/instruction   WePerfect;
- description of detail in the discourse   Nominal Sentence;
- emphasis on 'a detail of this kind'[3]   Imperfect.

---

1   Andersen, 1974, p. 71.
2   Talstra, 1982, p. 33.
3   It is not completely clear what he exactly means by this expression.

This is in line with his general approach in which he, following Schneider,[1] distinguishes between 'major' and 'minor' verbal forms within a particular type of text. De Regt, however, has already questioned whether such a distinction should be presupposed, when analyzing a textual corpus.[2] Indeed, in the fragments of Exodus 25 - 31 which we included in our analysis, we can distinguish, for the WePerfect-sentences only, among the following three roles:
a. Order/instruction for making the object or part of it.
b. Indication of certain details of the manufactured object.
c. Instruction for handling or using the object.
The roles a. and c. are in agreement with Niccacci's approach and can be found readily. Examples of role b. are present in Ex 25:20, 27:05, 27:07, all WePerfects of the verb היה. An example of the same form of another verb is 26:33 (with the hiph'il of בדל). So it appears that the indicative role, which Niccacci calls descriptive and which he restricts to the simple noun clause only, can also be fulfilled by verbal sentences, such as the WePerfect and the Imperfect. Examples of the latter can be found in Ex 25:15, 20, 27; 27:02. When used as instruction, these verbal forms usually are in the 2 m.s. (sometimes in the 3 m.p.) conjugation, but in the indicative role, their conjugation is in agreement with the object to which they refer. In a number of cases of this type, the 'counterpart' in the 'narrative account' in Ex 35 - 40 has the same verb-form; for example, 36:29 is identical to 26:24, and 36:30 to 26:25.

Considered purely formally, these sentences could be seen as 'narrative inserts' within a discourse-type of text,[3] along the same lines as it is assumed that discourse-like texts can be included in narratives.[4] At the same time, these indicative sentences seem to play a part in the instructions for the making of the objects. Even the NSs seem to carry an 'instruction-charge,' especially in fragments in which they constitute the main type of sentence, such as in Ex 27:09 - 19.

These preliminary observations show that the relation between sentence-type and role in the text requires more investigation. After our more detailed exploration of the structure of the various fragments in the three sections to come, we will consider this point again in section 8.5.6.

8.5.3. The objects for the cult.
8.5.3.1. Introduction.
Most of the fragments under this heading have a number of elements in common:

---

1   Schneider, 1985, p. 183.
2   De Regt, 1988, p. 52.
3   Schneider, 1985, p. 199.
4   see Niccacci, 1990, p. 102ff.

- General order for the construction of the object.
- Indication of the dimensions of the object.
- Instruction for additional processing.
- Instruction for making components.
- Final instruction for the place and use of the object.

The fragment on the lampstand forms an exception since it has a different structure and also shows a distribution of sentence-types which is different from the other fragments. We will therefore discuss it in a separate sub-section: 8.5.3.7.

The text-fragments for the other objects usually contain additional instructions for making auxiliary objects to be used in connection with the object. But despite these differences, a general pattern can be recognized in all these fragments and this will be discussed step by step in the subsequent sub-sections.

8.5.3.2. General order for construction.

The introductory sentence is of the form: V2P   NP   NP, in which:
 - V2P = וְעָשִׂיתָ;
 - the first NP refers to the object;
 - the second NP refers to the construction material.

Exceptions are:

a. the fragment on the altar of incense, which begins as follows:

V2P NP	וְעָשִׂיתָ מִזְבֵּחַ מִקְטַר קְטֹרֶת
NP V3P NP	עֲצֵי שִׁטִּים תַּעֲשֶׂה אֹתוֹ

This construction is remarkable because it introduces the construction material in a separate   Imperfect sentence. This may be due to the fact that the NP of the object is unusually long.

b. the fragment on the laver of bronze, which not only starts with a WaImperfect sentence, but where the construction material is connected with the object to form one NP only. Hence the structure for the general order of construction is: V2P   NP.

8.5.3.3. Dimensions of the object.

Usually the introductory sentence is followed by details of the dimensions, which are given in nominal sentences of the type: NP NP, in which the first NP denotes the size of the dimension concerned, and the second one the dimension concerned which is modified by a suffix referring to the object. The second and third sentence, if present, carry an initial וְ. For example the dimensions of the ark read (25:10):

NP NP	אַמָּתַיִם וָחֵצִי אָרְכּוֹ
C3 NP NP	וְאַמָּה וָחֵצִי רָחְבּוֹ
C3 NP NP	וְאַמָּה וָחֵצִי קֹמָתוֹ

The indications for both altars contain a separate sentence which refers to the fact that they are square; it has the structure NP   V3P, in which NP is רָבוּעַ, and the verb is הָיָה. In the case of the altar of burnt offering it also contains the grammatical subject הַמִּזְבֵּחַ, hence has the form: NP   V3P   NP. The text of this object also differs from the others by the fact that in the first two sentences the suffix to the dimension is missing.

The text for the breastpiece (see 8.5.5.) also contains a sentence telling that it is square; in this case, however, it precedes the sentences about the dimensions.

8.5.3.4. Additional processing.

For the objects to be made of wood, viz. the ark, the table, and both altars, after the intitial instruction and the details regarding the measures, there follow instructions for coating of the object. They start with a sentence of the structure V2P NP NP, in which the first NP refers to the object, and the second one to the material with which the object should be coated, זהב טהור for ark, table and altar of incense, and נחשת for the altar of burnt offering.

This main structure applies for the table only; the sections on coating for the other objects show the following additional characteristics:

- regarding the ark the main instruction is followed by a sentence specifying that the coating should cover both inside and outside of the ark; it has the structure (25:11):

PP C3 PP V3P NP   מבית ומחוץ תצפנו

- as far as the altar of burnt offering is concerned, it is noteworthy that the instruction for coating follows after the instruction for making the קרנת, which is made immediately after the general instruction for the construction of the altar.

- regarding the altar of incense the קרנת are also mentioned first in a nominal sentence, whereas the order for coating which has the usual form V2P NP NP, is followed by nominal sentences which read (30:03):

NP C3 NP NP   את־גגו ואת־קירתיו סביב
C3 NP   ואת־קרנתיו

Apparently this refers to a few extra components of the altar, including the קרנת. The role of סביב is not completely clear: it might be an additional phrase to the preceding NP or form an Adverbial Phrase to the process of the coating (see below, sub-section 8.6.2.5.).

8.5.3.5. Construction of components.
8.5.3.5.1. Introduction.

The instructions for making the objects contain in each case references to additional components. In this section we will discuss those components which occur in the instructions of two or more objects.

8.5.3.5.2. The golden molding (זר זהב).

The sections on the ark, the table and the altar of incense contain an instruction for making a golden molding, for example (25:24):

V2P PP NP NP   ועשית לו זר זנב סביב

The PP usually has the preposition ל (+suffix, referring to the object), with the exception of the text for the ark, where the preposition is על. But there is some textual evidence for ל as well. Again, סביב, can be understood in two ways: either as additional determination of זר זהב or as adverbial phrase with עשה.

For the table, the construction of another molding is ordered, attached to the frame (מסגרת), the construction of which has been ordered earlier. The structure of the two sentences reads (25:25):

V2P PP NP NP NP	ועשעת לו מסגרת טפח סביב
V2P NP PP NP	ועשעת זר־זהב למסגרתו סביב

The last NP, סביב, again can have a nominal or adverbial function. In the construction of the מסגרת the PP (לו) precedes the object to be constructed, whereas in the case of the זר the order is reversed and the whole object is mentioned: למסגרת. It is remarkable that for the מסגרת a dimension is given (טפח).

The function or use of זר and מסגרת is not mentioned, but both are included in PPs which indicate the place of the טבעת at the table and the altar of incense. In connection with the former the PP has the form: לעמת המסגרת, and with the latter: מתחת לזרו.

8.5.3.5.3. The rings (טבעת).

The order for constructing these components, which, for the objects grouped under this heading, is included in the fragments on the ark, the table, and both altars, is accompanied by a number of complications in the linguistic structure.

For the ark the instruction for making the rings is given as follows (25:12):

V2P PP NP	ויצקת לו ארבע טבעת זהב
V2P PP	ונתתה על ארבע פעמתיו
C3 NP PP	ושתי טבעת על־צלעו האחת
C3 NP PP	ושתי טבעת על־צלעו השנית

The two nominal sentences of the form NP PP contain further details for the placing of two of the טבעת.

In the case of the table, the instruction has the structure (25:26):

V2P PP NP	ועשית לו ארבע טבעת זהב
V2P NP PP	ונתת את־הטבעת על ארבע הפאת
C1 PP	אשר לארבע רגליו

Also in this case, there is additional information on the placing of the טבעת, but this is included in a V3P-sentence which also contains information regarding their use. It has the structure (25:27):

PP V3P NP PP PP	לעמת המסגרת תהיין הטבעת לבתים לבדים
V7 NP	לשאת את־השלחן

The final PPs in this sentence refer to the use of the rings.

For the altar of burnt offering it is ordered to make the טבעת on the רשת, a component which had been mentioned in the preceding sentence. The structure of the sentence reads (27:04):

V2P PP NP PP	ועשית על־הרשת ארבע טבעת נחשת על ארבע קצותיו

209

No separate sentences regarding the placing of the rings are given. A further PP has been added to the construction order which specifies the place: עַל אַרְבַּע קְצוֹתָיו, in which the suffix apparently refers to the רֶשֶׁת. What follows is an instruction for the placing and the position of the רֶשֶׁת, and the role of the טַבָּעֹת.

In the case of the altar of incense the instruction for making the טַבָּעֹת and their position consists of two V3P-sentences, which have the structure (30:04):

C3 NP V3P PP PP PP					וּשְׁתֵּי טַבְּעֹת זָהָב תַּעֲשֶׂה־לּוֹ מִתַּחַת לְזֵרוֹ
PP V3P PP					עַל שְׁתֵּי צַלְעֹתָיו תַּעֲשֶׂה עַל־שְׁנֵי צִדָּיו

This construction is peculiar for two reasons:
- The use of the imperfect of the verb עָשָׂה both for the instruction for making the טַבָּעֹת and for indicating their place.
- The use of a 'stepped formulation': in the first sentence only two טַבָּעֹת are mentioned, whereas the second sentence orders to construct these at two sides of the altar.[1]

8.5.3.5.4. The poles (בַּדִּים).

The construction of these components is ordered for the same objects as in the previous section. The parts of the text referring to them are given below:
a. the ark (25:13 - 15).

V2P NP NP			וְעָשִׂיתָ בַדֵּי עֲצֵי שִׁטִּים
V2P NP NP			וְצִפִּיתָ אֹתָם זָהָב
V2P NP PP PP			וְהֵבֵאתָ אֶת־הַבַּדִּים בַּטַּבָּעֹת עַל צַלְעֹת הָאָרֹן לָשֵׂאת
V7 NP PP			אֶת־הָאָרֹן בָּהֶם
PP V3P NP			בְּטַבְּעֹת הָאָרֹן יִהְיוּ הַבַּדִּים
AP V3P PP			לֹא יָסֻרוּ מִמֶּנּוּ

The order of the instruction for making the poles is very clear in this case: after the section on the rings, there follows the one on the poles with the sequence: construction - coating - function - position.

b. the table (25:28).

V2P NP NP		וְעָשִׂיתָ אֶת־הַבַּדִּים עֲצֵי שִׁטִּים
V2P NP NP		וְצִפִּיתָ אֹתָם זָהָב
V2P PP NP		וְנִשָּׂא־בָם אֶת־הַשֻּׁלְחָן

The same order is maintained, only the indication of the position is missing, but earlier, in the section on the rings, it has been stated that these function לְבָתִּים לְבַדִּים לָשֵׂאת אֶת־הַשֻּׁלְחָן

---

1   We assume that צֶלַע has the meaning 'side' throughout the whole of the text. See Fabry, 1987, p. 1064; Mulder, 1976, p. 103.

c. the altar of burnt offering (27:06 - 07).

V2P NP	וְעָשִׂיתָ בַדִּים לַמִּזְבֵּחַ
NP	בַּדֵּי עֲצֵי שִׁטִּים
V2P NP NP	וְצִפִּיתָ אֹתָם נְחֹשֶׁת
V2P NP PP	וְהוּבָא אֶת־בַּדָּיו בַּטַּבָּעֹת
V2P NP PP PP	וְהָיוּ הַבַּדִּים עַל־שְׁתֵּי צַלְעֹת הַמִּזְבֵּחַ בִּשְׂאֵת
V7 NP	אֹתוֹ

Here we find the same order as in a., but the statement on the position is different. The way to introduce the construction material by means of an extra NP which forms a separate NS, is unique.

d. the altar of incense (30:05).

V2P NP NP	וְעָשִׂיתָ אֶת־הַבַּדִּים עֲצֵי שִׁטִּים
V2P NP NP	וְצִפִּיתָ אֹתָם זָהָב

Whereas in this case the construction of the rings was ordered by Imperfect-sentences, for the poles the We-Perfect is used again. Indications both for function and position are missing, but they are implied in the section on the rings, which ends: וְהָיָה לְבָתִּים לְבַדִּים לָשֵׂאת אֹתוֹ בָּהֵמָּה.

8.5.3.6. Final instruction on using and placing the object.
These instructions vary to a great extent for the different objects. They may be relatively simple as in the case of the ark, the section on which ends as follows (25:16):

V2P PP NP	וְנָתַתָּ אֶל־הָאָרֹן אֵת הָעֵדֻת
Cl V3P PP	אֲשֶׁר אֶתֵּן אֵלֶיךָ

But they can also be quite complicated and extensive, as in the case of the altar of incense (30:06):

V2P NP PP	וְנָתַתָּה אֹתוֹ לִפְנֵי הַפָּרֹכֶת
Cl PP	אֲשֶׁר עַל־אֲרֹן הָעֵדֻת
PP	לִפְנֵי הַכַּפֹּרֶת
Cl PP	אֲשֶׁר עַל־הָעֵדֻת
Cl V3P PP AP	אֲשֶׁר אִוָּעֵד לְךָ שָׁמָּה

This place-indication is followed by a lengthy instruction on the offerings which should be brought to the altar, which we excluded from this fragment.

211

8.5.3.7. The lampstand.

The fragment on this object differs from the others under this heading in having a much higher proportion of NSs. This increases its "deskriptive Anlage."[1] McEvenue even formulated the hypothesis that the object had been present somehow (see above section 7.3.5.).

After the general order for construction, which has the same structure as the other fragments: V2P NP NP, there follows an additional instruction (25:31):

NP V3P NPL מקשה תעשה המנורה ירכה וקנה

This sentence is very similar to the following one in the fragment on the mercy seat (25:18):

V2P NP NP ועשית שנים כרבים זהב
NP V3P NP PP מקשה תעשה אתם משני קצות הכפרת

In the fragment on the lampstand a number of NSs and sentences with V6P follow, which indicate its shape in some detail. Two patterns can be distinguished in this respect. After having introduced the six קנים, verse 33 reads:

NP V6P PP NPL שלשה גבעים משקדים בקנה האחד כפתר ופרח
C3 NP V6P PP NPL ושלשה גבעים משקדים בקנה האחד כפתר ופרח
AP PP כן לששת הקנים
   V6P PP היצאים מן־המנרה

So this passage refers to the גבעים for one set of two קנים emerging from the main shaft of the lampstand, and indicates that its pattern should be repeated for all six of them.

But verse 35, which involves the position of the כפתרים, reads:

C3 NP PP PP וכפתר תחת שני הקנים ממנה
C3 NP PP PP וכפתר תחת שני הקנים ממנה
C3 NP PP PP וכפתר תחת־שני הקנים ממנה
PP לששת הקנים
V6P PP היצאים מן־המנרה

Here we have a complete description for all cases, which is achieved by repetition of the sentence referring to one pair of the קנים.

After these 'descriptive sentences' follows an instruction (with V2P) to make the lights of the lampstand, which also contains instructions for its use. A few special components are mentioned and the quantity of the construction material is specified. The latter seems to compensate for the complete lack of information on the size of the lampstand. Data on dimensions, such as height, are missing.

The fragment is closed by a statement which has a unique phrase structure, having two V5P-sentences, and which is the only passage in the instruction texts which refers to the תבנית mentioned in the introductory fragment of 25:1 - 9.

---

1   Görg, 1981, p. 23; see also Meyers, 1976.

8.5.4. The tabernacle and court.

8.5.4.1. Introduction.

As compared to those of the previous section, these fragments have a considerably higher proportion of NSs which creates the impression that they put heavy emphasis on indications of particular details of the objects concerned. In addition, their structure is not as uniform and shows many differences. Nevertheless, it is possible to distinguish within the fragments between the following structural elements, which will be discussed in the subsequent sub-sections:

8.5.4.2. The general order for construction.

8.5.4.3. The indication of dimensions.

8.5.4.4. The connection of components into a large construct.

8.5.4.5. The final comment.

The fragment on the veil does not fit within this framework and will be discussed separately in sub-section 8.5.4.6.

8.5.4.2. The general order for instruction.

The fragment on the tabernacle is the only one which starts its order of construction with two V3P-sentences (26:01):

C3 NP V3P NP NPL ואת־המשכן תעשה עשר יריעת שש משזר "

ותכלת ו

NP NP V3P NP כרבים מעשה חשב תעשה אתם

An additional feature is the indication of the components (the curtains of linen) to be used in the construction of the tabernacle. Similar indications can be found in the fragments on the curtains of goats' hair, the frames and the bars, but in all these cases the component is mentioned first and the whole only afterwards, for example in the fragment of the curtains of goats' hair (26:07):

V2P NP PP ועשית יריעת עזים לאהל על־המשכן

NP V3P NP עשתי־עשרה יריעת תעשה אתם

In the fragment on the court, the components (קלעים) are mentioned in the second sentence. This fragment has a unique structure since it contains only one finite verb form at its beginning and for the rest is composed of NSs and V6P-sentences.

As far as the veil is concerned, no components are specified, only the material is given.

8.5.4.3. The indications of the dimensions.

The dimensions for the curtains of linen are given as follows (26:02):

NP NP PP ארך היריעה האחת שמנה ועשרים באמה

C3 NP NP PP ורחב ארבע באמה

NP היריעה האחת

NP PP מדה אחת לכל־היריעת

In the fragment on the curtains of goats' hair a similar pattern is followed, whereas the one on the frames has the following structure (26:16):

213

NP NP   עשׂר אמות ארך הקרשׁ

C3 NP NP   ואמה וחצי האמה רחב הקרשׁ האחד

In the fragment on the court, the dimensions do not relate to the components but to the size of the court itself. For a number of its sides it is indicated how much length of קלעים is required, for example (27:12):

C3 NP PP NP   ורחב החצר לפאת־ים קלעים חמשׁים אמה

It is only at the end of that fragment that the dimensions of the court in general are given (27:18):

NP NP PP   ארך החצר מאה באמה

C3 NP NP PP   ורחב חמשׁים בחמשׁים

C3 NP NP NP   וקמה חמשׁ אמות שׁשׁ משׁזר

C3 NP NP   ואדניהם נחשׁת

Apart from the problem in the second phrase, where the Samaritanus and some textual witnesses of the Septuagint read באמה, this presentation of the dimensions is peculiar because it seems to use two systems of indicating the unit of size and because it includes the material of construction.

8.5.4.4. The connection of components into a large construct.

Both fragments on the curtains (linen and goats' hair) have a general instruction to connect them into larger units. In the case of the former, it reads (26:03):

NP V3P V6P NP PP   חמשׁ היריעת תהיין חברת אשׁה אל־אחתה

C3 NP V6P NP PP   וחמשׁ יריעת חברת אשׁה אל־אחתה

In the fragment on the curtains of goats' hair, a V2P-sentence is being used (26:09):

V2P NP PP   וחברת את־חמשׁ היריעת לבד

C3 NP PP   ואת־שׁשׁ היריעת לבד

V2P NP PP   וכפלת את־היריעה השׁשׁית אל־מול פני האהל

In both cases, the next instruction is to make the ללאת, which are used in the connecting process, together with the קרסים. The fragment on the curtains of goats' hair also refers to the hanging of the curtains.

In the fragment on the frames the statement on the dimensions is followed by an order for joining (26:17):

NP PP V6P NP PP   שׁתי ידות לקרשׁ האחד משׁלבת אשׁה אל־אחתה

AP V3P PP   כן תעשׂה לכל קרשׁי המשׁכן

The construction of the ידות is not mentioned, but the fragment continues with a repetition of the initial general order for the construction of the frames, followed by a specification of their number for a particular side of the tabernacle and an instruction to make auxiliary components (26:18 - 19):

V2P NP NP PP   ועשׂית את־הקרשׁים למשׁכן עשׂרים קרשׁ לפאת

                                  נגבן תימנה

C3 NP V3P PP   וארבעים אדני־כסף תעשׂה תחת עשׂרים הקרשׁ

NP PP PP   שׁני אדנים תחת־הקרשׁ האחד לשׁתי ידתיו

C3 NP PP PP   ושׁני אדנים תחת־הקרשׁ האחד לשׁתי ידתיו

The fragment continues with indications for other sides of the tabernacle, either with NSs or with V3P-sentences.

A similar structure for the instruction is also found in the fragments on the bars and the courtyard.

8.5.4.5. Final comments.

In some fragments, the final comment is very short, e.g. , in the one on the curtains of linen (26:06):

V2P NP NP   וְהָיָה הַמִּשְׁכָּן אֶחָד

The fragment on the curtains of goats' hair contains a much longer final comment, whereas the one on the bars sounds like a concluding remark concerning the construction of the tabernacle as a whole (26:30):

V2P NP AP   וַהֲקֵמֹתָ אֶת־הַמִּשְׁכָּן כְּמִשְׁפָּטוֹ

      Cl V1P PP   אֲשֶׁר הָרְאֵיתָ בָּהָר

The מִשְׁפָּט in this fragment seems to have the same role as the תָבְנִית in the fragment on the lampstand (see 8.5.3.7).

8.5.4.6. The veil.

The beginning of the fragment on the veil consists of a V2P-sentence as general order of instruction, specifying the material, and an additional V3P-sentence which indicates the pattern to be used.

It is followed by an extensive instruction mainly consisting of WePerfect sentences, which cover the placing of the veil, a description of its role as separating device between the 'Holy' and the 'Holy of Holies' and the placing within the tabernacle of the objects of the cult, the construction of which had been mentioned in chapter 25.

The fragment is concluded by a more or less separate instruction on the making of a curtain for the opening of the tent.

8.5.5. The garments.
8.5.5.1. Introduction.

The fragments under this heading are very different, which makes it difficult to discuss their contents under a limited number of categories. In any case, the first fragment needs separate discussion which will be given in sub-section 8.5.5.2. The other five have been included in the subsequent sections, which consider the following topics:

8.5.5.3. General order of construction.

8.5.5.4. Handling of stones and other solid material.

8.5.5.5. The connection of subparts.

8.5.5.6. Objects made of soft materials.

8.5.5.7. Instructions on the use of the objects.

8.5.5.2. The garments of the priests.

This fragment is unique, not only because of its first sentence having an imperative instead of the WePerfect, but in particular because the general

instruction for making the objects concerned is given three times, each time
followed by a secondary order which emphasizes a different aspect of the
making of the garments. All three general orders use a WePerfect, but the first
one is in 2 m.s., whereas the final two are in 3 m.p. Utzschneider uses this
difference as a supporting argument for the existence of a
"Volk-Heiligtum-Konzeption" (see above section 7.3.2.).

The first order is followed by the instruction to involve others (כל־חכמי־לב)
in the work, the second one is followed by a listing of all garments to be made,
and the third one by a listing of some of the materials to be used. In the latter
it should be noticed that the precious stones are not mentioned and that the
elements of the well-known combination of soft materials are given separately
(28:05): ואת־התכלת ואת־הארגמן ואת־תולעת השני ואת־השש.

Finally it should be noted that in all three general orders some reference is
made to the role of the garments.

8.5.5.3. General order for construction.

All the other fragments under this heading start with a WePerfect sentence
which involves the instruction of making the object and the pattern or material
to be used. In a few cases additional specifications are given in extra sentences
of the NS or V3P type. The fragment on the coat does not employ the general
verb עשה but the more specific שבץ piel.

In the fragment on the robe, the initial order is followed by a number of
detailed indications (with היה), whereas the one on the breastpiece gives its
dimensions.

The fragment on the chains explicitly specifies (28:22) that they are to be made
על־החשן, which also applies to the first set of rings. The final one has to be
placed על־שתי כתפות האפוד (28:27).

8.5.5.4. Handling of stones and other solid material.

The fragments on the ephod and the breastpiece contain instructions for
incorporating stones into these objects. The stones of the ephod have to be
engraved with the names of the sons of Israel, whereas in the breastpiece a
number of precious stones has to be fixed. For both operations detailed
instructions are provided in which various types of sentences are being used.
The following quotation from the fragment on the ephod will illustrate this (28:
9 - 11):

V2P NP	ולקחת את־שתי אבני־שהם
V2P PP NP	ופתחת עליהם שמות בני ישראל
NP PP PP	ששה משמתם על האבן האחת
C3 NP PP AP	ואת־שמות הששה על־האבן השנית כתולדתם
V6P	הנתרים
NP NP V3P NP PP	מעשה חרש אבן פתוחי חתם תפתח את־שתי
	האבנים על־שמת בני ישראל
V6P NP V3P NP	מסבת משבצות זהב תעשה אתם

216

The fragment on the breastpiece shows similar detail in which the contents of each row of stones is given exactly.

Engraving is also instructed for the golden plate (28:36):

V2P PP NP   ופתחת עליו פתוחי חתם

8.5.5.5. The connection of subparts.

This operation plays an important role in the fragments under this heading. The fragment on the chains (28:22 - 30) is almost completely dealing with it. Its beginning reads as follows:

V2P PP NP NP NP   ועשית על־החשן שרשת גבלת מעשה עבת
                                                   זהב טהור

V2P PP NP   ועשית על־החשן שתי טבעות זהב

V2P NP PP   ונתת את־שתי הטבעות על־שני קצות החשן

V2P NP PP PP   ונתתה את־שתי עבתת הזהב על־שתי הטבעת
                                               אל־קצות החשן

C3 NP NP V3P PP   ואת שתי קצות שתי העבתת תתן
                                                על־שתי המשבצות

V2P PP PP   ונתתה על־כתפות האפד אל־מול פניו

Here, as in the whole of this fragment, we see a clear predominance of the WePerfect-sentences. But in the other fragments we find other sentence-forms. After the introductory order, the fragment on the ephod continues (28:07):

NP V3P PP PP   שתי כתפת יהיה־לו אל־שני קצותיו

V6P   חברת

V2P   וחבר

8.5.5.6. Objects made of soft materials.

In the fragments under this heading, those on the robe and the coat contain references to objects of this category. In the first one, it is remarkable that the initial general order for construction is followed by four sentences with indications for details, three of which use the verb היה (28:32). It further contains the instruction for making the רמני and the פעמן, in which the word סביב occurs three times (28:33 - 34).

Apart from the order for making the coat, the fragment which we called after this object also contains instructions for making other objects, such as אבנט (28:39, 40) and מכנסי־בד (28:42). It is specifically said to make these articles both for Aaron and his sons.

8.5.5.7. Instructions on the use of the objects.

In all the five fragments which we consider in these sub-sections, it is specified that the objects shall be used by Aaron. In the case of the robe, the golden plate and the coat, the expression היה על is used, for example in the fragment on the robe (28:35):

V2P PP PP   והיה על־אהרן לשרת
  V7
V2P NP PP   ונשמע קולו בבאו
  V7 NP PP PP   אל־הקדש לפני יהוה
C3 PP   ובצאתו
  V7 NP
C3 AP V3P   ולא ימות

The verb נשא (see also below, section 8.6.4.) seems to be used in a more metaphorical way, as can be illustrated by the end of the fragment on the chains (28:30):

V2P PP NPL   ונתת אל־חשן המשפט את־האורים ואת־התמים
V2P PP PP   והיו על־לב אהרן בבאו
  V7 NP PP   לפני יהוה
V2P NP NP PP PP NP   ונשא ארהן את־משפט בני־ישראל על־לבו
לפני יהוה תמיד

8.5.6. The relation between sentence-form and role.
8.5.6.1. Introduction.
From the previous sections it will have become clear that Exodus 25 - 31 contains a limited number of sentence-types, but also displays an ability to use these types in a broad variety of ways. As announced already at the end of section 8.5.2., we now would like to elaborate a little more on the relation between the types of sentences and the roles they can play in the text. To this end, we will review a number of passages which employ different types of sentences but deal with situations which have a number of things in common.

In this comparison, we will also include the parallel passages in Exodus 35 - 40, if available. The first part of the concordance prepared by Postma et al.[1] provides a useful tool for this comparison. As already reported (see above section 8.5.2.), Niccacci assumes that in general the following 'conversions' take place between the various types of phrases in the two texts:

Exodus 25 to 31:	Exodus 35 to 40:
WePerfect	WaImperfect
Imperfect	Perfect
Nominal Sentence	Nominal Sentence

In the subsequent sub-sections, we will compare sentences with Imperfect and with WePerfect, Imperfect with Nominal Sentences, and WePerfect with other verb-forms.

In each case we start by giving the passages from Ex 25 to 31, followed in each case by the parallel passage in Ex 35 to 40. Our comments conclude each sub-section.

---

1   Postma, Talstra, Vervenne, 1983 I.

We believe that these comparisons will not be affected by the textual problems of Exodus 35 - 40 to which we referred earlier (see above section 7.3.1.). These problems mainly relate to the word order and general structure of the Greek text of the Septuagint and not to the word types and detailed structure of the Hebrew text of the Masoretes which we will include in our comparisons.

8.5.6.2. WePerfect and Imperfect.
<u>a</u>. Ark and mercy-seat.

25:16 ונתת אל־הארן את העדת אשר אתן אליך
25:21b ואל־הארן תתן את־העדת אשר אתן אליך

Of both passages no parallel texts in Ex 35 to 40 are available.

<u>b</u>. Table and altar of incense.

25:26a ועשית לו ארבע טבעת זהב
37:13a ויצק לו ארבע טבעת זהב

30:04a ושתי טבעת זהב תעשה־לו
37:27a ושתי טבעת זהב עשה־לו

25:27 לעמת המסגרת תהיין הטבעת לבתים לדבים לשאת את־השלחן
37:14 לעמת המסברת היו הטבעת בתים לבדים לשאת את־השלחן

30:04c והיה לבתים לבדים לשאת אתו בהמה
37:27b לבתים לבדים לשאת אתו בהם

<u>c</u>. The curtains of linen, those of goats' hair, and the ephod.

26:03 חמש היריעת תהיין חברת אשה אל־אחתה
וחמש יריעת חברת אשה אל־אחתה

36:10 ויחבר את־חמש היריעת אחת אל־אחת
וחמש יריעת חבר אחת אל־אחת

26:09a וחברת את־חמש היריעת לבד
ואת־שש היריעת לבד

36:16 ויחבר את־חמש היריעת לבד
ואת־שש היריעת לבד

28:07 שתי כתפת חברת יהיה־לו אל־שני קצוותיו
וחבר

39:04 כתפת עשו־לו חברת
על־שני קצוותו חבר

In example a., the use of the Imperfect in the second case may be related to the wish to put emphasis (25:21):
"You will place the mercy seat on the ark, above, but <u>in</u> the ark you will place ...."
This may also apply to the second instance of b. It is possible that the authors

wish to emphasize that in this case only two rings have to be constructed.

Whereas in the third instance, the position and purpose of the rings is indicated by an Imperfect of היה, the fourth one uses a WePerfect of the same verb. In this case, the parallel text in the description drops this verb-form and uses a Nominal sentence.

The first case of example c. is remarkable, because the 'instruction text' uses an Imperfect of היה and a participle of the verb חבר, whereas its parallel in the 'execution text' uses the 'equivalent' of the WePerfect. In the second instance of this example, we indeed find the WePerfect in the 'instruction' and the WaImperfect in the 'execution.' But in the third case we find in the instruction a combination of Imperfect of היה and a passive WePerfect of חבר, and in the execution a Perfect (= the equivalent of the Imperfect) of עשה.

8.5.6.3. Imperfect and Nominal Sentence.

a. Lampstand and court, curtains of linen and frames.

25:33b	כן לששת הקנים
37:19b	כן לששת הקנים

27:11a	וכן לפאת צפון בארך
38:11a	ולפאת צפון מאה באמה

26:04b	וכן תעשה בשפת היריעה הקיצונה
36:11b	כן עשה בשפת היריעה הקיצונה

26:17b	כן תעשה לכל קרשי המשכן
36:22b	כן עשה לכל קרשי המשכן

b. Within the fragment on the frames.

26:20	ולצלע המשכן השנית לפאת צפון עשרים קרש
36:25	ולצלע המשכן השנית לפאת צפון עשה עשרים קרשים

26:22	ולירכתי המשכן ימה תעשה ששה קרשים
36:27	ולירכתי המשכן ימה עשה ששה קרשים

26:23	ושני קרשים תעשה למקצעת המשכן בירכתים
36:28	ושני קרשים עשה למקמעת המשכן בירכתים

c. Altar of burnt offering and altar of incense.

27:02b	ממנו תהיין קרנתיו
38:02b	ממנו היו קרנתיו

30:02b	ממנו קרנתיו
37:25b	ממנו היו קרנתיו

Example a. contains two cases with Nominal Sentences and two with Imperfects with no significant differences between the parallel instruction and execution texts.

The second and third instance of example b. again contain Imperfect in the instruction text and Perfect in the execution text. But the first case has a Nominal Sentence in the instruction, whereas the execution has the equivalent of an Imperfect.

The same phenomenon is found in the second instance of example c.

8.5.6.4. WePerfect and other verb forms.
a. The ark and the table.

25:14b	לשאת את־הארן בהם
37:05b	לשאת את־הארן

25:27b	לשאת את־השלחן
37:14b	לשאת את־השלחן

25:28b	ונשא־בם את־השלחן
37:15b	לשאת את־השלחן

b. Within the fragment on the veil.

26:32	ונתתה אתה על־ארבעה עמודי שטים מצפים זהב וויהם זהב על־ארבעה אדני־כסף
36:36	ויעש לה ארבעה עמודי שטים ויצפם זהב וויהם זהב ויצק להם ארבעה אדני־כסף

26:37	ועשית למסך חמשה עמודי שטים וצפית אתם זהב וויהם זהב ויצקת להם חמשה אדני נחשת
36:38	ואת־עמודיו חמשה ואת־וויהם וצפה ראשיהם וחשקיהם זהב ואדניהם חמשה נחשת

Example a. contains formulations of the purpose of rings and poles. In five cases of both the instruction and execution text an Infinitive is used of נשא. In one case, however, the instruction text uses the WePerfect nif'al of this verb.

The instruction part of the first instance of example b. subsequently uses sentences of the type: WePerfect, Participle, Nominal Sentence. Its parallel in the execution text consequently uses three times the equivalent of WePerfect. This pattern (three times the WePerfect), using the same verbs, we find in the instruction part of the second instance of this example. The corresponding execution part, however, uses two NSs and one verbal sentence only, which has the equivalent of the Imperfect in the instruction text.

These examples, together with the preliminary observations already described at the end of section 8.5.2., make it probable that sentence-types have been considered as readily exchangeable within the text. This result does not support the idea of a strict connection between sentence-type and sentence-role.

8.5.7. General remarks.

a. Exodus 25 - 31 is a discourse which contains a limited number of sentence-types, in agreement with the suggestions of Niccacci.

b. As noted earlier (see sub-section 8.4.3.3.), WePerfect Sentences have a more or less rigid structure and do not allow for much variation. The results of this paragraph indicate that for information on details and complications of the objects, Imperfect and Nominal Sentences are used more frequently, though a series of WePerfect Sentences may occur as well (e.g. 28:29 - 30).

c. There is a certain fluidity as regards the relationship between the roles within the text and types of sentences. One type can fulfill a number of roles, and vice versa. So the situation is less rigid than proposed by Niccacci and others.

d. Nominal Sentences and sentences with WePerfect and Imperfect, especially of היה, which indicate particular details, can be included within the framework of a passage which constitutes an (extended) instruction.

e. The close connection between sentence-types and roles also seems problematic in view of the fact that different types of sentences are being used in more or less equivalent situations.

f. The general phrase structure of the different fragments also shows many variations. It seems that the linguistic structure of each fragment has been adapted to the specific requirements related to the object(s) concerned.

8.6. Referential functions, phrases and words.

8.6.1. Introduction.

So far, our analysis of the text has been rather broad. Apart from restricting ourselves to a limited number of fragments, namely to those within which we expect space and spatial aspects to play a substantial part, no particular attention has been paid to the ultimate objective of our investigation: the perception of space in the Old Testament.

But in this paragraph we will concentrate on this point. We will take our starting-point not so much in the text itself, but in the world to which it refers and will consider a number of spatial features of this world and investigate what phrases and words have been used to refer to them.

In view of the broad meaning of the expression 'referential function' and its intensive use in linguistics, it is useful to outline in some detail in what sense we will employ this concept. In our previous investigations of the more fundamental issues of language (see chapter 4, 5 and 6), we discovered that linguistic signs have at least three referring functions. Figure 7 on p. 124 shows all of them:

a. The text/language refers to the intentions and purposes of the sender. This aspect has been underlined in particular by the so-called 'speech-act' approach in linguistics, emphasizing the conscious side of this phenomenon.

b. There is also a referring of the text/language to the receiver, in whom they call into being a world, which is partly determined by them and partly by the

222

previous experience and structure (frame of reference) of the receiver himself.

c. The text/language refers to the world. This may be the 'real world,' the world 'out there,' or the 'projected world' which is based on it, as suggested by Jackendoff. In principle, this does not make any difference. We assume that there is a world, which is to a certain extent independent from the other elements in the triangle (sender, receiver and text/language), to which the text/language refers.

In addition to these three uses, the term 'reference' is also employed while remaining within the area of language/text. In this connection it describes the possibility that certain words point forwards or backwards to other words in the text. This is the case with deixis, demonstratives, etc., and is frequently used in grammars. Sometimes the distinction between the various types of reference is not strictly maintained.[1]

In this paragraph we will consider the type c of referring mentioned above. In this connection, we take our starting point in the world, concentrate on a number of spatial aspects and investigate what linguistic means are used to refer to them.

The aspects which we will investigate are:
- places;
- paths;
- distances.
- motion.

As we explained in our previous survey of the investigation of Jackendoff on the semantics of spatial expressions (see section 4.4.4.), he distinguishes between places and paths. During our analysis of the text, however, we discovered that within many fragments, places and paths cannot be distinguished properly. It is therefore not possible to separate these two topics in our analysis, so they will be discussed together in section 8.6.2. The reference to distances, which form a special category of paths, will be considered in section 8.6.3. The aspect of motion is discussed in section 8.6.4. In this case, verbs play an important role and in section 8.6.5., we make a few comments on the relation between sentence structure and referential role in general. As usual, the final section (8.6.6.) contains our general remarks concerning this step of the analysis.

This paragraph covers the same fragments of the text as paragraph 8.5. In the discussions to follow, we will occasionally refer to passages from the fragments of which we already presented the phrase structure and Hebrew text in this previous paragraph.

---

1   Compare the definitions of sense and reference in WO'C, p. 693 and the use of reference on p. 309.

8.6.2. Places and paths.
8.6.2.1. Introduction.
In his consideration of the place-concept, Jackendoff mentions two possibilities for its representation. It may "consist of an intransitive preposition alone, such as 'here,' 'thataway,' 'forward,' or 'downstairs.' Alternatively, it may explicitly mention a reference object as the object of the preposition, as in 'on the table,' 'under the counter,' or 'in the can.' It may even mention two reference objects, as in 'between the square and the circle' ..... The place referred to is distinct from the reference object, since one can refer to a variety of places, such as 'under the table,' 'near the table,' 'on the table,' and 'inside the table,' holding the reference object constant."[1]

Regarding paths, Jackendoff distinguishes between path-roles and path-types. He describes three path-types:

- bounded paths, which include "source paths for which the usual preposition is 'from,' and goal paths for which the preposition is 'to.' In bounded paths, the reference object is an endpoint of the path."[2]

- directions; in this case "the reference object or place does not fall on the path, but would if the path were extended some unspecified distance."[3]

- routes, where "the reference object or place is related to some point in the interior of the path."[4]

Regarding the roles of paths Jackendoff also makes a threefold distinction:
- a path may be traversed by a thing.
- a thing may extend over a path.
- a thing may be oriented along a path.

Combining types and roles Jackendoff arrives at 9 possible combinations.[5]

Of course, it remains to be seen whether all these forms occur in the text. In addition, it should be borne in mind that this scheme for representing the various spatial aspects of place and paths originates from a study of a European language. It puts emphasis on the coordination of prepositions and nouns. In his investigation of the prepositions in Ugaritic, Pardee spends more attention to the coordination of verbs and prepositions.[6] But it looks worth while to see what the approach of Jackendoff offers for the study of a text in OTH.

References to places and paths occur in the various fragments in particular in a number of situations relating to the objects or parts of them. They may specify where they are located or where and how they should be placed. As already explained above (see section 8.5.7.), it is often difficult to distinguish sharply between these two, because descriptive phrases seem to have a prescriptive

---

1   Jackendoff, 1985, p. 161.
2   o.c. , p. 165.
3   o.c. , p. 165.
4   o.c. , p. 165.
5   o.c. , p. 168.
6   Pardee, 1975.

purpose as well. In addition, references to places or paths are used to indicate on which parts and in what way processes involving certain objects should be carried out.

These references may have a simple structure and consist of one Prepositional Phrase only or of a few complementary phrases. These cases will be discussed in the next sub-section. Frequently, however, references of this type are complex, consisting of two, or sometimes even more, independent phrases. The review of these cases is made in sub-section 8.6.2.3. The subsequent sub-section considers the use of more complex noun phrases within the PPs. Finally, a few special cases of places and paths will be considered in sub-section 8.6.2.5.

8.6.2.2. Simple references.

These occur relatively rarely in the fragments of the text which we selected for analysis.

References to places where objects have to be placed can be found in 25:16 and 25:21 (see above 8.5.6.2. example a.) which refer to the placing of the עדת. Another example concerns the breastpiece (28:30):

V2P PP NPL   ונתת אל־חשן המשפט את־האורים ואת־התמים

Details regarding processes can also be given by a simple reference to a place or path. Examples are
- the coating of the ark (25:11B, see 8.5.3.4.);
- the making of the rings in the fragments on the ark and the table (25:12A, 26A, see 8.5.3.5.3.)
- the making of the chains in the one on the breastpiece (28:22A, see 8.5.5.5.).

Whereas in the latter example, the preposition על is used, the two preceding ones use ל. This preposition is also used to indicate the object for which auxiliary parts have to be constructed, as in the fragment on the curtains of goats' hair (26:07A, see 8.5.4.2.) and in the one on the veil (26:37A):

V2P PP NP   ועשית למסך חמשה עמודי שטים

A similar phrase may also be used to refer to the person(s) for whom objects are to be made, as in the fragments on the garments. In most cases, however, extra PPs have been added, which complicate the structure of the sentence. An example of a sentence in which a PP of this type stands alone, can be found in the fragment on the coat (28:40A):

C3 PP V3P NP   ולבני אהרן תעשה כתנת

It should be noticed that the 'accusative of place' which is mentioned in the grammars[1] does not occur frequently within the text. Perhaps 29:11A (see also 29:32, 42.) and 28:25 can be considered as examples. The former reads:

V2P NP PP NP   ושחטת את־הפר לפני יהוה פתח אהל מועד

But in this case an extra PP has been added.

The use of an 'intransitive preposition' (Jackendoff) to denote a place can be found in 30:18D:

V2P AP NP   ונתת שמה מים

The addition of the ה-locativus seems to emphasize the directional rather than the local aspect.[2]

8.6.2.3. Complex references.

In many cases, the reference to places and paths is of a complex nature, both in instructions how objects should be made or where they should be placed. As an example, we will consider in some detail the passages which deal with the rings (הטבעת).

In paragraph 8.5., we already presented most of the sentences concerned. Sub-section 8.5.3.5.3. contains the passages in the fragments on the ark, the table, the altar of burnt offering and the altar of incense. Sub-section 8.5.5.5. contains the initial references to the rings in the fragment on the chains. To these sentences the following ones should be added (28:26 - 28):

V2P NP   ועשית שתי טבעות זהב
V2P NP PP PP   ושמת אתם על־שני קצות החשן על־שפתו
         Cl PP NP   אשר אל־עבר
         האפד ביתה
V2P NP   ועשית שתי טבעות זהב
V2P NP PP PP PP PP PP   ונתתה אתם על־שתי כתפות האפוד
         מלמטה ממול פניו לעמת מחברתו ממעל לחשב האפוד
V8P NP PP PP PP PP PP   וירכסו את־החשן מטבעתו אל־טבעת האפד
         בפתיל תכלת להיות
         V7 PP   על־חשב האפוד
C3 AP V3P NP PP   ולא־יזח החשן מעל האפוד

In addition to the fragments mentioned above, rings also occur in the fragments on the frames and the bars. In the first one we find the following sentences (26:24A, B):

V8P NP PP   ויהיו תאמים מלמטה
C3 NP V3P NP PP PP   ויחדו יהיו תמים על־ראשו אל־הטבעת האחת
AP V3P PP   כן יהיה לשניהם
PP V3P   לשני המקצעת יהיו

The fragment on the bars reports the following on the rings (26:29):

---

1   see WO'C, p. 169 - 170; GKC, p. 373.
2   see Hoftijzer, 1981, p. 144 - 150.

C3 NP V3P NP   ואת־הקרשים תצפה זהב

C3 NP V3P NP   ואת־טבעתידהם תעשה זהב

NP PP   בתים לבריחם

V2P NP PP   וצפית את־הבריחם זהב

When we compare these statements on the rings in the various fragments, we can make a number of observations.

a. As verbs for the construction are used either יצק or עשה with ל or על as prepositions preceding the object to which they are to be made.

b. For objects mainly made of wood, the making of the rings seems to be closely related to the coating process.

c. With one exception (the frames), all fragments contain separate instructions for the making of the rings and for placing them.

d. Whereas the instruction for the making of the rings usually has a simple structure, the instruction for placing them is complex, consisting of a number of sentences and employing two or more PPs. These PPs, which refer both to places and paths, may use a number of elements of the objects concerned, such as: פאה table; פעם ark; צד altar of incense; צלע ark, altar of incense; קצה altar of burnt offering (the network), the breastpiece; רגל table. This point will be discussed in detail in the next sub-section.

e. Though possibilities are available (see below 8.6.3.), no reference to distances of fixed measure is made in the indications for placing the rings.

Similar observations can be made when investigating other fragments, for example: the mercy seat (the placing of the cherubim) and the lampstand (the whole construction). In the details of the construction no distances are used but mainly series of PPs.

8.6.2.4. The use of complex Noun Phrases in Prepositional Phrases.

The PPs used for referring to places and paths often have the objects themselves as the NP which is governed by the preposition. Examples are: 25:20: אל־הכפרת; 25:30: על־השלחן; 25:35: מן־המנרה.

Quite frequently, however, components or aspects of the objects are mentioned. Sometimes the instruction for making these components has been given before, but it is also possible that they are used without any prior introduction. It looks as if it is assumed that they are present 'immediately,' as soon as the object concerned has been constructed. Table 8;4 gives a survey of them, together with the prepositions and the objects in connection with which they are used.

Geographical directions may be used to indicate more precisely what component of the object (e.g. צלע, פאה) is intended. Other words which are used in this respect are numerals, such as אחד, שנית, or substantives as קצון (26:04, 10) or תיכן (26:28).

In addition the preposition מן can be used in this case in a paired phrase construction, more or less similar to that of בין. For example in the fragment on the mercy seat (25:19A + B):

C3 V5P NP PP PP   ועשׂה כרוב אחד מקצה מזה
C3 NP PP PP   וכרוב־אחד מקצה מזה

The other cases occur in the fragment on the curtains of goat hair (26:13, see below under 8.6.3. for the phrase structure and Hebrew text).

Table 8;4

	comp.	prep.	objects
1	ירכה	ב, ל	dwelling
2	כתף	ל	dwelling, ephod
3	פאה	ל, על	table, dwelling
4	פנה	ל, על	altar of burnt offering, court
5	פעם	על	ark
6	צד	מן, על	lampstand, dwelling, altar of incense
7	צלע	ל, על	ark, dwelling, altar of burnt offering, altar of incense
8	קצה	אל, ב, מן	curtains of linen, bars
9	קצה	אל, מן, על	mercy seat, curtains of linen, altar of burnt offering, ephod, breastpiece
10	רגל	ל	table
11	שפה	ב, על	curtains of linen, curtains of goat hair, breastpiece, robe
12	שׁול	על	robe

This construct of phrases seems to refer to a spatial arrangement involving two different locations from which paths originate which indicate the position of the objects involved. It is remarkable that in all these cases the particle זה is used which in this case plays the role of a locative adverb. The two locations seem to have equal value, as in the similar use of בין.[1]
Finally, words as מול or עבר can be used as in the fragment of the lampstand (28:37C):
V2P PP   והאיר על־עבר פניה
or in that of the chains (28:25B):
V2P PP PP   ונתתה על־כתפות האפד אל־מול פניו

8.6.2.5. A few particular cases.
At first, we consider a few cases in which two objects (or components of them) have a (physical) connection with each other. Auxiliary parts may be used to bring about these connections, such as rings, hooks or a cord.
In the phrases used to refer to these connections, the preposition מן plays an

---

1   see Barr, 1978.

228

important role. This preposition occurs about 80 times in the text and is used in particular to refer to source-paths. Sometimes it governs a more or less specified place, such as in 25:22: מְבֵּין שְׁנֵי הַכְּרֻבִים. But often it is combined with an NP and in these cases it seems to refer to some form of connection between two objects or between an object and a part of it. This is quite obvious when verbs which involve joining are used, as in 26:28:

C3 NP PP V6P PP PP   וְהַבְּרִיחַ הַתִּיכֹן בְּתוֹךְ הַקְּרָשִׁים מַבְרִחַ
מִן־הַקָּצֶה אֶל־הַקָּצֶה

But it can also occur with verbs like יָצָא and הָיָה, as illustrated by the following examples from the fragment on the lampstand:
- 25:33C and C1:

AP PP   כֵּן לְשֵׁשֶׁת הַקָּנִים
    V6P PP   הַיֹּצְאִים מִן־הַמְּנֹרָה

- 25:31C:

NPL PP V3P   גְּבִיעֶיהָ כַּפְתֹּרֶיהָ וּפְרָחֶיהָ מִמֶּנָּה יִהְיוּ

In both cases the PP with מִן seems to indicate that there is some form of fixed connection between the parts concerned and the lampstand. A similar use of this PP can be found in other fragments: the mercy seat (25:19), the altar of burnt offering (27:02), the ephod (28:08) and the altar of incense (30:02). In the case of the mercy seat, additional information is given on the position of the parts (the כְּרֻבִים) in relation to the object.

Another expression which is used in referring to connections is אִשָּׁה אֶל־אֲחֹתָהּ . This phrase and its equivalent (אִישׁ אֶל־אָחִיו) occur 6 times in the text, including four times in the fragment on the curtains of linen. In all these cases a verbal form with the meaning of some form of joining is involved, as in 26:03A:

NP V3P V6P NP PP   חָמֵשׁ הַיְרִיעֹת תִּהְיֶיןָ חֹבְרֹת אִשָּׁה אֶל־אֲחֹתָהּ

The same applies to its occurrence in the fragment on the frames in 26:17A:

NP PP V6P NP PP   שְׁתֵּי יָדוֹת לַקֶּרֶשׁ הָאֶחָד מְשֻׁלָּבֹת אִשָּׁה אֶל־אֲחֹתָהּ

In the fragment on the mercy seat the masculine equivalent occurs in a Nominal Sentence referring to the position of the faces of the cherubim (25:20C + D):

C3 NP NP PP   וּפְנֵיהֶם אִישׁ אֶל־אָחִיו
PP V3P NP   אֶל־הַכַּפֹּרֶת יִהְיוּ פְּנֵי הַכְּרֻבִים

It is clear that this phrase involves two objects (or parts of them) which are similar and in a certain way belong together. They may be 'physically connected' (as in the first five cases), or have a fixed spatial position towards each other (as in the final case).

In the execution text of Exodus 35 - 40, all feminine expressions have been transformed into אַחַת אֶל־אֶחָת. The masculine form used in the fragment of the mercy seat is maintained.

It is noteworthy that this expression can be used in case of such diverse objects as curtains, frames and cherubim.

The second special situation which we consider in this sub-section is the reference to paths of a closed shape. In this respect the word סָבִיב seems to be

229

important.[1] As we already noticed above (see 8.5.3.4. and 8.5.3.5.2.), its role is not completely clear. It can be considered as an additional phrase to an object, or as an Adverbial Phrase to a process, as in a sentence such as 25:11C:

V2P PP NP NP   ועשית עליו זר זהב סביב

In sentences of this type it occurs five times in the fragments on the objects of the cult. In addition, it is used in the fragment on the court (27:17A):

NP NP V6P NP   כל־עמודי החצר סביב מחשקים כסף

In this case it seems reasonable to assume that it is connected with the preceding NP, although the Masoretic accents connect it with the following participle. In any case, it is used here in a situation where larger distances are involved. In the fragment on the robe, the word סביב is used with smaller distances, e.g. in 28:33A+B:

V2P PP NP PP NP שׁני   ועשית על־שוליו רמני תכלת וארגמן ותולעת
                                                    על־שוליו סביב

C3 NP PP NP   ופעמני זהב בתוכם סביב

Outside the fragments which we investigate in detail, it occurs in Exodus 25 - 31 in the instructions for the procedures of the cult, e.g. in 29:16B+C:

V2P NP   ולקחת את־דמו

V2P PP NP   וזרקת על־המזבח סביב

From these examples, it is clear that סביב is a versatile word that can be used for referring to spatial patterns which have a closed shape but need not to be exactly circular.[2] It is used in connection with objects and processes of many types.

Another expression used in this case is the complex preposition בתוך. It occurs two times in passages together with סביב, and one time in the fragment of the frames (26:28).

8.6.3. Distances.

A distance can be described as the "measure of space, between two points, places, etc."[3] In the fragments, the most important use of them is in providing the dimensions of objects. Examples have been mentioned already in paragraph 8.5, in particular in the sub-sections 8.5.3.2. and 8.5.4.3.

All cases in the first sub-section use nominal sentences of the type as present in 25:16B:

NP NP   אמתים וחצי ארכו

The first NP refers to the number of units and the unit, whereas the second NP refers to the dimension of which the size is given (length, width or height).

This sentence-type is also found in the dimensions of the breastpiece (28:16).

In the second sub-section, we find a different type of nominal sentence. In this

1   Hurvitz, 1982, p. 84 - 87.
2   Garcia López, 1986, p. 731.
3   Hornby, 1981, s.v.

case, we give the following example (26:08A):

NP NP PP   ארך הריעה האחת שלשים באמה

Now the first NP refers to the dimension of which the size is given, the second NP refers to the number of units and the sentence is closed by a PP which refers to the unit itself.

The fragment on the frames (26:16) seems to use the type as shown in sub-section 8.5.3.2., but the reference to the width shows irregularities in structure. In most cases, the unit for giving the distances is the cubit, but in the case of the breastpiece, the span (זרת) is used (28:16). The handbreadth (טפח) is used in 25:26, as an additional NP to the מסגרת which has to be constructed to the table. No dimension is given in this case, but it is generally assumed that it refers to the width of this part of the object.

The reference to distances, otherwise than to indicate dimensions of objects, can also be found in two other passages. The first one occurs in the fragment of the curtains of goats' hair, and reads as follows (26:12 - 13)[1]:

C3 NP PP   וסרח העדף ביריעת האהל
    V6P

NP V3P PP   חצי הריעה העדפת תסרח על אחרי המשכן
    V6P

C3 NP PP   והאמה מזה
C3 NP PP   והאמה מזה

PP PP V3P NP PP C3 PP PP   בעדף בארך יריעת האהל יהיה
     V6P PP   סרוח על־צדי המשכן מזה ומזה לכסתו
       V7 NP

The distance of one cubit seems to be strictly bound to the (long) side of the curtains. At the same time, the word ארך is used as a physical entity, as indicated by its parallel position to עדף.

A similar phenomenon can be seen in the second passage where distances are used without referring to dimensions. In the fragment on the court, distances are used to indicate the amount of קלעים, for example in 27:12:

C3 NP PP NP   ורחב החצר לפאת־ים קלעים חמשים אמה

In this passage, altogether seven sentences with distances (27:09, 11, 12, 13, 14, 15{?}, 16;) occur, which seem to perform a similar function. The words ארך and רחב are used as if they refer to physical parts of the court.

8.6.4. Motion.

As we reported in section 4.4.4., Jackendoff discusses explicitly the verbs used

---

1   In the presentation of this text, all the words within the Hebrew text at the right hand side have been given in linear order, whereas in the phrase structure at the left, the phrases of embedded sentences have been written on separate lines, as usual.

to refer to this concept and we will follow him in this respect. In the fragments of the text, the analysis of which we consider in this paragraph, a number of these verbs occur and the most important of these will be discussed below in alphabetical order (Hebrew).

a. בוא.

The hiph'il of this verb occurs three times and the hoph'al one time. The בדים have to be brought בטבעת (25:14, 27:07) and the קרסים בללאת, (26:11); the ark as a whole has to be brought שמה, but in this case an additional PP is added.

The infinitive of the qal is used in referring to Aaron performing his service (28:29, 30, 35, 43).

b. לקח.

This verb plays an important role in the fragments of the text which refer to cultic procedures, especially in chapter 29. It seems to involve a more or less ceremonial taking of objects, animals, etc. in connection with sacrifices.[1] In the same line its use in 28:05 could be understood, where it is described that the 'skilled men' should take the materials for making the garments of the priests. In the fragments on the objects, the verb is used only once: 28:09 which refers to the taking of the stones for the ephod.

In both cases no preposition is used. In the 'ceremonial use,' the preposition מן frequently occurs together with it.

c. נשא.

In the fragments on the ark, the table and both altars, this verb occurs with the meaning of carrying the object concerned. Four times it has the form of the Infinitive; one time, in the fragment of the table, where it occurs twice, it has the form of the WePerfect nif'al.

In the structure of the sentence, the object is included as an accusative, whereas in three cases the poles are referred to in an additional PP with ב, as in 30:04C1:

    V7 NP PP   לשאת אתו בהמה

The verb נשא is also used in metaphorical sense (see above sub-section 8.5.5.7.).

d. נתן.

This is the verb which is used most frequently (20 times) in the fragments, when they refer to putting or placing an object somewhere. With one exception, the destination is indicated by a PP. על is widely used and seems to include both the meaning 'on' (as in 25:21) and 'at' (as in 25:12). In the latter case, it seems to refer to a fixed connection in a sense, similar to the one for מן, which we mentioned above (see sub-section 8.6.2.5.). The preposition אל is used with the ark and the breastpiece and apparently refers to placing things 'in' these objects. It is also used twice in the meaning of giving something 'to' a person (25:17, 21). Other prepositions used with this verb are: בין''בין, לפני, תחת.

In 30:18D, in the fragment on the laver, an AP of location is used for referring

---

1   Seebass, 1984, p. 590 - 91.

to the destination:

V2P AP NP

e. שִׂים.

וְנָתַתָּ שָׁמָּה מַיִם

This verb occurs four times in the fragments in a role which is very similar to that of נתן. Three times it uses the preposition עַל, and in one case (26:35), which refers to the placing of the table in the dwelling, the complex phrase מִחוּץ לַפָּרֹכֶת.

From this review of the verbs used for indicating motion, it appears that two verbs are available for referring to placing/putting, which is the most important form of motion that we can expect in a text on the constructing of objects. Of course, the concept of motion covers a much wider area, but our choice of limiting the analysis to Exodus 25 - 31 does not enable us to study it in more detail.

8.6.5. Type of sentence and reference role.

In the course of our investigation we have tried to discover possible regularities between the structure and type of sentences and their role in referring to specific aspects of the world, e.g. motion, location and construction.

Whereas Jackendoff and Talmy, in their studies of English, were able to describe a number of detailed relations, we could make very general observations only. For example, the verb which is used most frequently in referring to location (places and paths), הָיָה, has a higher proportion of Imperfect Sentences than the verb which is used most frequently for referring to construction, עָשָׂה: 60% of a total number of occurrences of 55, against 43% out of a total of 107.

Attempts to go into more detail, for example taking into consideration the order of the various sorts of phrases (VP, NP, PP, AP) in the sentences, failed to reveal any consistent regularity. These attempts also suffered from the low number of occurrences, which limited the mathematical significance of the results in general.

At the same time, it must be said that this outcome seems to be in agreement with the lack of rigid rules in the general coordination of sentence-types and roles, which we described above (see sub-section 8.5.6.4.). In this connection, it is also worth while to note that comparison of the instruction text (Exodus 25 - 31) and its execution parallel (Exodus 35 - 40) reveals that many alterations occur in the verbal forms (see 8.5.6.4. for a few examples), whereas the number of changes in the Prepositional Phrases remains very limited.

8.6.6. General remarks.

a. OTH provides many possibilities for referring to space and spatial aspects.

b. These possibilities are used in a broad variety of phrase and sentence structures.

c. A rigid linkage between sentence type and role could not be ascertained, both in a general sense and in referring to space and spatial aspects.

d. Though the use of certain (technical) terms is limited to the fragments on particular objects, there is a remarkable range in the employment of more general words involving space and spatial relations.

e. Distances are used only in a limited way, namely to indicate dimensions of objects along straight lines which coincide with sides of objects.

f. The dimensions of a more complex object, like the lampstand, are not given. The size is roughly indicated by mentioning the weight of the raw material to be used in its construction.

g. A more precise reference to places which are not located on lines of this type is accomplished by using a number of Prepositional Phrases.

h. The same applies to the reference to directions which do not follow lines of this type.

i. Words for dimensions, such as אֹרֶךְ and רֹחַב, appear to refer also to physical aspects of objects.

j. It appears that Prepositional Phrases have a certain degree of 'permanency.' Both within the fragments of Exodus 25 - 31 and in the shift from the instruction account to the construction account in Exodus 35 - 40, they show relatively few changes, as compared to Verb Phrases.

k. The concepts 'left' and 'right' are not used in reference to ordering in space. In addition to geographical directions, numerals and phrases, which do not allocate any 'spatial priority,' are used to refer to 'paired opposite' locations or parts of objects.

8.7. Summary.

8.7.1. Introduction.

In this paragraph we summarize the main findings of our investigation of Exodus 25 - 31. We will base our observations in particular on the general remarks which we made at the end of each step of the analysis.

To begin with, in section 8.7.2., we consider in what way the text uses OTH for the structuring of space and spatial relations. The next section (8.7.3.) uses the results of these considerations for devising an idea of the perception of space involved. Finally, in section 8.7.4., we pay attention to some general aspects of our investigation.

Before starting this summary, it is wise to underline two limitations of our investigation:

a. It uses a particular method of analysis.

b. Only a small pericope of the Old Testament has been investigated.

Its results should be considered, bearing in mind these limitations.

8.7.2. The structuring of space and spatial relations.

Our analysis shows that the language of the text has many possibilities for the structuring of space and spatial relations. These possibilities cover both main aspects of language:

234

- the lexicon: many words of various types (verbs, substantives, prepositions) are available for referring to space and related phenomena.
- the structure: a wide variety of structural possibilities, both at the phrase level and at the sentence level, are used in this respect.
We feel that this is the main result of our analysis. The author of the text found that OTH offers many and diverse possibilities for referring to space and spatial relations and he used these possibilities in a variety of ways.

Indications were obtained that, as far as the employment of verbs is concerned, his language allowed him a certain flexibility. The same applies to the fine-structure of sentences, e.g. the order of the various phrases within them. The coordination of prepositions to nouns seems to be more strict, however.

The separate fragments of the text, which refer to the construction of the various objects, display different structures as far as the types of sentences are concerned and their order and number. The fragments on objects which apparently require more detailed indications, contain a higher proportion of Imperfect and Nominal Sentences. So linguistic and textual structure has been adapted to the specific requirements of the objects.

On the basis of these data, we conclude that in general the possibilities of OTH for referring to space and spatial relations, and the use made of them by the author of the text, are comparable to that of modern European languages and their users.

At the same time, we noticed a few points in the use of certain types of words and expressions of OTH, which are remarkable, at least as compared to the use of modern European languages in this respect:

a. The use of distances, measured lines between two positions, seems to be limited to those cases in which these lines follow more or less straight sides of objects. At least, we were unable to find any application of distances for referring to 'unmarked positions,' for example, on the surface of the flat side of an object, by indicating its distances to the two sides.

b. A dimension of an object, such as length, seems to refer to some physical aspect of it. The meaning of the word אֹרֶךְ in particular includes the concept of 'the long (straight) side of an object.' It cannot be used independently from that for any other distance.

c. The concepts of left and right are not used for referring to spatial relations in general. In Exodus 25 - 31 the word יָמִין is used, but only for referring to parts of the body (29:20, 22). When dealing with equivalent aspects (for example, sides) of objects, other linguistic constructions are used (see above sub-section 8.6.2.5.).

8.7.3. The perception of space.

In this section, we use the results of our analysis to arrive at some statements about the perception of space by the author of the text. In this respect, we should bear in mind the difficulties which accompany the formulation of ideas about mental phenomena of other persons on the basis of linguistic data alone

235

(see above chapter 4, 5 and 6).

Based on the broad agreement between the possibilities of OTH and its use by the author of the text, and the possibilities of modern, Western languages and their use, we conclude that in general, there is agreement in the perception of space between the people involved.

We also believe that the few differences which we found (see above section 8.7.2.), allow us to modify this general picture to a certain extent. Our analysis points to the following data:

a. In OTH, linguistic means are available for referring to distances.

b. The author of the text did not use distances for referring to 'unmarked positions.'

c. For that purpose, he used other means (e.g., one or more Prepositional Phrases). From c. it follows that the need for referring to 'unmarked positions' was felt by the author. Apparently, he did not consider phrases referring to distances, which would have been a useful tool in this case, to be an acceptable possibility. This phenomenon can be reasonably explained by assuming that he did not perceive space as an entity which can be quantified in general and under all conditions. His use of distances was restricted to straight edges and fringes of objects, all of them being lines with a clear (physical) appearance. It looks as if in his perception, space could only be quantified when attached to a more or less smooth border area which could easily be distinguished, and perceived in a material shape.

This assumption is in agreement with another result of the analysis, namely, that words which in Western languages are generally used for dimensions of objects were used in the text in contexts not involving measurement, only for referring to aspects of objects which have a clear physical and material form.

It may be, however, that the differences described in the previous section and discussed above, can be explained in a different way. In this connection, it is necessary to consider in detail a point which we mentioned in paragraph 7.4., at the end of our discussion of the literature on Exodus 25 - 31.

According to a number of exegetes, the author of this text did not refer to a real tabernacle, but to an imaginary one which should be considered as a kind of theological construction. If this were true his use of language might be neither completely technical nor purely theological.

As we already made clear in paragraph 7.4., we believe that the available evidence is insufficient for deciding definitely in favour or against this idea. So we did not consider it strong enough to force us to abandon Exodus 25 - 31 altogether and look for another text for our study of the perception of space in the Old Testament. In our opinion, the results of our analysis, which aims primarily at the linguistic characteristics of the text, do not change that position.

Our investigation shows that the text can be read adequately as if referring to real physical objects. A detailed analysis of all technical terms involved falls outside the scope of our study, so it is possible that not every special aspect of each object is clear. But our results provide no reason to assume that the text

236

refers to imaginary objects. Regarding the remarkable way (from the point of view of the use of modern Western languages) for referring to unmarked positions, it seems sufficiently technical to be perfectly suitable for reference to real objects. So this point does not provide a particular reason for supposing that the author referred to an imaginary tabernacle.

Other possible explanations of this remarkable use of language can be excluded as well, e.g.:

- The author did not think it necessary to write a detailed technical text, because he supposed his readers to be familiar with the objects he referred to.

- He omitted certain technical details because they did not serve his objective.

Both explanations do not make clear why the author maintained a way of referring which has technical features. But they suggest another possibility. It could be that the author of Exodus 25 - 31 used older material which he did not understand completely. In his editing of the original text, he made alterations according to his personal knowledge and experience, thereby changing the original text and linguistic structure.

So it could be that the author replaced the more advanced (according to Western ideas), technical description which he found in his (written?) source by a different one with which he was more familiar. A factor, which is of influence in this respect, is the level of what in Western terms would be called science and technology, in the cultural environment from which the text originated. We will explore this point in more detail in paragraph 9.2.

But for the time being, basing ourselves on the investigation of the text of Exodus 25 - 31, we believe that this remarkable use of language for referring to this particular spatial aspect, can best be accounted for by assuming a small difference in the perception of space by the author of the text and by modern, Western people.

8.7.4. Some general aspects of the investigation.

The first point which we will consider, is the method of analysis used in our investigation. It is true that the X-Bar theory was devised in particular for English, a modern, Western language, but since the basis for its analysis is formed by the different types of words of that language, it proved possible to use it for a different language such as OTH. It was, of course, necessary to adapt it to the types of words used in OTH, but this did not present many difficulties. A further fundamental step in the formulation of the structure of the text is the grouping of words into phrases. In this step, the 'sense-of-language' and intimate familiarity with its usage are extremely important. In the case of an extinct language, both are not readily available, so it is necessary to rely on alternatives. Usually, the sense-of-language of the investigator receives a predominant influence. In our investigation, we tried to compensate for that, at least partly, by incorporating a different 'sense-of-OTH,' namely the one expressed in the Masoretic accents. Apparently these accents have not been added to the text with the sole purpose of bringing about a purely linguistic structuring of it.

237

Hence, its use in our analysis presented a number of problems and limitations (see paragraph 8.3.). Despite these, we feel that this additional step provided a valuable contribution to our analysis.

At a number of points, it led to a structure which was different from what we expected to find on the basis of our modern sense-of-language. This led us to consider alternative possibilities, which otherwise might have escaped attention. It appeared that most differences were connected with the higher constructs in the structure, the grouping of phrases into sentences. At the basic level, the coordination of words to a phrase 'headed' by one of them, there proved to be much agreement between the approach of the Masoretes and that of modern linguistic science.

One of the objectives of our investigation was the use of an analytical method which would not impose a structure from outside upon the text, but would handle it carefully, and be as open as possible to both the text and its language. It is impossible to determine exactly whether this objective has been achieved or not. In any case, both in performing and presenting the analysis, this point has received permanent attention. The method we used, should be considered as an attempt to obtain a careful research tool for investigating ancient texts, which is able to cover both comprehensive and detailed aspects.

A second point to consider is the relation between the complicated method which we used in our analysis of the text and the rather straightforward result which we obtained. It seems appropriate to ask ourselves: Would it have been possible to achieve a corresponding result with a simpler analytical tool?

In scientific study, as a rule, the method of investigation is chosen beforehand, on the basis of the assessment of the level of complexity of the problem at hand. From our summary of the prior evidence in chapter 6, we concluded that the investigation of the perception of space in the Old Testament involves many methodological problems. In addition, the work of Jackendoff and Talmy on the structuring of space and spatial relations by modern, Western languages suggested that a relation between linguistic fine-structure and details of referring to space might exist. The consideration of both aspects made us decide to use a comprehensive and detailed method of analysis.

From section 8.7.2., it appears that, according to our analysis of Exodus 25 - 31, the most characteristic points relating to the structuring of space by the language of that text are found not so much in the detailed and complex structure of the sentences and the text but in the presence or absence of certain types of phrases in certain parts of it. Perhaps the use of a simpler method of analysis might have given a similar result, but we would not have been certain of the existence of other and more complex relations within the text. The use of a thorough method of analysis in our investigation enables us to say that, within the framework of our application of it, such more complex relations are not readily detectable, and hence, improbable.

Our final point concerns a more general result of our investigation. It appears that the sentence structure of Exodus 25 - 31, in particular as regards the verb-type, is in general agreement with what might be expected for discourse-type of texts on the basis of recent publications in this field.[1] At the same time, it shows that a number of rules outlined in these publications should not be applied in a rigid way. When the relation between sentence- and verb-type on one hand, and their role or function in the text on the other, is considered in more detail, it appears to be quite flexible (see above 8.5., in particular 8.5.6.). In this sense, our result provides a confirmation of a comment by de Regt.[2]

---

1   Schneider, 1985; Niccacci, 1990.
2   De Regt, 1988, p. 52.

9. THE PERCEPTION OF SPACE IN THE OLD TESTAMENT.

9.1. Introduction.
In this final chapter we consider the results of our investigation in wider perspective. In the next paragraph, we take into account a number of relevant aspects of the world of the ANE as a whole. Some data concerning Palestine and the Old Testament which so far have been left out of consideration will be included. A comparison of the result with previous work on the perception of space in the Old Testament is given in section 9.3. The final paragraph 9.4. pays attention to the role of the perception of space within the wider concept of the (general) experience of space in the Old Testament.

9.2. Comparison with the perception of space in the Ancient Near East.

9.2.1. Introduction.
As mentioned in paragraph 1.3., we assume that the perception of space in the Old Testament is somehow connected with the perception (and general experience) of space in the ANE as a whole. For a number of reasons, we decided to postpone a survey of this area until after completing our investigation. This has the advantage that we are now able to pay special attention to those aspects which are relevant in view of the result of our study. So, on one hand, this paragraph aims to cover more or less the whole field, whereas on the other hand it is directed to a few particular items.
In section 9.2.2. we consider a few publications which discuss the general role of space in the world of the ANE. The study of the pictorial art and general aspects of science for obtaining an idea of the use of space in the thought patterns of the ANE is reviewed in section 9.2.3. The more quantitative aspects, which relate in particular to disciplines such as metrology and construction technology, are explored in section 9.2.4. This section also covers archeological findings and related data from the Old Testament and Palestine. The final section of this paragraph (9.2.5.) summarizes the results of the various sections.

9.2.2. The experience of space in general.
In most publications which we were able to find, the role of both space and time in certain parts of the ANE is discussed. The only exception is Brunner's

article on the concept of space of the ancient Egyptians.[1] He distinguishes between the "Raum des Alltags" and the "mythische Raum" and describes the attitude of the Egyptians to them as follows: "Der Raum des Alltags wird ebenso empfunden wie bei uns. Die Teile dieses Raumes sind meßbar, wahrnehmbar, eindeutig lokalisierbar, der Mensch kann über sie verfügen. Der andere, der Mythische Raum dagegen ist nur bedingt wahrnehmbar, kaum meßbar und keinesfalls eindeutig lokalisierbar. Er begegnet uns im eigentlichen Mythos, also in Göttererzählungen, ferner realisiert im Kult und im Tempel als dem Rahmen des Kultes."[2] After an extensive review of the concept of the mythical space, he considers its relation to the concept of 'every-day-space.' It appears that mythical space takes the dominant position, which in a number of cases leads to contradictions between ideas from the mythical space and observations from daily life. Brunner concludes his article with the following comment: "Krasse Widersprüche, für unser wissenschaftlich bestimmtes Denken unerträglich, läßt der Ägypter einfach stehen: Bis in die Spätzeit findet er kein Ärgernis darin, daß die Quellen des Nils bei Asuan und bei Altkairo liegen, wenn man die Sache religiös-mythisch betrachtet, daß aber der Nil von weit oben aus dem Sudan kommt, wenn man einen geographisch-politischen Maßstab anlegt. Mythos und Arbeitswelt widersprechen einander, doch ist das im allgemeinen erst für die klassischen Griechen und die von ihnen abhängigen Kulturen ein Grund zum Anstoß, nicht für Menschen, die noch mit dem Mythos lebendigen Umgang pflogen. Ja die Ägypter benutzten sogar mythische Begriffe, die ihrem Wesen nach widersprüchlich sind, um wissenschaftliche Erkenntnisse auszudrücken, und zwar gerade bei Fragen des Raumes."[3]

The same point has been made by Leclant who, using an expression of Frankfort, writes: ".... c'est par la 'multiplicité des approches' que l'Egyptien appréhende la réalité. Selon le point de vue où il se place, celle-ci peut lui apparaître différente, voire même ce que nous nommerions 'contradictoire,' avec ce que lui offrirait un autre angle de vue."[4] The influence of theology on the logical and rational thought processes of the ancient Egyptians has been emphasized by Reineke.[5] In another publication, dealing with the boundaries of space and time with the Egyptians, Brunner also emphasized the importance of influences of this nature: "Wer die Grenze zwischen der religiösen Intention der Mythen und der modernen Erkenntnis eines naturwissenschaftlichen Weltbildes verwischt, wird zu schweren Fehldeutungen kommen."[6]

In both publications, Brunner notices that space within the confines of the

---

1   Brunner, 1957.
2   o.c. , p. 615.
3   o.c. , p. 620.
4   Leclant, 1969, p. 218.
5   Reineke, 1982, p. 102.
6   Brunner, 1954 - 56, p. 141, n.1.

creation has an ordered nature, whereas outside creation, it is chaos.[1] The same observation has been made by Leclant.[2] The latter also remarks that the Egyptian vocabulary seems to indicate "que les catégories pour nous fondamentales de l'espace et du temps n'ont pas été reconnues d'une façon semblable à la nôtre par les anciens Egyptiens."[3]

As far as ancient Persia is concerned, Duchesne-Guillemin has pointed to the close identity of the roles of Zurvan, the god of time, and Vayu, the god of space.[4] In her review on space and time in ancient Mesopotamia, Cassin also writes on the similarity of certain features of time and space: "Dans le mythe et dans la vie sociale par le moyen des fêtes, il y a équivalence ou identité entre le jour, le mois, l'année; de même nous trouvons ici équivalence ou identité entre un espace aux dimensions réduites et la terre dans sa totalité."[5]

From this review, it is clear that our search of the literature on the role of space in the ANE does not yield any publications which are directed in particular to the perception of space.

9.2.3. The role of space in the pictorial art and science of the Ancient Near East.

In our literature search, we found a number of publications on these two aspects of the ANE, which also pay attention to the role of space in them.

In her study of "Frühformen des Erkennens," Brunner-Traut discusses ancient Egyptian art as a source of knowledge on ancient thought. Her starting point is the impression which this art makes on the modern viewer: "Das seit den Griechen der klassischen Zeit .... an tiefenräumlich-perspektivische Darstellweise gewöhnte Auge sieht in ägyptischen Bildern flächig ausgebreitete Gebilde, denen Körperlichkeit und Raumtiefe fehlen und die Lösungen anbieten, welche mit der Sehbild-Wirklichkeit nicht übereinstimmen."[6] According to her, this way of presentation can be found with all archaic cultures before the Greek classical period, but also, among others, with children and uneducated painters in our own time. People who use this approach "zeichnen in der Weise, daß sie einzelne (Binnen-)Teile eines Gegenstandes (möglichst) unverkürzt wiedergeben, aber diese Teile nur gradweise zum Bildganzen in Beziehung bringen. Das Bildganze ist Teil um Teil (richtig) er-faßt, bzw. diese Teile sind addiert zu einem gefälligen Ganzen. Nicht etwa zu einem Mosaikbild; es genügt, so viele Teile ins Bild zu bringen, wie zum Verständnis des Ganzen nötig sind. Da das ganze Aspekt um Aspekt gelesen ist, habe ich diese Darstellweise die aspektivische genannt, in Abhebung von der perspektivischen. ....

Addition ist in Ägypten freilich an sinnbedingte Position gebunden, das

---

1   o.c. , p. 142.
2   Leclant, 1969, p. 223.
3   o.c. , p. 218 -19.
4   Duchesne-Guillemin, 1969, p. 267f.
5   Cassin, 1969, p. 251.
6   Brunner-Traut, 1990, p. 7.

Benachbartsein ist als Relation er-faßt, Lage und Maße, aber nur bedingt die Richtung sind dem Ganzen angepaßt."[1]

After a short description of the historic growth of the perspective way of presenting, she comments on its relation to its aspective counterpart: "Perspektive ist jene Darstellweise, die der Aspektive entwicklungsgeschichtlich folgt und eine sprunghaft veränderte Wahrnehmungsweise signaliert; nicht die optische Wahrnehmungsweise, denn diese ist, solange wir den Homo sapiens kennen, die gleiche geblieben ...., sondern in die erkenntnismäßige, die kognitiv-psychische Verinnerlichung."[2]

At this point Brunner-Traut touches upon the general distinction between perception and experience. In view of the importance of this distinction for our investigation (see above paragraph 1.3.), it is worth while to take notice of her ideas on this topic. According to her, it is beyond doubt that human beings can and could perceive optically in the same way. "Meine Behauptung ist aber die, daß sich die kognitiv-psychische Wahrnehmung, die zur Gewinnung des Gegenstandes führt, die Apperzeption, generell gewandelt hat. ....

Die Gegenstandsgewinnung hat zur Voraussetzung die niedere Stufe der auch 'Perzeption' genannte Aufnahme von Eindrücken, die über die Sinnesorgane gewonnen werden. Damit diese Eindrücke operationell, d.h. für eine Darstellung verfügbar werden, müssen sie selektiert, organisiert, gegliedert, geordnet, kurz: beurteilt werden. Dieser psychisch-intellektuell-willensmäßige Prozeß, der zu dem konzept 'dieser Gegenstand' führt, ist eine die Bedeutungssysteme durchlaufende, auf sensomotorischer Aktivität beruhende Leistung und ist das, was uns hier als Gegenstandsgewinnung interessiert. Das seelische, erkennende Verhalten gegenüber neu auftretenden Bewußtseinsinhalten, die Art der Einordnung neuer Wahrnehmungen und Erfahrungen, die Auslese und Ordnung des Gegebenen, die Weise der Verinnerlichung, kurz: die Einbindung in den Empfindungs- und Kenntniszusammenhang nennen wir 'Apperzeption', und diese steht hier zur Diskussion. Also nur, auf welche Weise der Mensch die Perzeption zur Apperzeption umbildet, ist für unsere Fragestellung zunächst von Belang."[3]

After this explanation of more fundamental issues involved, she describes the main difference between the two modes of presenting (aspective and perspective) as follows: "Die Ägypter und ihre Geistverwandten gewinnen ihren Gegenstand im schrittweisen Nacheinander-Erfassen der Teile; die Griechen entdeckten die (optische) Zusammenschau des Ganzen."[4]

To illustrate the two approaches, Brunner-Traut discusses a number of examples; at the end of this exposition, she confirms her initial explanation of the phenomena. After she has emphasized once more: "Aspektivische Bilder wollen

---

1   o.c. , p. 7 - 8.
2   o.c. , p. 11.
3   o.c. , p. 12 - 13.
4   o.c. , p. 13.

nicht simultan überblickt werden, sondern Element für Element wie eine Art Bildersprache gelesen werden. Die Elemente sind nur auf die nächste Nachbarschaft bezogen, nicht allseitig verknüpft," she gives the following more detailed comment on the spatial aspect involved: "Das sensomotorische, psychisch-intellektuelle Verarbeiten des Seherlebnisses 'Raum', genauer: der Dinge im Raum, gehört zu den Höchstleistungen des Menschen. Bekanntlich können Blindgeborenen, die im Erwachsenenalter durch Operation sehfähig werden, niemals mehr ein vollständiges räumliches Wahrnehmen erwerben. Stellt bereits die Raumwahrnehmung ein komplexes Phänomen dar, an dessen Zustandekommen viele Faktoren beteiligt sind, so ist die Raumvorstellung (und entsprechend -darstellung) ein vielgestaltig durchgegliederter Endzustand psycho-physischen Geschehens, für den intentionale Aktivität aufgebracht werden muß."[1]

She continues with a summary of the work of Piaget on space experience in general and at the end of the chapter on art, gives a comment, which can be regarded as a kind of programme for the remainder of her book: "Da sich zeigen wird, daß sich das parataktische Nach- und Nebeneinander wie in der Kunst so in der hierarchischen Gesellschaftsordnung, auf den Gebieten der Wissenschaft ...., in der durch Polytheismus und Mythen gekennzeichneten Religion, in Sprache, Literatur, Geschichtsauffassung, im Rechtswesen, kurz in den Vorstellungs- und Denkformen aller kulturellen Sparten wiederfindet, wird die These, daß die bildnerische Artverschiedenheit ein Grundverhalten der Alten Ägypter und der Vergleichsgruppen zu erkennen gibt doch wohl zur Gewißheit."[2]

It cannot be denied that Brunner-Traut provides a thorough and comprehensive discussion of a problem which had been identified earlier. In 1951, Groenewegen-Frankfort also signalled that "Ancient Near Eastern art .... shares .... a way of rendering objects which differs fundamentally from [ways of representing objects whereby the surface space surrounding them is two- or three-dimensional]."[3] She calls this approach 'non-functionalism,' and explains it as follows: "Non-functionalism .... is a logical concept, not an aesthetic or a psychological one. It is a characteristic of nonfunctional representations that the surface is neither a completely dominant factor nor reduced to a mere opportunity for spatial illusion, but that the conflict between the three-dimensional object to be rendered and the two-dimensional opportunity given has not been solved in favour of either."[4]

As compared to this earlier approach, Brunner-Traut seems to opt for the predominance of the two-dimensional surface, without specifying exactly the mutual relationship between the various 'aspects' of the picture, and the

---

1   o.c. , p. 68.
2   o.c. , p. 70.
3   Groenewegen-Frankfort, 1951, p. 7.
4   o.c. , p. 7.

relationship of the aspects to the whole.

The application of this approach for elucidating the broader cognitive structures of the ancient Egyptians has been attacked by Reineke: "Man darf aber m.E. nicht das aus der Entwicklung der bildlichen Darstellung hergeleitete Element auf die Erkenntnisstruktur schematisch übertragen. Die Aspektive würde m.E. die Entdeckung von Kausalitäten verhindern, die die Ägypter zweifelsohne gemacht haben."[1]

A similar problem seems to exist in modern assessment of the 'science' of ancient Mesopotamia. Its results consist mainly of extensive lists of expressions, as described by Von Soden: "Die sumerische Wissenschaft ist satzlos und reiht nur nominale Ausdrücke ohne jede Erläuterung eindimensional aneinander."[2] But similar to Reineke for ancient Egypt, Von Soden does not conclude to serious limitations of Mesopotamian science: "Daß Schlüsse und Erkenntnisse ebenso wie die Prämissen nicht formuliert wurden, darf uns nun freilich nicht zu der Folgerung verführen, die Babylonier waren an solchen Erkenntnisse nicht interessiert gewesen. Vor allem ihre Mathematik zeigt deutlich, daß ein die vielen Einzelheiten übergreifendes Wissen für sie verfügbar war, ohne daß es in Sätzen formuliert wurde."[3]

This idea can be illustrated by the data on the theorem of Pythagoras, which was used in practical applications both in Egypt and Mesopotamia. Although its general formulation so far has not been found in the ANE, its employment in more theoretical exercises has been established for Mesopotamia.[4] It is true that in these exercises dimensions like width or length are being used, but on the basis of the specific numbers involved, Neugebauer suggests that they "are hardly more than a convenient guide to illustrate the underlying general process. Thus it is substantially incorrect if one denies the use of a 'general formula' to Babylonian algebra."[5]

The relation between the separate aspects and the whole which they form together presents another problem within Brunner-Traut's approach. The elements which she distinguishes in pictures, and which appear to be depicted in a reasonably correct way (as seen from the 'perspective approach'), can be considered as more or less separate entities which form 'wholes of some size' on their own. Apparently the Ancients were able to consider these smaller wholes in an appropriate way. Perhaps their appreciation of space and spatial arrangements was restricted to small areas.

In this connection a few remarks made by Keel seem to be relevant. In his treatise on the world of Ancient Eastern picture symbolics and the Old

---

1   Reineke, 1982, p. 102, n. 4; see also Reineke, 1980, p. 1238.
2   Von Soden, 1985, p. 139.
3   o.c. , p. 145.
4   see Neugebauer, 1957, p. 43 - 48; Oelsner, 1982, p. 58 - 60; Ronan, 1983, p. 29.
5   Neugebauer, 1957, p. 43 - 44; see also Oelsner, o.c. , p. 58.

Testament, he includes a paragraph on 'technical presentations' of the 'Weltganzen'. Its opening sentence reads: "Das technische Verständnis der Welt, ihre Durchsichtigkeit und Machbarkeit sind aufs engste mit ihrer Quantifizierbarkeit verbunden."[1]

With this comment, Keel touches upon the quantitative aspects of space experience. We will come back to this point in the next section, in which we will investigate these aspects in more detail.

9.2.4. The quantitative aspects of space experience; metrology and archaeology.

As already announced, this section will cover data from the ANE in general and from Palestine and the Old Testament. The measuring of dimensions, surfaces, weights, etc. was an important activity in the ANE, not only in terrestrial affairs but also in cosmic relations[2] and in the world of the gods.[3] Different systems of measuring units were in use in the various ancient societies and much attention has been paid to the clarification of individual details and the elucidation of their mutual relationships. This applies to the ANE as a whole[4] and to the Bible and Palestine.[5] It is clear that the diversity of units presents a problem when scholars wish to compare the various data with each other. In particular, the length of the cubit has been the topic of much investigation.[6] In connection with our interest in the perception of space, these publications prove to be less relevant. We would like to know more about the technical aspects of measuring. But in the literature which we were able to collect, no detailed descriptions of measuring techniques are given. As far as the Old Testament is concerned, De Vaux, after having explained that in his opinion, very detailed calculations for the various measures of length, such as the cubit, are "pointless because there was no official standard," writes: "In practice, the architects, masons and craftsmen measured with their own arms, their extended hands, their palms and their fingers."[7] At the same time he describes various measuring instruments, like the rod (קָנֶה) and various cords, but points to the fact that we do not know whether they were standardized.[8]

In connection with our interest in measuring methods, it is useful to know that 1 Kings 7:23 describes that such a cord was used to measure the circumference of a round object. But, in agreement with what we found in our investigation of Ex 25 - 31 (see section 8.7.4.), it is again a solid rim which is measured. It would

---

1   Keel, 1977, p. 13.
2   see Houtman, 1974, p. 211.
3   see Korpel, 1990, p. 463.
4   see Lorenzen, 1966; Helck, 1980; Vleeming, 1980; Powell, 1987 - 1990; Van den Hout, 1987 - 1990.
5   see Sellers, 1962; Schmitt, 1977; Huey, 1976.
6   Scott, 1959, p. 23 - 27; Kaufman, 1984.
7   De Vaux, 1974, p. 197.
8   o.c. , p. 196.

be interesting to know whether cords were used to measure distances across surfaces or in space. The 'man with a linen cord and a measuring stick in his hand' of Ezechiel 40:03 ff, also seems to measure along 'solid lines' only. The plumb-line (אֲנָךְ), mentioned in Amos 7: 7, 8, which also might be used in this respect, apparently was only applied for checking the condition of walls. There are references to the stretching out of a measuring cord on surfaces (2 Kings 21:13; Jeremiah 31:39; Zechariah 1:16; Job 38:05), but no further details are given. As with the plumb-line, its purpose might be to control the quality of buildings and towns (see Isaiah 28:17; 34:11, 17). From Isaiah 44:13, it appears that a similar cord was also used on a smaller scale, but again, no details are given.

For ancient Egypt, Wilsdorf reports that already in the Old Kingdom, the use of plumb-line and measuring rod by ship constructors has been depicted.[1] He also refers to the use of "Baugrundrisse und kartographische Skizzen" which is not limited to Egypt, but also includes Mesopotamia.[2] Regarding the construction activities, Baines and Malek write that we still know very little of how the Egyptians prepared the locations and made the necessary measurements.[3] In their survey of Egyptian masonry, Clarke and Engelbach report the finding of a mason's cord-and-reel,[4] and discuss the use of squared surfaces in architecture. According to them the Egyptians "dimensioned their plans more or less, but, to our eyes, the dimensions are very meagre."[5]

Lorenzen refers to grids which apparently were applied to surfaces on which pictures had to be made, and which were usually removed afterwards. In a number of cases, however, traces of them have been found.[6] Iversen and Shibata include the function of these grids in their discussion on Egyptian art and believe them to play a role in the proportioning of the figures to be depicted. But, as with other means used by the Egyptians, they "were never, as in Greece, systematized into general laws of optics and perspective."[7] Together with proportion, these authors use two other terms in the canonical analysis of Egyptian art: "Proportion, for the correct adjustment of the parts to the anthropometric standardizations of the canon, Symmetry, for the commensurability of the parts, and Eurhythmy, for the coordination of proportions and symmetry into a harmonious unity in accordance with the established aesthetics of numbers."[8]

Whatever their role may have been, these grids indicate that the artists had some idea of structuring the empty two-dimensional space prior to using it for

---

1   Wilsdorf, 1982, p. 134.
2   o.c. , p. 136.
3   Baines, Malek, 1988, p. 64.
4   Clarke and Engelbach, 1930, p. 65.
5   o.c. , p. 48.
6   Lorenzen, 1966, p. 20; see also Baines, Malek, 1988, p. 61.
7   Iversen, Shibata, 1975, p. 11.
8   o.c. , p. 13; see also Davis, 1985.

depicting figures, scenes, etc. This is a form of seeing (a limited) space as an independent entity.

As regards Mesopotamia, Keel, whose book shows a number of pictures of plans of towns and houses, comments: "Den Bewohnern Mesopotamiens war es um 1500 v. Chr. also möglich, ein Gebiet von ca. 900 x 800 m. relativ genau zu erfassen. Seine Welt, die Stadt, war von ihm ausgedacht, geplant und gebaut, und er war für ihren Unterhalt verantwortlich. .... War ein Gebiet nicht eben und größer als ein paar Quadratkilometer, so wurde es für den AO schon schwierig, sich von ihm eine technische und genaue Vorstellung zu machen."[1]

A comprehensive picture of his ideas can be found in the following quotation: "Worauf hier insistiert wird, ist nicht die Unfähigkeit des ao Menschen, ein größeres Gebiet von einem einheitlichen - sei es technisch-künstlichen ...., sei es perspektivisch-natürlichen ....- Gesichtspunkt aus darzustellen. So gut wie sicher handelt es sich hier ja gar nicht um eine technische Unfähigkeit, sondern um eine instinktive Abneigung, die Dinge so wiederzugeben, wie man sie von einem einzigen zufälligen Gesichtspunkt aus sieht, oder positiv, um die tiefsitzende Notwendigkeit, die Dinge so zu zeigen, wie man sie in langem Umgang und mit allen seinen Sinnen erfahren hat und nun in sich herumträgt (Denkbild)."[2]

Heinrich and Seidl published details on a number of plans of buildings from Mesopotamia, in some of which the measure of the dimensions concerned had been written at the proper place. They comment: "Der Umstand, daß in mehreren Fällen die eingeschriebenen Maße zwar richtig sind und sich auftragen lassen, jedoch die Figur, die sich dabei ergibt, nicht mit der Zeichnung identisch ist, läßt mit Sicherheit darauf schlieszen, daß es sich nicht um Entwürfe (für die der Maßstab überdies zu klein wäre), sondern um Aufmaße handelt, für die sich der aufnehemende Architekt auch heute eine Handskizze anzufertigen pflegt, in die er die Maße einträgt."[3]

In his discussion of architectural planning in ancient Israel, Isserlin also refers to the use of drawings and sketches. After reviewing their use in Mesopotamia, Egypt and Israel, he concludes: "In view of the measurements for the Temple of Solomon, preserved in 1 Kings 6 2ff, one may assume that Israelite plans were provided with figures for dimensions, as were the Egyptian and Mesopotamian plans ...."[4]

In this connection, it is important to pay special attention to the Siloam tunnel, as constructed under king Hezekiah.[5] The inscription found within the tunnel not only shows that longer distances were measured (the accuracy of the result

---

1   Keel, 1977 , p. 14.
2   o.c. , p. 14 - 15.
3   Heinrich, Seidl, 1967, p. 45.
4   Isserlin, 1984, p. 175; see also Wright, 1985, 464 - 466.
5   see Simons, 1952, p. 157 - 94; Barrois, 1962, p. 352 - 55

is a separate problem), but also that the digging of the tunnel started from its two ends: from within the city and from the well outside the walls. It is clear that such an approach requires some insight into the spatial arrangement of the area concerned and careful planning in advance of the whole operation, in order to achieve that the workers from both sides meet each other somewhere underground. An additional problem is presented by the curved shape of the tunnel. Amiran discusses two groups of theories aiming to explain these problems: the first one is based on a suggestion by Clermont-Ganneau, "who believed the curved course of the tunnel to be due to the desire to avoid the 'Tombs of the Davidic Kings' in the City of David," and the second one based on ideas of Hecker, "who believes that the engineers and hewers followed a stratum in the rock which was of a medium hardness, known as meleke."[1] She herself adopts a variant from the second group of theories, based on an idea of Sulley, who suggested that "the curved course of the tunnel indicates the former existence of a natural subterranean stream which ran from the spring through the hill, emerging at the bottom of the valley on the west of the Mount Zion spur."[2] In her opinion, this theory is able to clarify many points in relation to the tunnel, among others the problem referred to above, how the hewers working from both sides, were able to meet in the middle. In addition, she suggests that "the word zdh in the third line of the inscription, the etymology of which remains obscure, can now be explained as a technical term for a crack in the rock through which water and air could pass."[3] Her suggestion has been accepted by Mazar,[4] whereas Kenyon and Moorey are more careful and write that the workers "probably exploited natural fissure lines and crevices in the rock."[5]

It is difficult to decide whether this explanation is correct. Perhaps additional and directed archeological investigations may provide more, and conclusive, evidence. In any case, the inscription indicates that the construction of the tunnel was experienced as a major technical achievement. But it also shows that the precise recording of the length of the tunnel presented a problem.

9.2.5. Summary.

Having completed our survey of the general background of the ANE as far as space experience is concerned, we summarize three points:

a. It appears that within certain limits, the perception of space in the ANE is considered to be more or less similar to that of modern, Western culture. The limits are formulated in different ways by different authors, e.g. :

---

1   Amiran, 1975, p. 77.
2   o.c. , p. 77.
3   o.c. , p. 78.
4   Mazar, 1990, p. 484.
5   Kenyon and Moorey, 1987, p. 113.

- Brunner: within the space of everyday;
- Brunner-Traut: within the elements of the figures or phenomena;
- Keel: within a restricted, geographical area.

b. As far as the experience of space is concerned and the use of spatial concepts in the expression of other subjects, many authors point to differences between the ANE and modern, Western culture. Most of them believe this phenomenon to be due to the influence of other factors, but they differ in opinion as regard, what they are:
- Brunner: mythical space;
- Brunner-Traut: the aspective way of presentation;
- Keel: the sensibility for the things "in ihrer Eigenheit und Eigenständigkeit."[1]

Brunner seems to emphasize the influence of world-view and religion, which leads people in the ANE to consider some spatial aspects in a way which is unacceptable to people from modern, Western culture. He restricts himself to noticing the difference.

Brunner-Traut pays more attention to cognitive and psychological factors, but the use of her approach for areas other than pictorial art has been heavily attacked.

Keel believes that no technical aspect is concerned, but "eine tiefsitzende Notwendigkeit."[2] Unfortunately, he gives no reasons for this statement.

In this respect, it is necessary to keep in mind that recent research shows that the relation between mental imagery and spatial cognition is rather complicated.[3]

In particular, when it comes to the practical use of spatial images (and their 'material parallels': maps), people show many individual differences. Some are very able in working with them, others seem to lack this ability almost completely. In addition, an adequate psychological model of all aspects of the experience of space and the use of spatial aspects in other areas of life does not seem to be available. Hence, we believe that it is not wise at this moment to elaborate on detailed 'explanations' of possible differences between people of the ANE and of modern, Western culture.

c. It appears that science in the ANE mainly tries to solve practical problems. At the same time there are a number of examples of generalizations and attempts to formulate rules.

What we believe to be possible and useful at the end of this summary is to consider the question: how do our results relate to the generally-accepted aspects of the picture of the perception of space? On one hand, they underline the agreement in the perception of space between the ANE and our time. On the other hand, the differences which we found led us to assume that the author of Exodus 25 - 31 lacked the possibility of seeing and employing 'space in general'

---

1   Keel, 1977, p. 15.
2   o.c. , p. 15.
3   Anderson, 1980, p. 86 - 93; Klein, 1983.

as a quantifiable entity. The results of our literature search as reported in this paragraph, suggest that it is highly improbable that this has been the case for everybody in the ANE including Israel. Architects and construction engineers must have had the knowledge and experience to use 'space and spatial aspects' which were not bound to 'organized and easily surveyable surfaces.' Perhaps this knowledge and ability were restricted to a small group of professionals only and had little or no influence on the majority of the population. This could explain why the author of Exodus 25 - 31 referred to these spatial aspects in the remarkable way he did, as outlined in section 8.7.2.

It seems difficult to relate this difference in the perception of space directly to the approaches by Brunner-Traut and Keel. But it seems possible that the absence of a 'quantified image' of space facilitates the remarkable flexibility of people in the ANE in accepting that certain events were connected with more than one location, as noticed by Brunner. In the experience of space in the Old Testament, something similar has been described, which we will consider in the paragraph 9.4.

9.3. Comparison with previous work on the perception of space in the Old Testament.

In the comparison of our results with those of previous work in this area, we should keep in mind the limitations of our investigation (see our discussion in paragraph 8.7.). In this connection there is another point to remember. From our final assessment of the literature on the experience of space in the Old Testament (see paragraph 6.3.), it appears that in particular the publication of Boman is relevant in connection with space perception. But his method must be assessed as very weak (see above section 3.2.5. and paragraphs 3.3, 3.5. and 6.3.). This led us to consider his ideas as working hypotheses only. But it cannot be denied that they are based on an investigation which covers the whole of the Old Testament.

Despite these points, we believe that a comparison of the results of both investigations is useful, in order to see how they relate to each other.

The idea of Boman which seems to be most relevant to the perception of space in the Old Testament is the one under point b of section 3.2.1. It states that the Hebrews do not have an abstract concept of space and see objects as they are, without auxiliary lines such as contours and boundaries.

It appears that our results do not support both parts of this statement. Regarding the latter part, it is indeed probable that imaginary auxiliary lines, connected with some mathematical, geometric grid, were unknown to the people of the Old Testament. At least, in our analysis, no indications relating to their use could be found. But as a positive result, we found that boundaries and solid contours, especially straight ones, are important as 'bearers' of the dimensions of objects.

As far as the first part of Boman's statement is concerned, our results do not provide support either. The conclusion that, in general, there is agreement in the perception of space between people of the Old Testament and of modern,

251

Western culture might be seen as an indication that the reverse is true.

Our results also do not support another idea of Boman, namely, that the Hebrews are not interested in an accurate description of what things look like, but in the way they have been constructed (item d. on page 33). In our analysis of Ex 25 - 31, it appears that it is extremely difficult to distinguish between sentences giving instructions for the construction of objects and those providing more detailed indications of them.

On the basis of this comparison, we conclude that our results do not confirm the main ideas of Boman on the perception of space in the Old Testament.

It can be said that Boman makes a number of correct observations as far as the wider area of the experience of space in the Old Testament is concerned. But he used these points primarily for drawing conclusions on the more fundamental issue of the perception of space. It is this procedure which creates confusion and leads to general statements which cannot be defended. In addition to the inadequate use of linguistic data, as demonstrated by Barr, the book of Boman also suffers from this confusion.

Our search of the literature of the ANE shows that as far as the wider concept of space experience is concerned, a more or less generally accepted pattern exists: People in the ANE perceived space in a way similar to that of modern Western people, but in the experience and use of space and spatial concepts they were influenced by factors which originated from their cultural background and usually are alien to modern Western culture. It seems worth while to consider these factors as far as the Old Testament is concerned. This will be attempted in the next paragraph.

9.4. The experience of space in the Old Testament.

It seems possible to relate a number of data in the experience of space in the Old Testament with the ideas of Brunner on the experience of space in ancient Egypt, which we reported above (see section 9.2.3.). According to him, the ancient Egyptians accepted a way of relating events with locations which seems contradictory and impossible to modern man. In their experience, certain events (e.g., the beginning of the river Nile) can be connected with more than one location. Brunner connects this attitude with the influence of mythical space.

So it comes as no surprise that there seems to be a relation to what Childs writes about mythical space, in which, according to him, certain experiences seem to be attached to certain limited areas. If we understand him rightly, he thinks that one of the characteristic features of the Old Testament' way of using the concept of mythical space was that it believed that God Himself was bringing into existence in history (i.e. in the world of time and space) a new spatial reality (see above section 3.2.2.). This seems to imply that certain locations 'receive,' or rather, become the 'bearers' of, events of a new nature. In this connection, we mention Levenson (see above paragraph 2.5.), who speaks about the extraterrestrial quality attached to the mountain Horeb, and Gorman (see above paragraph 2.6.), who describes how some places within the tabernacle

252

take specific qualities with specific meanings in the Priestly ritual system.

We also point to a phenomenon described by Patte in his study of early Jewish hermeneutics, which he calls 'telescoping.' At its basis is an interpretation of Scripture by Scripture which leads to "a synthetic view of Scripture and sacred history. This is an expression of the unity of Scripture which manifests itself as 'telescoping' of all elements of Scripture around a limited number of locations, dates and personages."[1] Within the framework of his study, he concentrates on the occurrence of this process in post-biblical exegesis, and refers to a number of examples from the Targum, in which places from the Scriptures were identified with certain locations.[2] But he emphasizes that this attitude is already present in the Hebrew Bible itself. As an illustration, he refers to 2 Chr. 3:1, in which the mount Moriah is located in Jerusalem.[3]

These examples make it probable that the remarkable flexibility regarding space which Brunner noticed in ancient Egypt also applies to the Old Testament. And in agreement with our comment at the end of section 9.2.5., it seems justified to see a relation with one of the results of our investigation: the absence of a 'quantitative, strictly structured perception of space' may facilitate such a flexible experience of space.

For practical reasons, our investigation had to be restricted to one passage of the Old Testament. Hence, the statement given above is supported by evidence from limited sources only and should be seen as an invitation for further research in this area. We hope that in this respect our methodological explorations will be of some help.

---

1   Patte, 1975, p.67 - 68.
2   o.c. , p. 62.
3   o.c. , p. 68.

SUMMARY.

Having completed the written account of our investigation, it seems appropriate to conclude by considering it as a whole. Hence, this summary is not intended primarily as a survey of its contents (see above paragraph 1.4. for a short form of of this), but as an attempt to discuss its internal structure.

Our investigation can be divided roughly into five parts:

a. Chapter 1 provides the background and objective of our investigation. In order to expand our knowledge of the role of the concept of space in the Old Testament, we set as its objective: to investigate and describe how space was perceived in the Old Testament.

b. The next part consists of the result of our search for what is known already about this topic. From chapter 2, it appears that space and spatial aspects are indeed used in current reflection on the theological ideas of the Old Testament. Chapter 3, however, not only shows that relatively little is known about the perception of space in the Old Testament, but also makes clear that there is much discussion and confusion on the methods to be used in the investigation of a subject-matter like this. The underlying question in this debate is: "To what extent is it possible to draw conclusions on thought patterns of people on the basis of their (use of) language only?"

Unfortunately, even an extended search in the literature of the study of the Old Testament in a wider sense, in particular on the use of modern linguistics in it, did not provide an adequate answer to this question.

c. The third part of our investigation is described in chapter 4, 5 and 6. It reports and reviews our attempts to obtain an answer to the question formulated above by exploring the literature of relevant areas within linguistics, psychology, anthropology and philosophy. At the end, we had to conclude that our question touches upon a domain which is characterized by complicated relations and which requires a cautious approach and careful methods of investigation. Quick and easy results cannot be expected.

The outcome of our literature search led us to a critical examination of what has been written so far on the perception of space in the Old Testament and made us decide to undertake a further investigation of it.

In this search, we had also found a few publications which examine in what way language and its structure within texts are related to space and spatial aspects. It seems possible to indicate a relation between certain aspects of the fine structure of the language of a text and the spatial characteristics of the world to which this text refers.

So, for our investigation, we chose a text from the Old Testament referring to a part of the world which has clear, physical, spatial features, namely Exodus

25 - 31. In addition, we used a method of analysis which seems careful and detailed enough to enable us to assess the scope of possible relations between the fine structure of that text and the spatial aspects of its world, namely the X-bar theory as applied by Jackendoff.

d. In the fourth part, we report the course of our investigation. Chapter 7 contains a short survey of previous study of Exodus 25 - 31. So far, this text has not been used in an investigation like ours which uses it in order to study mental phenomena such as the perception of space by its author.

Subsequently, chapter 8 describes our analysis of Exodus 25 - 31. Its results lead us to conclude that the language of the text shows possibilities for referring to space and spatial relations which are comparable to those of modern European languages. In addition, we assume that its author made use of his language in a way which is similar to the ways in which modern users apply their languages.

These conclusions make us assume that, as far as the perception of space is concerned, there is general agreement between users of modern, Western languages and the author of the text. However, in our investigation, we also detected a few points in which the author used his language in a remarkable way as compared to modern users. On the basis of these points, we believe that there is a small difference in the perception of space: unlike most modern, Western people, the author did not perceive space as an entity which can be quantified in general and under all conditions.

e. In the final part of our investigation which is included in chapter 9, we discuss the result of our analysis of Exodus 25 - 31 in view of a few other phenomena.

At first, we compare it with what is known of the perception of space in the Ancient Near East in general. According to most scholars who have studied the science and technology of this period, there is similarity in the perception of space between the ANE and modern Western culture. This is in agreement with our results. The differences between the two cultures are assumed to relate to a large extent to the wider area of the experience of space. On the basis of the additional evidence from the ANE as a whole, we have to consider the possibility that the difference in the perception of space, which we discovered in our investigation, does not apply to the whole population, but that those involved professionally in technology had a perception of space which did not show this difference.

We also compare our results with previous work on the perception of space in the Old Testament and conclude that they differ considerably from earlier views. Contrary to prior statements, our results indicate that in general there is agreement in the perception of space between people of the Old Testament and of modern, Western culture. It is in the wider area of the perception of space that there exist important differences.

Finally, we make a few preliminary remarks on the relation between this broader concept and the result of our investigation. We assume a relation between the absence of a quantitative, strictly structured perception of space and the flexible experience of space which is characteristic for the ANE as a whole, including the world of the Old Testament.

It is clear that a conjecture like this requires support by more extensive investigation. It is also true that our study of the perception of space in the Old Testament is of limited scope only. It is based on the analysis of a small pericope only and uses one specific method.

At the same time, it shows that it is possible to investigate this phenomenon in some detail and arrive at a proper description of it.

ABBREVIATIONS.

The following abbreviations have been used:
a. In the text:

ANE   Ancient Near East.
LRH   Linguistic Relativity Hypothesis.
OTH   Old Testament Hebrew.

b. In the notes:

GKC   Kautzsch, E. , Cowley, A.E. , 1910, Gesenius' Hebrew grammar,
       2nd ed. of the English translation of the 28th German
       edition, Oxford.
WO'C   Waltke, B.M. , O'Connor, M. , 1990, An Introduction to Biblical
       Hebrew Syntax, Winona Lake.

c. In the Bibliography:

GWDA   Jürss, F. , et al. , 1982, Geschichte des wissenschaftlichen
       Denkens im Altertum, Berlin.
IDB   Buttrick, G.A. , et al. (eds.) , 1962, The Interpreter's Dictionary
       of the Bible, Nashville.
TWAT   Botterweck, G.J. , Ringgren, H. , et al. (eds.) , 1973 -   ,
       Theologisches Wörterbuch zum Alten Testament,
       Stuttgart / Berlin / Köln / Mainz.
VT   Vetus Testamentum, Leiden.
ZAW   Zeitschrift für die Alttestamentliche Wissenschaft,
       Berlin / New York.

BIBLIOGRAPHY.

Albrektson, B. , 1967, History and the Gods, Lund.

Amiran, R. , 1975, The Water Supply in Israelite Jerusalem, in: The Israel Exploration Society, Jerusalem Revealed, Archeology in the Holy City, 1968 - 1974, p. 75 - 78, Jerusalem.

Andersen, F.I. , 1970, The Hebrew Verbless Clause in the Pentateuch, Nashville.

Andersen, F.I. , 1974, The Sentence in Biblical Hebrew, The Hague / Paris.

Anderson, J.R. , 1980, Cognitive Psychology and Its Implications, San Francisco.

Apel, K-O. , 1974, Zur Idee einer transzendentalen Sprach-Pragmatik, in: J.Simon (ed.), Aspekte und Probleme der Sprachphilosophie, p. 283 - 326, Freiburg / München.

Bachelard, G. , 1969, The poetics of space, translated from the French, Boston.

Baines, J., Malek, J. , 1988, Atlas van het oude Egypte, translated from the English, Amsterdam.

Barr, J. , 1961, The semantics of biblical language, Oxford.

Barr, J. , 1978, Some notes on ben "between" in Classical Hebrew, Journal of Semitic Studies 23 (1978), 1 - 22.

Barrois, G. , 1962, Siloam, in: IDB, vol.4, p. 352 - 355.

Bartelmus, R. , 1990, רהב, in: TWAT, Band 7, Lieferung 3 - 5, p. 449 - 460.

Berlin, B. , Kay, P. , 1969, Basic color terms: their universality and evolution, Berkeley / Los Angelos.

Bernstein, B. , 1970, A sociolinguistic approach to socialization. With some reference to educability, in: F.Williams (ed.), Language and poverty: Perspectives on a theme, p. 25 - 61, Chicago.

Blackburn, S. , 1984, Spreading the Word. Groundings in the Philosophy of Language, Oxford.

Blum, E. , 1990, Studien zur Komposition des Pentateuch, Berlin / New York.

Boman, T, 1977, Das hebräische Denken im Vergleich mit dem Griechischen, 6. Aufl. , Göttingen.

Brockelmann, C. , 1956, Hebräische Syntax, Neukirchen.

Brown, R. , Lenneberg, E.H. , 1954, A study in language and cognition, Journal of Abnormal and Social Psychology 49, p. 454 - 462.

Brunner, H. , 1954 - 56, Die Grenzen von Zeit und Raum bei den Ägyptern, Archiv für Orientforschung 17, p. 141 - 145.

Brunner, H. , 1957, Zum Raumbegriff der Ägypter, Studium Generale 10, (1957), p. 612 - 620.

Brunner-Traut, E. , 1990, Frühformen des Erkennens: am Beispiel Altägyptens, Darmstadt.

Bühler, K. , 1982, Sprachtheorie. Die Darstellungsfunktion der Sprache,

Ungekürzter Neudruck der Ausgabe Jena, Fischer, 1934, Stuttgart / New York.

Cassin, E. , 1969, Cycles du temps et cadres de l'espace en Mésopotamie Ancienne, Revue de Synthèse, IIIe Sér. , 55 - 56, p. 241 - 257.

Cassirer, E. , 1985, Philosophie der Symbolischen Formen. Teil 1. Die Sprache, 8. unveränd. Aufl. ,reprogr. Nachdr. d. 2. Aufl., Darmstadt.

Childs, B.S. , 1962, Myth and Reality in the Old Testament, London.

Childs, B.S. , 1974, Exodus, a commentary, Old Testament Library, London.

Clark, H.H. , 1973, Space, time, semantics, and the child, in: T.E.Moore (ed.), Cognitive Development and the Acquisition of Language, p. 27 - 63, New York / London.

Clarke, S. , Engelbrecht, R. , 1930, Ancient Egyptian Masonry. The building Craft, London.

Cooper, D.E. , 1973, Philosophy and the nature of language, London.

Cotterell, P. , Turner, M. , 1989, Linguistics and Biblical Interpretation, London.

Crites, S. , 1987, The spatial dimensions of narrative truthtelling. in: G.Green (ed.), Scriptural Authority and Narrative Interpretation, p. 97 - 118, Philadelphia.

Cross, F. M. , 1947, The Tabernacle. A study from Archaeological and Historical Approach, Biblical Archaeologist 10, 3, p. 45 - 68.

Cross, F. M. , 1981, The Priestly Tabernacle in the Light of Recent Research, in: A.Biran (ed.), Temples and High Places in Biblical Times, Proc. of the colloquium in honour of the centennial of HUC-Jew. Inst. Religion, Jerusalem.

Davis, W.M. , 1985, The Canonical Tradition in Ancient Egyptian Art, PhD. Thesis, Harvard University, Cambridge, Mass.

Deist, F. , 1977, Stilvergleichung als literarkritisches Verfahren, ZAW 89, p. 325 - 357.

Derrida, J. , 1967, De la Grammatologie, Paris.

Devitt, M. , Sterelny, K. , 1987, Language and reality. An Introduction to the Philosophy of Language, Oxford.

Duchesne-Guillemin, J. , 1969, Espace et temps dans l'Iran ancien, Revue de Synthèse, IIIe Sér. , 55 - 56, p. 259 - 280.

Eichrodt, W. , 1959, Theologie des Alten Testaments, Teil I., 6. Aufl. , Stuttgart / Göttingen.

Elliger, K. , 1952, Sinn und Ursprung der priesterlichen Geschichtserzählung, in: K.Elliger, Kleine Schriften zum Alten Testament, ThB. 32, p. 174 - 98, München, 1966.

Fabry, H.-J. , 1989, צלע, in: TWAT, Band 6, p.1059 - 1064.

Fish, S. , 1980, Is There a Text in This Class? The Authority of Interpretive Communities, Cambridge / London.

Fishman, J.A. , 1982, Whorfianism of the third kind: Ethnolinguistic diversity as a worldwide societal asset, in: J.A. Fishman, Language & Ethnicity in minority sociolinguistic perspective, p. 564 - 579, Philadelphia, 1989.

Fraine, J. de, 1959, Adam et son lignage. Etudes sur la notion de 'personalité corporative' dans la Bible, Paris.

Fretheim, T.E. , 1968, The priestly document: anti-temple?, VT 18 , p. 313 - 329.

Friedman, R.E. , 1980, The Tabernacle in the Temple, Biblical Archaeologist, Fall 1980, p. 241 - 248.

Friedrich, G. , 1970, Zum Problem der Semantik, Kerygma und Dogma 16 , p. 41 - 57.

Friedrich, P. , 1986, The language Parallax. Linguistic Relativism and Poetic Indeterminacy, Austin.

Fritz, V. , 1977, Tempel und Zelt: Studien zum Tempelbau in Israel und zu dem Zeltheiligtum der Priesterschrift, Neukirchen-Vluyn.

Galling, K. , 1939, Die Anordnungen für den Kultus (25 - 31), in: G.Beer, K.Galling, Exodus, Handbuch zum Alten Testament, Tübingen.

Gamberoni, J. , 1989, קוֹם, in: TWAT, Band 6, p. 1251 - 1274.

Garcia López, F. , 1986, סבב, in: TWAT, Band 5, p. 730 - 744.

Gibson, A. , 1981, Biblical semantic logic. A preliminary analysis, Oxford.

Gipper, H. , 1972, Gibt es ein sprachliches Relativitätsprinzip? Untersuchungen zur Sapir-Whorf-Hypothese, Frankfurt am Main.

Gipper, H. , 1976, Is there a Linguistic Relativity principle? in: R.Pinxten (ed.), Universalism versus Relativism in Language and Thought. Proceedings of a Colloquium on the Sapir-Whorf Hypotheses, p. 217 - 228, The Hague / Paris.

Gölz, W. , 1970, Dasein und Raum. Philosophische Untersuchungen zum Verhältnis von Raumerlebnis, Raumtheorie und gelebtem Dasein, Tübingen.

Görg, M. , 1967, Das Zelt der Begegnung. Untersuchungen zur Gestalt der sakralen Zelttraditionen Altisraels, Bonn.

Görg, M. , 1981, Zur Dekoration des Leuchters, Biblische Notizen 15, p. 21 - 29.

Gooding, D.W. , 1959, The account of the tabernacle, Cambridge.

Gorman, F. , 1990, The ideology of ritual: Space, time and status in the priestly theology, Sheffield.

Gosztonyi, A. , 1976, Der Raum : Geschichte seiner Probleme in Philosophie und Wissenschaften, 2 Bände, Freiburg.

Gottwald, N.K. , 1985, The Hebrew Bible - a socio-literary introduction, Philadelphia.

Grace, G.W. , 1987, The linguistic construction of reality, Beckenham / North Ryde.

Groenewegen-Frankfort, H.A. , 1951, Arrest and Movement. An essay on space and time in the representational art of the ancient Near East, London.

Gross, W. , 1987, Die Pendenskonstruktion im biblischen Hebräisch, St. Ottilien.

Haran, M. , 1978, Temples & Temple Services in Ancient Israel, Oxford.

Hardmeier, C., Talstra, E. , 1989, Sprachgestalt und Sinngehalt. Wege zu neuen Instrumenten der computergestützten Textwahrnehmung., ZAW 101, p. 408 - 428.

Harris, R. , 1981, The language myth, London.

Hasel, G.F. , 1975, Old Testament Theology. Basic issues in the current debate, 2nd ed. , Grand Rapids.

Heinrich, E., Seidl, U. , 1967, Grundrißzeichnungen aus dem Alten Orient, Mitteilungen der Deutschen Orientgesellschaft 98, p. 24 - 45.

Helck, W. , 1980, Maße und Gewichte, in: Lexikon der Agyptologie, Band 3, p. 1199 - 1209, Wiesbaden.

Henton Davies, G. , 1962, Tabernacle, in: IDB, vol 4, p. 498 - 506.

Heschel, A.J. , 1951, The Sabbath. Its meaning for modern man, New York.

Hickmann, M. , 1987, Introduction: Language and Thought Revisited, in: M.Hickmann (ed.), Social and Functional Approaches to Language and Thought, p. 1 - 13, London.

Hockett, C.F., 1954, Chinese versus English: an Exploration of the Whorfian Theses; in: H.Hoyer (ed.), Language in Culture: Proceedings of a Conference on the Interrelations of Languages and Other Aspects of Culture, p. 106 - 123, Chicago.

Hoftijzer, J. , 1981, A search for method. A study in the syntactic use of the H-locale in classical Hebrew, Leiden.

Hornby, A.S. , 1981, Oxford Advanced Learner's Dictionary of Current English, Third ed., Oxford.

Hout, Th.P.J. van den, 1987 - 1990, Maße und Gewichte: bei den Hethitern, in: Reallexikon der Assyriologie, Band 7, p. 457 - 517, Berlin.

Houtman, C. , 1974, De hemel in het Oude Testament: een onderzoek naar de voorstellingen van het oude Israel omtrent de kosmos, Franeker.

Houtman, C. , 1980, Inleiding in de Pentateuch, Kampen.

Houtman, C. , 1986, Exodus, deel 1, Commentaar op het Oude Testament, Kampen.

Huey Jr, F.B. , 1976, Weights and Measures, in: The Zondervan Pictorial Encyclopedia of the Bible, Vol. 5, p. 913 - 924, Grand Rapids.

Hurowitz, V. , 1985, The priestly account of building the tabernacle, Journal of the American Oriental Society 105, p. 21 - 30.

Hurvitz, A. , 1982, A linguistic study of the relationship between the priestly source and the book of Ezechiel. A new approach to an old problem, Paris.

Hurvitz, A. , 1988, Dating the Priestly Source in Light of the Historical Study of Biblical Hebrew. A Century after Wellhausen., ZAW 100, Supplement, p. 88 - 100.

Isserlin, B.S.J. , 1984, Israelite architectural planning and the question of the level of secular learning in ancient Israel, VT 34, p. 169 - 178.

Iversen, E. , Shibata, Y. , 1975, Canon and Proportions in Egyptian Art, 2nd ed. , Warminster.

Jackendoff, R.S. , 1985, Semantics and cognition, 2nd ed. , Cambridge / London.

Jacob, E. , 1955, Théologie de l'ancien Testament, Neuchatel / Paris.

Janowski, B. , 1982, Sühne als Heilsgeschehen, Neukirchen-Vluyn.

Johnson, B. , 1979, Hebräisches Perfekt und Imperfekt mit vorangehendem we, Gleerup.

Johnson-Laird, P.N. , Wason, P.C. (eds.), 1977, Thinking. Readings in Cognitive Science, Cambridge.

Joüon, P. , 1947, Grammaire de l'Hébreu Biblique, 2me ed. , Rome.

Kaufman, A.S. , 1984, Determining the length of the medium cubit, Palestine Exploration Quarterly, 116, p. 120 - 132.

Kautzsch, E. , Cowley, A.E. , 1910, Gesenius' Hebrew grammar, 2nd ed. of the English translation of the 28th German edition, Oxford.(abbreviation: GKC)

Kayser, W. , 1969, Das sprachliche Kunstwerk. Eine Einführung in die Literaturwissenschaft, 13. Aufl. ,Bern / München.

Kearny, P.J. , 1977, Creation and Liturgy: The Redaction of Ex 25 - 40, ZAW 89, p. 375 - 387.

Kedar, B. , 1981, Biblische Semantik. Eine Einführung, Stuttgart.

Keel, O. , 1977, Die Welt der altorientalischen Bildsymbolik und das Alte Testament: am Beispiel der Psalmen, 2. Aufl. , Zürich / Neukirchen-Vluyn.

Kenyon, K.M. , Moorey, P.R.S. , 1987, The Bible and Recent Archeology, rev. ed. , London.

Klein, W. , 1983, Deixis and spatial orientation in route directions. in: H.L.Pick, L.P.Acredolo (eds.), Spatial Orientation. Theory, Research and Application, p. 283 - 311, New York / London.

Koch, K. , 1959, Die Priesterschrift. Von Exodus 25 bis Leviticus 16. Eine überlieferungsgeschichtliche und literarkritische Untersuchung, Göttingen.

Koch, K. , 1968, Gibt es ein hebräisches Denken? Pastoralblätter 108, p. 258 - 276.

Koch, K. , 1974, Was ist Formgeschichte? Neue Wege der Bibelexegese, 3. Aufl. , Neukirchen.

Koch, K. , 1991, Die hebräische Sprache zwischen Polytheismus und Monotheismus, in: K.Koch, Spuren des hebräischen Denkens. Beiträge zur alttestamentlichen Theologie, Gesammelte Aufsätze, Band 1, Neukirchen-Vluyn.

Korpel, M.C.A. , 1990, A rift in the clouds. Ugaritic and Hebrew Description of the Divine, Münster.

Lakoff, G. , Johnson, M. , 1980, Metaphors We Live By, Chicago / London.

Langacker, R.W. , 1976, Semantic representations and the linguistic relativity hypothesis, Foundations of Language 14, p. 307 - 357.

Leclant, J. , 1969, Espace et temps, ordre et chaos dans l'Egypte Pharaonique, Revue de Synthèse 55 - 56, p. 217 -239.

Leech, G. , 1981, Semantics. The Study of Meaning, 2nd ed. , Harmondsworth.

Lettinga, J.P. , 1976, Grammatica van het Bijbels Hebreeuws, 8ste druk, Leiden.

Levenson, J.D. , 1985, Sinai and Zion. An entry into the Jewish Bible, Minneapolis.

Levine, B.A. , 1965, The descriptive tabernacle texts of the Pentateuch, Journal of the American Oriental Society 85, p. 307 - 318.

Licht, J., 1978, Storytelling in the Bible, Jerusalem.

Liere, van, F.A. , 1985, Mens,taal en wereld. Een anthropologische studie, Assen / Maastricht.

Lohfink, N. , 1978, Die Priesterschrift und die Geschichte, in: VT Suppl. XXIX, p. 187 - 225, Leiden.

Lorenzen, E. , 1966, Technological studies in ancient Metrology, Copenhagen.

Lucy, J.A. , Wertsch, J.V. , 1987, Vygotsky and Whorf: A Comparative Analysis, in: M.Hickmann (ed.), Social and Functional Approaches to Language and Thought, p. 67 - 86, London et al.

Lundin, R. , Thiselton, A.C. , Walhout, C. , 1985, The responsibility of hermeneutics, Grand Rapids.

Lyons, J. , 1981, Language and Linguistics. An Introduction, Cambridge.

Mazar, A. , 1990, Archeology of the Land of the Bible; 10.000 - 586 BC, New York.

McEvenue, S. , 1971, The narrative style of the Priestly Writer, Rome.

McEvenue, S. , 1974, The style of a building instruction, Semitics 4, p. 1 - 9.

Meyer, H. , 1957, Raumgestaltung und Raumsymbolik in der Erzählkunst, Studium Generale 10, p. 620 - 630.

Meyers, C.L. , 1976, The Tabernacle Menorah; A synthetic study of a Symbol from the Biblical Cult, Missoula.

Moor, J.C. de, 1977 - 78, Realiteit en relevantie. Visies op de werkelijkheid in de wereld van de Bijbel, unpublished lectures, Theological University, Kampen.

Mulder, M.J. , 1976, Einige Bemerkungen zur Beschreibung des Libanonwaldhauses in I Reg 7,2f, ZAW 88, p. 99 - 105.

Neugebauer, O. , 1969, The exact sciences in Antiquity, 2nd ed. , New York.

Niccacci, A. , 1990, The syntax of the verb in Classical Hebrew prose, translated from the Italian, Sheffield.

Nida, E.A. , 1972, Implications of contemporary linguistics for biblical scholarship, Journal of Biblical Literature 91, p. 73 - 89.

Noth, M. , 1948, Überlieferungsgeschichte des Pentateuch, Stuttgart.

Noth, M. , 1959, Das zweite Buch Mose, Exodus, Das Alte Testament Deutsch, 5. Aufl. , Göttingen.

Nuchelmans, G. , 1978, Taalfilosofie. Een inleiding, Muiderberg.

Oelsner, J. , 1982, Vorderasiatische Mathematik und Astronomie, in: GWDA, p. 50 - 70.

Paran, M. , 1989, Forms of the Priestly Style in the Pentateuch. Patterns, linguistic usages, syntactic structures. [Hebrew, with summary in English], Jerusalem.

Pardee, D.G. , 1975, The Preposition in Ugaritic, Ugarit-Forschungen 7, p. 329 - 378.

Pater, W. de, 1986, Filosofie van de taal; een historisch-systematische inleiding, Leuven.

Patte, D. , 1975, Early Jewish hermeneutics in Palestine, Missoula.

Pelzl, B. , 1975, Das Zeltheiligtum von Ex. 25ff. Die Frage nach der Möglichkeit seiner Errichtung, Ugarit-Forschungen 7, p. 379 - 387.

Penn, J.M. , 1972, Linguistic relativity versus innate ideas. The origins of the Sapir-Whorf Hypothesis in German thought, The Hague / Paris.

Pinxten, R. , 1976, Epistemic Universals. A Contribution to Cognitive Anthropology, in: R.Pinxten (ed.), Universalism versus Relativism in

Language and Thought. Proceedings of a Colloquium on the Sapir-Whorf Hypotheses, p. 117 - 175, The Hague / Paris.

Pinxten, R. , Dooren, I. van, 1983, Anthropology of space. Explorations into the Natural Philosophy and Semantics of the Navajo, Philadelphia.

Plessner, H. , 1975, Die Stufen des Organischen und der Mensch. Einleitung in die philosophische Anthropologie, 3. Aufl. , Berlin / New York.

Polzin, R. , 1976, Late Biblical Hebrew. Toward an historical typology of Biblical Hebrew Prose, Missoula.

Postma, F. , Talstra, E. , Vervenne, M. , 1983 I, Exodus. Materials in Automatic Text Processing, Part I, Morphological, Syntactical and Literary Case Studies, Amsterdam / Turnhout.

Postma, F. , Talstra, E. , Vervenne, M. , 1983 II, Exodus. Materials in Automatic Text Processing, Part II, Concordance, Amsterdam / Turnhout.

Powell, M.A. , 1987 - 1990, Maße und Gewichte, in: Reallexikon der Assyriologie, Band 7, p. 457 - 517.

Rad, G. von, 1931, Zelt und Lade, in: G. von Rad, Gesammelte Studien zum AT, ThB 8, München, 1965.

Rad, G. von, 1934, Die Priesterschrift im Hexateuch, Stuttgart / Berlin.

Rad, G. von, 1975, Theologie des Alten Testaments, Band II, 6. Aufl. , München.

Regt, L.J. de, 1988, A parametric model for syntactic studies of a textual corpus, demonstrated on the Hebrew of Deuteronomy 1 - 30, Assen / Maastricht.

Reineke, W.F. , 1980, Mathematik, in: Lexikon der Agyptologie, Band 3, p. 1237 - 1245, Wiesbaden.

Reineke, W.F. , 1982, Agypten, in GWDA, p. 91 - 132.

Reventlow, H. Graf, 1982, Hauptprobleme der alttestamentlichen Theologie im 20. Jahrhundert, Darmstadt.

Richter, W. , 1971, Exegese als Literaturwissenschaft. Entwurf einer alttestamentlichen Literaturtheorie und Methodologie, Göttingen.

Richter, W. , 1985, Untersuchungen zur Valenz althebräischer Verben, Band 1, 'rk, St. Ottilien.

Richter, W. , 1986, Untersuchungen zur Valenz althebräischer verben, Band 2, gbh, 'mq, qsr II, St.Ottilien.

Ridderbos, N.H. , 1964, Is het Hebreeuws een van de bronnen van de Openbaring? Gereformeerd Theologisch Tijdschrift 64, p. 209 - 229.

Robins, R.H. , 1976, The Current Relevance of the Sapir-Whorf Hypothesis, in: R.Pinxten (ed.), Universalism versus Relativism in Language and Thought. Proceedings of a Colloquium on the Sapir-Whorf Hypotheses, p. 99 - 107, The Hague / Paris.

Ronan, C.A. , 1983, The Cambridge illustrated history of the World's Science, Cambridge.

Rosch, E. , 1977, Linguistic Relativity, in: P.N.Johnson-Laird, P.C.Wason (eds.), Thinking. Readings in Cognitive Science, p. 501 - 519, Cambridge.

Sawyer, J.F.A.., 1967 -1968, Spaciousness. (An important feature of language about salvation in the Old Testament), Annual of the Swedish Theological Institute

VI, p. 20 - 34.

Sawyer, J.F.A. , 1972, Semantics in Biblical Research. New Methods of Defining Hebrew Words for Salvation, Naperville.

Sawyer, J.F.A. , 1976, A modern introduction to Biblical Hebrew, London.

Scherer, A. , 1957, Die Erfassung des Raumes in der Sprache, Studium Generale 10, p. 574 - 582.

Schmitt, G. , 1977, Maße, in: K.Galling (ed.), Biblisches Reallexikon, 2. Aufl. , Tübingen.

Schmitt, R. , 1972, Zelt und Lade als Thema alttestamentlicher Wissenschaft, Gütersloh.

Schneider, W. , 1985, Grammatik des biblischen Hebräisch: ein Lehrbuch, 6. Aufl. , München.

Scholten, T. , Evers, A. , 1981, Inleiding in de transformationeel-generatieve taaltheorie, Groningen.

Schweizer, H. , 1981, Metaphorische Grammatik. Wege zur Integration von Grammatik und Textinterpretation in der Exegese, St. Ottilien.

Scott, R.B.Y. , 1959, Weights and Measures of the Bible, Biblical Archaeologist 22, 2, p. 22 - 40.

Seebass, H. , 1984, לקח, in: TWAT, Band 4, p. 588 - 594.

Sellers, O.R. , 1962, Weights and Measures, in : IDB, vol.4 , p. 828 - 839.

Simon, J. , 1981, Sprachphilosophie, Freiburg / München.

Simons, J. , 1952, Jerusalem in the Old Testament. Researches and theories, Leiden.

Sklar, L. , 1974, Space, time and spacetime, Berkeley / Los Angeles.

Slobin, D.I. , 1971, Psycholinguistics, Glenview / London.

Soden, W. von, 1985, Einführung in die Altorientalistik, Darmstadt.

Stadelmann, L.I.J. , 1970, The Hebrew conception of the world. A philological and literary study, Rome.

Stam, J.H. , 1980, An historical perspective on 'linguistic relativity', in: R.W.Rieber (ed.), Psychology of Language and Thought. Essays on the Theory and History of Psycholinguistics, p. 239 - 262, New York / London.

Stegmüller, W. , 1978, Hauptströmungen der Gegenwartsphilosophie. Eine kritische Einführung, Band I, 6. Aufl. , Stuttgart.

Stegmüller, W. , 1986, Hauptströmungen der Gegenwartsphilosophie. Eine kritische Einführung, Band II, 7. Aufl. , Stuttgart.

Steinfatt, T.M. , 1989, Linguistic Relativity. Toward a Broader View, in: S.Ting-Toomey, F.Korzenny (eds.), Language, communication and culture. Current directions. International Intercultural Communication Annual, vol. XIII, p. 35 - 75, Newbury Park / London.

Struppe, U. , 1988, Die Herrlichkeit Jahwes in der Priesterschrift, Klosterneuburg.

Talmy, L. , 1983, How language structures space, in: H.L.Pick, L.P.Acredolo (eds.), Spatial Orientation. Theory, Research, and Application, p. 225 - 282, New York / London.

Talstra, E. , 1978, Text Grammar and Hebrew Bible. I: Elements of a Theory,

Bibliotheca Orientalis 35, p. 169 - 174.

Talstra, E. , 1982, Text Grammar and Hebrew Bible. II: Syntax and Semantics, Bibliotheca Orientalis 39, p. 26 - 38.

Terrien, S.L. , 1978, The elusive presence. The heart of biblical theology, San Francisco.

Tesfai, Y. , 1975, This is my resting place. An inquiry into the role of time and space in the Old Testament, Chicago.

Thiselton, A.C. , 1980, The two Horizons. New Testament hermeneutics and philosophical description with special reference to Heidegger, Bultmann, Gadamer and Wittgenstein, Grand Rapids.

Utzschneider, H. , 1988, Das Heiligtum und das Gesetz. Studien zur Bedeutung der sinaitischen Heiligtumstexte (Ex 25 - 40; Lev 8 -9), Freiburg / Göttingen.

Vaux, R. de, 1974, Ancient Israel. Its Life and Institutions, translated from the French, London.

Vernon, M.D. , 1977, The psychology of perception, 2nd ed. , Harmondsworth.

Vleeming, S. , 1980, Maße und Gewichte in den demotischen Texten, in: Lexikon der Agyptologie, Band 3, p. 1209 - 1214, Wiesbaden.

Waltke, B.K. , O'Connor, M. , 1990, An Introduction to Biblical Hebrew Syntax, Winona Lake.(abbreviation: WO'C)

Weimar, P. , 1973, Untersuchungen zur Exodusgeschichte, Würzburg.

Weimar, P. , 1984, Struktur und Komposition der priesterschriftlichen Geschichtsdarstellung, Biblische Notizen 23, p. 81 - 134, 24, p. 138 - 162.

Weimar, P. , 1988, Sinai und Schöpfung. Komposition und Theologie der Priesterlichen Sinaigeschichte, Revue Biblique 95, p. 337 - 385.

Wells, P.R. , 1980, James Barr & the Bible. Critique of a new liberalism, Phillipsburg.

Werlen, I. , 1989, Sprache, Mensch und Welt. Geschichte und Bedeutung des Prinzips der sprachlichen Relativität, Darmstadt.

Wheeler Robinson, H. , 1980, Corporate Personality in Ancient Israel, rev. ed. , Philadelphia.

Whorf, B.L. , 1956, Language, Thought and Reality. Selected writings by B.L.Whorf, edited by J.B.Carroll, Cambridge.

Whybray, R.N. , 1987, The Making of the Pentateuch: a methodological study, Sheffield.

Wilsdorf, H. , 1982, Technisches Denken in Agypten, in: GWDA, p. 133 - 140.

Wolters-Noordhoff, 1988, De Grote Bosatlas, 50ste druk, Groningen.

Wright, G.R.H. , 1985, Ancient Building in South Syria and Palestine. Volume 1, Leiden / Köln.

Yeivin, I. , 1980, Introduction to the Tiberian Masorah, Missoula.

Zevit, Z. , 1982, Converging Lines of Evidence Bearing on the Date of P., ZAW 94, p. 481 - 511.

NAMES.

Niccacci, A. 177, 182, 192ff, 201, 203ff, 218, 222, 239
Nida, E.A. 64
Noth, M. 158f
Nuchelmans, G. 116f
O'Connor, M. 182ff, 191, 198, 213, 223, 226
Oelsner, J. 245
Paran, M. 151ff, 178
Pardee, D.G. 224
Pater, W. de. 78
Patte, D. 253
Peirce, C.S. 114f
Pelzl, B. 175
Penn, J.M. 76
Piaget, J. 83ff, 96, 244
Pinxten, R. 82ff, 96, 100, 109ff
Plato, 42, 112
Plessner, H. 89
Polzin, R. 176f
Popper, J. 156
Popper, K.R. 118
Postma, F. 145, 177, 180, 218
Powell, M.A. 246
Quine, W.V.O. 118f
Rad, G. von. 20, 26, 156ff, 161f, 172, 174f
Regt, L.J. de. 206, 239
Reineke, W.F. 241, 245
Rendtorff, R. 159, 163, 171
Reventlow, H.G. 20
Richter, W. 53, 155
Ricoeur, P. 118
Ridderbos. N.H. 60ff
Robins, R.H. 85ff
Ronan, C.A. 245
Rosch, E. 91ff, 96, 109f, 138
Sapir, E. 58, 60, 74f, 85
Sawyer, J.F.A. 49f, 55f, 65f, 71, 144, 184, 191
Scherer, A. 100
Schmitt, G. 246
Schmitt, R. 165

Schneider, W. 182, 191f, 206, 239
Scholten, T. 190
Schweizer, H. 184, 191
Scott, R.B.Y. 246
Seebass, H. 232
Seidl, U. 248
Sellers, O.R. 246
Shibata, Y. 247
Simon, J. 117
Simons, J. 248
Sklar, L. 15
Slobin, D.I. 76f
Soden, W. von. 245
Sperber, H. 65
Stadelmann, L.I.J. 51ff, 55f, 71, 144f
Stam, J.H. 74f
Stegmüller, W. 117
Steinfatt, T.M. 77, 95ff, 109f, 138
Sterelny, K. 119, 121ff, 125, 131, 136
Ströker, E. 14
Struppe, U. 174
Talmy, L. 103ff, 108f, 131, 138, 146, 233
Talstra, E. 145f, 177, 180, 182, 205, 218
Terrien, S.L. 21, 28ff, 38f
Tesfai, Y. 21, 25ff, 38f
Thiselton, A.C. 68ff, 71, 128f, 151
Turner, M. 66f
Ullmann, S. 61
Utzschneider, H. 148ff, 174, 203, 216
Vaux, R. de. 246f
Vernon, M.D. 138
Vervenne, M. 145, 177, 180, 218
Vleeming, S. 245
Voss, H. 14
Vygotsky, L.S. 96
Walhout, C. 69f, 71, 128, 151
Walkenhorst, K.H. 159
Waltke, B.K. 182ff, 191, 198, 201, 223, 226
Warren, A. 149
Wason, P.C. 139

Weimar, P. 159, 161f, 164f, 174f, 177
Weinrich, H. 193
Weisgerber, L. 79
Wellek, R. 149
Wellhausen, J. 154, 156, 165
Wells, P.R. 62f
Wenham, G.J. 36
Werlen, I. 78, 91
Wertsch, J.V. 96
Westerman, C. 163
Wheeler Robinson, H. 61

Whorf, B.L. 58, 60, 67f, 74ff, 85, 91, 96ff, 109ff, 119
Whybray, R.N. 156
Wilsdorf, 247
Wittgenstein, L. 68f, 118f
Wolters-Noordhoff. 135
Wright, G.R.H. 248
Yeivin, I.184
Zenger, 153
Zevit, Z. 167

SUBJECTS

altar of burnt offering 206ff, 220
altar of incense 206ff, 219f
Ancient Near East 11, 17f, 57, 240ff
anthropology 88ff
aphasics 97
appearance of Yahweh 29f, 161f
archaeology 246ff
architecture 24734ff
ark 161ff, 206ff, 219, 221
bars 213ff
bilingualism 97f
breastpiece 215ff
cartography 137
chains 215ff
children 102f, 149, 242
city 27
coat 215ff
cognition 73f, 109f, 138f
   see also: language and cognition
cognitive dissonance 98f
coherence 155f, 164
cohesion 155f, 169ff
colours 93f
cosmos 51f, 100, 144
court 213ff, 220
cult 36f, 163
cultural distance 137f

curtains of goats' hair 213ff, 219f
curtains of linen 213ff, 219f
Dani 94
deaf 98
dimensions 207f, 213f, 235f
distances 230ff, 235f
Documentary Hypothesis 153ff, 178
Eden 47ff
Egypt 240ff
ephod 215ff, 219
frames 213ff, 220
garments 215ff
Greek, see: Hebrew
grids 247f
Hebrew and Greek thought 41ff, 56ff, 90f
hermeneutics 68f, 128ff, 137
history 11, 20f, 25ff
Hopi 79ff
Jerusalem 47ff
lampstand 212, 220
land 26, 50
language, see also: space
language and cognition 56, 71f, 74f, 105f, 130ff
language, figurative aspects of 78, 87f, 100

DATE DUE

D 27 14			

HIGHSMITH 45-220